The Rulings of the Night

The Rulings of the Night

An Ethnography of Nepalese Shaman Oral Texts

Gregory G. Maskarinec

THE UNIVERSITY OF WISCONSIN PRESS

The University of Wisconsin Press
114 North Murray Street
Madison, Wisconsin 53715

3 Henrietta Street
London WC2E 8LU, England

1 3 5 4 2

Printed in the United States of America

Parts of Chapter 2 appeared in an essay in *Social Sciences and Medicine* 35:723–34. Reprinted courtesy of Pergamon Press Ltd., Headington Hill Hall, Oxford OX3 OBW, U.K.

Library of Congress Cataloging-in-Publication Data
Maskarinec, Gregory Gabriel.
The rulings of the night: an ethnography of Nepalese shaman oral texts /
Gregory Gabriel Maskarinec.
288 p. cm.
Includes bibliographical references and index.
ISBN 0-299-14490-9 ISBN 0-299-14494-1 (pbk.)
1. Shamanism—Nepal. I. Title.
BL2033.5.S52M37 1995
299'.1495—dc20 94-23024

what is it called, your country
behind the mountain, behind the year?
—Paul Celan

Contents

Illustrations

Illustrations

Figures

Map

Acknowledgments

In writing this work, I draw upon ethnographic material that I have collected over the past fifteen years in Jājarkoṭ and Rukum Districts of Nepal. I lived in western Nepal for six years, from 1977 until 1983, returning for a few months in both 1989 and 1992. From the beginning, so many people have helped me in so many ways that a complete list of acknowledgments would be impossible. I recall countless acts of hospitality, assistance, kindness, and patient teaching, all helping guide me through the intricacies of Nepalese society and language, all contributing in some ways to my research. To all, I press together my palms and bow my head.

Within that enormous domain, in this book I concentrate on material supplied by fourteen shamans, without whose cooperation this study would have been impossible. Throughout the text, I have identified them, as they insisted, by their true names and real villages. Two deserve special acknowledgment: the late Gumāne Mohār Kāmī of Syāulā Village and Karṇa Vīr Kāmī of Churī Village. Both assisted with this study from its earliest to its final stages. Śiva Bahādur Kāmī, Abi Lal Kāmī, Kamāro Kāmī, Nar Siṅgh Kāmī, and Gore Sārkī also deserve an additional word of thanks.

I am particularly indebted to Śrī Yogiśwar Kārki, who supplied endless examples of word use from local songs, proverbs, riddles, and reported speech, without which my translations would be flat and lifeless. To my considerable advantage, Yogiśwar widely circulated an ironic remark made by a local official who called me the Vyāsa of shamans, referring to the legendary compiler of the Mahābhārata. Much of my early rapport with shamans was built on Yogiśwar's argument that Brāhmans have their texts written down in books, but shamans don't, so that their extensive learning goes unappreciated.

Amar Rokāya and Citra Prasād Śarmā did most of my preliminary transcriptions, a task that drove others to near madness. In different years, I lived with families of Śāhs and Kārkis of Jājarkoṭ Khalaṅgā, Rokāyas of Saru, and Kāmīs of Lahā, all of whom were true hosts. Deserving particular acknowledgment for their generous help are Nirālā Kārki, Rājeśwar Kārki, Nar Bahādur Rokāya, Amar Śāh, Mohan Vikram Śāh, and Kesāb Juṅg Śāh.

The complex of shamans in western Nepal was first recorded by John T. Hitchcock. Thanks to his very gracious generosity, I have had access to texts that he collected thirty years ago in the Bhujī Valley, a five days' walk east of Jājarkoṭ. His material includes more than twenty-five hours of tapes made in 1961/62 and 1967, along with extensive supplementary notes. It provides a geographic range and a time depth that clearly would have been otherwise impossible for me to obtain. Hopefully, his material will appear in a complete edition elsewhere, but with Professor Hitchcock's kind permission, I have included some selections from it in this work.

My interests in these topics grew as I worked as a Peace Corps volunteer teaching high school math and science, first in Jājarkoṭ and later in Paīk. Not only was time consumed by my research always tolerated by my supervisors, headmasters, colleagues, and students, but many of them actively and enthusiastically contributed to it. For two years, I was honored to be King Mahendra Scholar of Tribhuvan University. Later, the East West Center, Honolulu, provided me with four years of financial support. To each of these institutions I offer my gratitude for the indulgent trust that they showed toward me.

This study has gone through many drafts, one of which was my dissertation in anthropology at the University of Hawai'i. My committee chair, Jack Bilmes, earned my respect for both his firm encouragement and his detailed suggestions. Robert Desjarlais, John T. Hitchcock, and Gabe Maskarinec offered much helpful advice for improving the entire manuscript. Remarks at different times by András Höfer, Peter Manicus, Caspar Miller, Mark Oppitz, and Anne de Sales have helped me enormously with particular issues. Were it but possible to incorporate all of their comments, this work would be far better. I thank all of them for their efforts.

My family has patiently tolerated my long absences, out of touch in the field or lost in reflection, as I have worked on this project. There is clearly no way I can ever repay them, but as a small gesture, a hint and nudge, this book is for them.

The Rulings of the Night

1
Words as Cures

Mahādev brushed a white yak tail at the head,
brushed a black yak tail at the feet,
with a powerbolt staff delivering seven blows,
"Speak, man," he said, "Hā̃, hā̃, hũ hũ," it went.
"Go and die," said Mahādev, gave a curse.

(1.1)

When Lord Mahādev created the first man, he fashioned a series of homunculi from different durable materials such as gold, silver, and copper. Each time he commanded his creation to speak. None did, so he destroyed each in turn. Finally he tried a mixture of sandalwood ash and chicken dung, and man managed to mumble, "hā̃, hā̃, hũ hũ." Although this response was sufficient to convince Mahādev that his latest model was indeed a human male (females have a separate, divine origin, 2.6) its ineloquence infuriated the creator, as my first selection from a shaman's recital tells us. In wrath, he cursed man and his descendants with seven times of natural death, fourteen times of unnatural death. Compassionate Sitā intervenes, and Mahādev agrees to create different intercessors empowered to postpone or alleviate human fate—to speak for us in different ways—Brāhman priests, astrologers, oracles, seers, counselors, fortune-tellers, and, most successfully, shamans (local Nepali: *jhāṅgarī;* standard Nepali: *jhā̃kri*) on whom in this study I concentrate.

Jhāṅgarīs are Himalayan shamans, intercessors who rely upon extensive training in oral texts to diagnose and treat afflictions that trouble their clients. Jhāṅgarīs accomplish their intercessions through diverse rituals, ceremonies that prominently incorporate throughout every stage of activity both long, publicly chanted recitals and short, whispered, secretive incantations. When I first encountered a shaman's ceremony, both forms of texts appeared to me utterly submerged in the spectacle of performance, in which drumming, dancing, and dramatic ritual, now frenzied, now subdued, contend with apparently incomprehensible mumbling, babbling, shouting, and whispering—utterances that seemingly resemble man's original speech that so angered his creator. My confusion as to who was speaking, and who was being spoken to, further obscured the language. Frequently, in various possession events throughout the Himalayas, participants say that the agents of possession communicate through their chosen vehicle, either with each other, or with the shaman, or with the audience, or, conversely, that the shaman is ecstatically and spontaneously communicating with the spirits. Postulating specifically supernatural or private languages, each of these explanations diminishes the possibility that a noninitiate can ever really understand what jhāṅgarīs say in their ceremonies, and certainly argues strongly against any suggestion that what they are saying could possibly provide the most comprehensive understanding of what they are doing.

All of these confusions were part of my initial understanding of Himalayan shamans, whose performances I first experienced in 1977 during my second month of training as a Peace Corps volunteer preparing to teach mathematics in a village high school. Eager to immerse myself in local culture, the first time that I became ill I chose to be treated by a shaman. My meager grasp of Nepali naturally contributed to my initial impression that a shaman's speech was completely incomprehensible. The training staff of sophisticated Kathmandu Brāhmans and Newars explicitly confirmed this conclusion. They were self-consciously embarrassed by the event, as were Peace Corps officials, not at all amused that I had a chicken sacrificed to counter a witch attack marked by spectacular, relentless vomiting. Though I often attended shaman ceremonies, several years lapsed before I attempted to understand the recitations within their performances. I was long misled by various additional commentaries, including those of local schoolteachers, government officials, and especially, circumspect, wary villagers. Each affirmed that this was an inaccessible discourse that could not conceivably be understood, not really language at all. Such remarks convinced me that shaman texts were privileged knowledge known only by special-

Illustration 1.1. Jhāṅgarī Karṇa Vīr Kāmī

ists—the shamans themselves. Incomprehensible to common men and women, their utterances apparently left patients simply (and literally) spellbound. It seemed that the audiences who overhear them no more expect to understand the text than they would a Brāhman's Sanskrit recital at a Rudri Pātha (3.17, below) or the pages of tiny English print wrapped around an expensive vial of allopathic pharmaceuticals. Any effort to penetrate the sense, or meaning, of these texts seemed alien to their use. The texts apparently supplied a backdrop of rhythmic sound overshadowed by the spectacular, dramatic curing ceremonies. As Eliade suggests at the end of his pioneering study, shamans produce a "*spectacle* unequaled in the world of daily experience . . . where the 'laws of nature' are abolished" (1964:511, italics in original). Impressed by that wonder-filled spectacle, I prematurely concluded that the drama of the cure, not its script, interested the audience. These misconceptions were further reinforced by popular views (both Western and orthodox Hindu) of "mantras" that it is crucial to achieve the right sound, not the right sense, that the words themselves have no real meaning, that they provide sonic envelopes of private enlightenment. Discovering that all of these ideas were completely untrue motivated me to write this work. Like all poetry, shaman texts do construe words "for their shape and their sensuous emanations, not only for their meaning" (Artaud 1958:125), but like the best poetry, they voice serious meanings deserving extended exploration and analysis.

Utterly distinct from the disgracefully ineloquent mutterings of the original man, both the long public recitals and the short private *mantar*s (standard Nepali: *mantra*) of Himalayan shamans are polished, well-constructed, orally preserved texts, meticulously memorized through years of training. These texts constitute the core of every shaman's knowledge. By their accurate recitation, shamans intervene to manipulate and change the world. In learning them, shamans acquire the knowledge necessary for their profession and obtain a complete, detailed view of the world and its participants. What you learn to say is what you learn to do. Shaman texts create shamans.

To become a shaman (a topic of Chapter 6), one first formally requests another shaman to teach you his texts. Instruction begins with the *rāyā sarsu* mantar, named after two varieties of mustard seeds. This mantar is used to potentiate mustard seeds, which the shaman throws to the six directions at the beginning of every ceremony. The seeds bind in place the surrounding universe and fill it with the shaman's power. In some versions, this mantar begins with the correct form of the formal request itself, as Nar Siṅgh Kāmī first taught it to me:

> First, at the beginning, "Teach me rāyā sarsu."
> Say, "Guru Father, Guru Father, all honor to you."
> Say, "Guru Father, all honor to the soles of your feet."
> Say, "Nourishing guru, nurturing guru,
> teaching guru, training guru."
> Say, "When did rāyā sarsu arise?"
> Say, "In that age, on that day, they arose."
> Say, "Jaya Jaya Guru, in the Age of Truth, you arose."
> Say, "In the Kali Yuga, the Age of Murder, they arose."
>
> (1.2)

The transition from request into the text proper in the sixth line is seamless, as instructions how to address your guru shift directly to the mantar's opening line: "When did mustard seeds arise?" Instructions to the novice continue to be woven into the text as "you say," an informally conjugated imperative that reflects the predominant mood of verbs throughout the mantar itself. Pupils carefully learn their texts, convinced at least initially that words lose their efficacy if distorted. Later, though, they manipulate their texts deliberately. For example, many replace the homage toward their human guru originally expressed at the beginning of the Mustard Seeds Mantar with homage for Guru Gorakhnāth, whom many shamans regard as the "highest" spiritual authority (see 4.12).

Mustard seeds metonymically represent the natural world and its powers of generation and transformation. They are simultaneously symbol and physical device, standing for and spreading the power of the shaman's speech. They not only protect the space surrounding his performance, they transform the mundane world into an ideal universe rooted in the golden age of divine creation. Their textual sprouting exemplifies the shaman's control over growth, aging, decay, and rejuvenation. The Mustard Seeds Mantar details the seeds' origin, involving major deities of creation in their cultivation, connecting the miraculous and transcendent with the everyday experiences of local agriculture:

> Reversed mustard, straight mustard,
> seed mustard, leaf mustard,
> where did this mustard originate?

Across the Triśūl River, Ayodhyā City,
in Rām Lakṣmaṇ's deep field they originated.
Who did the plowing, who did the leveling?
Śrī Mahādev did the plowing, master oxen the fertilizing,
Mottled Ox and Spotty Ox pulled the plow.
A boa constrictor plow upright, a python plow beam,
a viper snake yoke, a wind snake whip,
a cobra yoke fastener, blunt-tailed snake yoke bars they made.
His own lord Mahādev pierced the seven levels of the earth.
Sitā Pārvatā weeded and tended,
breaking the clods she made a great field.
At first, on the premier Thursday,
this mustard, plowing, planting,
pierced the seven levels of the earth.
This mustard, on the second day, became fertilized,
on the third day it arose.
In what form did it arise?
Moving the earth, its roots met the world of death.
Like a pillar of a tree, it was a green plant.
A second branch, a second leaf, a third branch, a third leaf,
a fourth branch, a fourth leaf, a fifth branch, a fifth leaf,
a sixth branch, a sixth leaf, a seventh branch, a seventh leaf.
How did this mustard bloom?
The fields were yellow, the forests were yellow.
The flying bees were out, the honey bees were out.
It was a pleasant sight.

(1.3)

Shaman texts not only tell stories of the origin of men and of mustard seeds, they also relate the creation of the universe and of its elements. They tell of the origins of worldly disorder and the histories of malevolent forces, stories that explain why people suffer, grow old, and die. They tell of extraordinary events and exceptional individuals. When treating cases of witchcraft, shamans chant the Recital of the Nine Little Sisters, a story of the first witches. This text culminates in their subjugation by the original shaman, who seals an agreement with the youngest sister that still binds their contemporary descendants. The shaman allows her to survive and perform her tricks in the world, so that he is guaranteed a profitable career, an extraordinarily candid explanation of why the world needs shamans:

"Don't kill me, O Jhāṅgarī Jhiṅgrātamau, Rammā Purācamau,
I will cause illness, you will cure it,
you will receive wealth, you will receive grain,
I will apply reversed knowledge,
you will apply straightened spells,
I will obey your assigned times and assigned cures,
I will put frogs and turtles into victims,
you will cure them . . .
throughout the world, I'll cause illness,
you'll cure it, don't kill me.
First go to a crossroads, first recite my story,
your meeting place and mine will be the crossroads,
don't kill me, O *jhāṅgrīyau*,
throughout the world, I'll cause illness, you'll cure it,
don't kill me," said the witch.
"All right, you apply curses, I'll apply cures.
If you cross a river, your curses will turn to ash.
If you cross the black waters,
I will strike your mouth with an iron rod,
your knowledge will turn to ash," said the jhāṅgarī,
and he allowed one sister to survive.

(1.4)

This is not just to guarantee a career, however. As I will show, shamans create the conditions that they treat. As part of their treatment, shamans replace the chaotic, unbalanced, inexpressible suffering of a patient with orderly, balanced, grammatical, and eloquently expressible states. Taking responsibility for the orderliness of affliction as well as for the balance of its cure, shamans accept their role in the prevalence of evil, including that done by witches.

Many passages of both public recitals and private mantars are simultaneously directions and narratives. As the previous two examples indicate, artfully embedded as parts of the stories themselves are precise expositions of what else shamans need to know. This includes lists of symptoms attributable to different agents of affliction, the identities of those agents, and the places where such agents may be found. Directions, such as meeting witches at crossroads and striking at them with an iron rod, are not only parts of the story but prescriptions followed by the shaman as he performs his profession.

The private mantars, as I shall demonstrate, are compact, intense, but entirely discursive supplements to the recitals, directly addressing unseen audiences with promises, threats, injunctions, and commands. Intended to manipulate the causes of affliction, the mantars closely resemble the recitals given to human audiences, structurally, thematically, and pragmatically. Jumping ahead to the final subject that a shaman teaches his pupils, consider a mantar to raise spirits of dead humans *(masān)*, used to drum up some business for the shamans:

> Wake up, masān, wake up!
> Go to the east, go to the west!
> Go to the north, go to the south!
> Go in the middle of the night,
> stay in the village,
> whoever takes your fancy, strike them!
> Go, masān, go!
>
> (1.5)

Unambiguous, grammatical, and filled with detail, texts such as this one not only bring to life spirits of the dead, they animate the shamans themselves. Without an understanding of these texts, one cannot understand what it is that a shaman undertakes to do. The words shape and give purpose to the rituals, establishing new orders in the world. The language of the texts is coextensive with professional competence, with the ability to be a proper shaman. To reverse a psychoanalytic observation of Julia Kristeva (1989:11), the discourse itself forms and transforms the subject. It is communicated to him as though he were truly an "other," and transforms him into a specialist who can actively intervene in the world with cures and curses; these texts are themselves the ways by which that intervention is undertaken.

This study discursively analyzes several complete repertoires of such texts. (To discuss conveniently passages from the texts, I have sequentially numbered each selection throughout this work, in the order that they occur.) I identify the knowledge required to be a shaman, how they negotiate the relations between language, action, and social realities. I show what it is that shamans say as they perform ceremonies and the ways that those words make their rituals significant. I situate these concerns within more general questions: When examined through texts and ceremonies, what precisely are shamans and what is it that they do? How do they satisfy their client's expectations and preserve their social position?

Most jhāṅgarī performances take place at night. The shaman, dressed in an elaborate costume, enters a physical frenzy, a corybantic state perceived by his audience to demonstrate his possession by spirits *(deutā lāgnu)*. As he drums, dances, and engages in various ritual activities, he speaks, sings, chants, whispers, and shouts: that is, he does diverse things with words. In these nightlong performances, which continue to attract both a significant clientele and a large audience undeterred by familiarity, what do the participants expect to accomplish? This is a central theme that I explore in this work. To do so, I range through various corollaries, such as, "What does one need to know to be a jhāṅgarī?"; "What kinds of afflictions can they treat?"; "How is the cure expected to work?"; and, most important for my approach, "What exactly is it that shamans are saying in these performances?" By answering this last question at three levels, lexical, semantic, and pragmatic, I undertake to answer each of the other questions. I demonstrate that these oral texts themselves provide a well-constructed and thoroughly consistent intentional universe. Only in that particular universe can all shaman actions and beliefs be systematically comprehended. What shamans say within their rituals informs and clarifies what they do in those rituals. The oral texts, whose memorization forms the primary training needed to become a shaman, taken as a whole, form a coherent world that both defines and explains all shaman activities. Moreover, not only do these texts teach the shaman about the world in which he intervenes, they also, simultaneously, provide him with the resources needed for that intervention: the texts are the interventionary resources. By learning these texts, the shaman learns how the world in which he finds himself is constructed, as well as the critical points at which his mediation is possible. He learns how the present disorders have come about, a knowledge that provides him with starting points from which to remedy those disorders. As he learns to identify specific causes of worldly disorder, the agents of afflictions, he concurrently learns ways to appease, pacify, or neutralize those sources and thereby reestablish universal order. He learns of the roles of shamans, of their position in the extended social order, which includes not only kings and priests, blacksmiths and merchants, but also witches and disembodied souls, gods and demons. By publicly reciting the texts, the shaman affirms his mastery not only of this material but also of its topics. He displays his enormous cosmological and theoretical knowledge and shares it with his audience, giving them a perspective on their misfortunes that provides hope of possible relief. The texts give reassurance that the role of shamans is precisely to reassert order in the world, and that a shaman who knows them retains his capacity to do so. Hence, listening carefully to these texts is to hear both the self-image and the public persona of the shaman, how he has learned to articulate his professional self and how he portrays that profession to clients. To analyze the discourse of such texts is to answer conclusively (but with polyphonic diversity) the question: "What is a shaman?"

Analyzing the language of oral texts, this work looks beyond the specificity of shamans to meditate on more general properties of language and social action. Acknowledging one of Wittgenstein's best-known witticisms, I argue that since languages are commensurate with forms of life, to analyze a particular language is to unpack the particular form of life that it permeates and vitalizes. We do not live in private worlds, or speak private languages. In language resides our social being. Language is not only the technical means by which we can inquire whether reality is intelligible, but also the encompassing medium in which we investigate the relations between thought, action, and reality. The seemingly exotic events of spirit possession are as firmly part of the everyday, social world of Nepalese villagers as they are not of the daily reality of most Americans. While not insisting that language in any absolute sense determines perceptions, I do maintain that when we want to talk about those perceptions, we can do so only within the current limits of our language. Conversely, it is within the medium of social life that language lives. Not only is language the primary means by which people are socialized, the chief way that they learn to participate in a society, it is also a primary means by which they participate in society. For these reasons, language is not only the most accessible social phenomenon but the most central social phenomenon. As Vāc (speech deified) declares in Ṛg Veda X.125.4: "Hear! You who are heard. Though not aware of it, you dwell in me."

To analyze shaman texts, I do not apply a fully preconceived, inflexible theory. Rather, I have begun with particular philosophic dispositions, perspectives that have helped me discover what I am doing as my inquiry progressed. Throughout, I accept an indissoluble unity of narrative and theory. While I will elaborate this perspective subsequently, a concise summary is Richard Rorty's argument for the contingency of language: since languages are human constructions, and sentences are constructed in particular languages, and truth is a property of sentences, it follows that we cannot profitably seek a perspective outside language from which to evaluate a form of life—and crucially, we cannot profitably seek a position outside a particular language game from which to begin any such evaluation. As Rorty puts it: "The world is out there, but descriptions of the world are not. Only descriptions of the world can be true or false. The world on its own—unaided by the describing activities of human beings—cannot" (1989:5).

My alternative to beginning from a priori epistemological abstractions of a fully developed theory is to address actual social phenomena. Following Alfred Schutz (1966), I "bracket" such a set of phenomena (the texts), which are clearly and demonstrably, in Harold Garfinkel's phrase, "anthropologically strange." I then analyze the content and structures of those phenomena to uncover a stock of knowledge specific to shamans, what it is that they use to construct their social world, what its factual properties are. Wittgenstein observed: "Only in a stream of thought and life do words have meaning" (1967:173). If we initially accept his suggestions that meaning results from custom and training, oral texts such as these offer the perfect starting point to analyze semantically and pragmatically the traditional society in which they have prominence and continuing importance. To do so identifies how accurately Wittgenstein's observations on the nature of language fit an actual set of social phenomena, and whether their application can explain how "strange" phenomena like spirit possession events make sense to those who participate in them.

One way to approach this problem would be through a logico-grammatical analysis of events (Coulter 1979; Winch 1958). It seems to me, however, unnecessarily limiting to rely only on the insights of ordinary language philosophy. Based as they are on abstract ("arm-chair," or "jet-lounge") speculation, they form an insecure basis for concrete anthropological research. However, the body of sociological research collectively known as ethnomethodology (in which I include for my purposes not only the work of Garfinkel and his associates, but also the work of the conversation analysts, particularly Harvey Sacks) has developed specific programmatics for these situations. Ethnomethodologists study ordinary activities to reveal the tacit reasoning that makes up their orderliness. They seek to discover, within actual settings, the formal properties that organize those settings, the techniques that are known, used, and taken for granted. Garfinkel insists that we must try to see "objective reality as an ongoing accomplishment of the concerted activities of daily life," directing our focus to "the ordinary, artful ways of that accomplishment . . ." (1967:vii).

My chief initial modification to this agenda is to study events that the participants themselves claim are, in a traditional way, extra-ordinary, requiring powers absent from daily life. By choosing to look at such events, we can even more vividly identify and open up to analysis their "seen but unnoticed" details, so that the practices of commonsense reasoning become even more apparent. I privilege the meanings that emerge through the uses to which expressions are put, though at the narrative level I also contrast the meanings that situationally emerge with lexical and etymological ones. At both narrative and pragmatic levels of analysis, I attempt to clarify interconnections of meaning and event, of sense and reference, to secure a convincing exposition of the material itself. Although I naturally aspire for coherency, I do not seek a conclusiveness that would deny the plurivocality of language. Consequently, I hope that readers will judge my results by standards of consistency and cohesiveness, not by either transcendental or empirical theories of "Truth."

Within both texts and ceremonies, I seek details that explain how spirit intercession becomes a practical activity, what the discursive resources available to intercessors and clients are, and how they make use of those details and resources to give sense to the actions in which they participate. To use an apt phrase attributed to Alfred Schutz, I investigate the "fact of the fact": how it is that for both intercessors and their clients, spirit possession becomes and remains part of their everyday, factual world.

Why do this analysis for shaman texts? One ambitious (and perhaps misplaced) goal might be to uncover what ritual speech and ritual action contribute to healing, though I confess making little progress on that complex point. Some people "get better," "improve," or are "cured" by a shaman's intervention, just as some people are apparently sometimes "cured" by allopathic, homeopathic, Ayurvedic, and probably every other form of medicine. Although I am familiar with the usual theories that try to answer *why* they are cured, none of the available explanations seem satisfactory to me. I suspect that questions of "why it works" possibly must remain outside the scope of social science, perhaps forever beyond the subjects of which we can speak. We may have to settle for an analysis of the "what is done" (Bilmes 1986:6) and its poetics, for any discourse is inadequate to encompass the body, with its solid, persistent proofs that language is born of acts of violence toward reality. To echo the Buddha's radical conclusion, our very existence may be a disease. Still, in later chapters, I offer some ideas about what seems to be going on at ontological levels of healing within shaman ceremonies, and I at least achieve a discussion of healing in the terms in which the shaman texts themselves discuss it.

Throughout, I show how ritual language constructs a public universe in which the use of precisely that language is required, how it sustains itself and its users. Concisely, I accept that the primary locus of rational processes is public language, of which most thought is merely an internalized version. I am studying reasoning, but not "mind." It is not what shamans feel in their heads or think in their hearts that interests me, but what they say to others: my perspective is sociological, not psychological. Events in public, not thoughts in private, form the basis of my study. With Wittgenstein again my starting point, I seek meaning within public discourse, not in private languages or "internal" states. Situating meaning in public avoids the too frequently indulged temptation to "psychologize" the study of shamans. It allows a complete circumvention of questions of "mind" or "private" experiences. These play a necessarily important part in our commonsensical reasoning about the world, but remain inaccessible information for ethnographers. Social realities are intersubjectively constituted, creatively negotiated. This negotiation takes place through the actions and interests of participants themselves, using resources provided by language. To understand these realities, we must examine specific uses of language, language manifesting itself in social action. Language spins entangling webs of signification, but we ourselves participate in weaving the contemporary meanings of words, even as the meanings of our lives are woven by the past use of words. I suggest that we can usefully apply Wittgenstein's concept of finitism—that past meanings never strictly determine future meanings—not only to semantics, but to our understandings of texts as well. The meanings of a text are no more ostensible features of the given world than are the meanings of the expressions that we use. Like expressions in any intentional world, texts must be indexical and reflexive, not just open to, but relying upon, active negotiations that temporally anchor sense in them.

To find the meanings of ritual texts, or of rituals, one must explore the multiple dimensions of discourse. I begin with Foucault's concise definition of discourse: practices that systematically form the objects of which they speak (1972:49). But, attempting to emulate Foucault's own meticulous methodology rather than his aphoristic excesses, I will not leap beyond words too quickly, and, crucially, I will argue that discourse equally speaks both subject and object. As do other contemporary hermeneuticists, I examine as discourse the workings of language at four interpenetrating levels:

1. signs—as parts of systems of contrast, as parts of lexicons: the texts themselves as monuments built of words;
2. semantics, including syntax and grammar—the empirical reduction of language to an "object" consisting of structure/event, by systemic constraints: a shamanic ethnolinguistics;
3. pragmatics—the uses to which speech acts are put: the contribution to persons, to rituals, and to society that particular texts make at particular times;
4. ontology—the level of inquiring into the ways that the comprehension of signs relates to the comprehension of the self, the multiple ways that being is spoken: shamans and spirits as linguistic events.

Unlike many philosophical hermeneuticists, however, I have unusually direct access to extratextual contexts, provided by the ceremonies in which the texts appear, the audiences who hear them, the patients for whom they are recited, and, of course, by their immediate enunciators, the shamans. In an immediate sense, these are vibrantly living texts, and this is the way that I have striven to understand them. Finding them to be filled with life has led me to supplant abstract ontological or epistemological speculations with concrete pragmata—real incidents in created life worlds—so that, effectively, the first three levels above subsume the final one. Consequently, I explore labyrinths of nuance, layers of metaphor, refusing to privilege the literal over the figurative, refusing to pretend that I've found what the text "eternally means." I remain instead content with a "mobile army of metaphors, metonymies, and anthropomorphisms," as Nietzsche provocatively defined "truth." This, as Rorty (1989:27) observes, "amounted to saying that the whole idea of 'representing reality' by means of language, and thus of finding a single context for all human lives, should be abandoned." Satirically playing with Hegel's insistence that Truth (capitalized) is not a minted coin that can be pocketed readymade (Hegel 1966:58), Nietzsche undermined that metaphor to argue that "truth" is "in short, a sum of human relations which have been poetically and rhetorically intensified, transferred and embellished . . . coins which have lost their embossing and are now considered as metal and no longer as coins" (Nietzsche 1973:374–75).

Nietzsche's early infatuation with positivism led him to conclude from these insights that all nondenotative postulates were null. An anthropologically more interesting conclusion is, as Richard Shweder (1991:40) argues, the existence of multiple objective worlds, each with an internally consistent, rational structure. This is a position consonant with that of Garfinkel, who, following Schutz in this matter, reached the same conclusion. Every exploration of a world of human relations is hermeneutically cyclic. Although this work is noninterpretive (a position I discuss in Chapters 3 and 7), I follow what Garfinkel (1967:78) calls the "documentary method of interpretation," by which any action (such as an utterance) becomes the "document of" some underlying pattern, while at the same time the underlying pattern is seen as "giving sense to" the action. Not only does this circularity free us from the objectifying deadliness of fixed conclusions, it also limits excesses of interpretive solipsism. Anthropologists must explore the dialectical polarities summarized by Paul Ricoeur (1976:23) under the four poles of event and meaning, sense and reference, whose grid forms the linguistics of discourse. It is the texts that speak, to which we listen. By we I mean not just the ethnographer (and others ordinarily not participating in Nepalese events), but also the full participants, the shamans and their audiences. The semanticity of the texts binds their users, who struggle to re-create their meanings at the same time as their performances are made meaningful by those texts. Binding is not just an appropriate trope, it is a major theme of shaman texts:

> Wherever you strike, there you bind.
> Bind, bind, first bind this house, first bind this home.
> Putting its own ancestral spirits away,
> bind the secondary ancestral spirits,
> foundation stones, boundary markers, the house mother,
> this hearth, this drying rack, these rafters, plastered eaves,
> golden door, silver doorway, bind cow sheds, bind buffalo barns,
> bind babies, adults, white-haired elders,

nursing infants, newborn babies,
bind hands that strike, bind tongues that speak, . . .
tricks, deceits, minor witches, major witches,
striking, killing, pulling out eyes of the living,
breaking arms, I drive into hell!

(1.6)

Language like this passage from the Mustard Seeds Mantar does not just create dramatic effect, it holds in place the shaman himself, who assumes responsibility for the world around him (see 5.9). This has led me to withdraw radical applications of Garfinkel's suggestions, for I have gradually concluded that the indexicality and reflexivity of the texts are rigidly circumscribed within their range of possible meanings. Social realities are creatively negotiated, but not everything is up for negotiation at all times. As another concrete example, consider the choice of animal to be sacrificed in a shaman's healing session, a thoroughly pragmatic issue. As he distances the deadly star obstructions, the shaman knows that he must offer

Blood measured out for blood,
flesh measured out for flesh,
sense measured out for sense,
breath measured out for breath.

(1.7)

He negotiates with the maternal ancestors of various animals to find a voluntary substitute who will go in place of man. Each insists that it already has sufficient responsibilities and recalls its obligations in contemporary society, its roles in sacrifices performed by others as well as by shamans:

"I will give you sacrifice in place of man.
Barren cows, lame oxen, buffalo flesh,
I will give you in sacrifice," he said.
"Mother Buffalo, you must go to the star obstructions,
you must go to satisfy the Time of Death," he said.
"This is not my share, this is not my sacrifice,
my male buffalos I will give at the goddess's post,
I will not go," she said.
"Mother Cow, you must go to the star obstructions,
you must go to satisfy the Time of Death," he said.

"This is not my share, this is not my sacrifice,
my milk is a pure offering to Nārāyaṇ,
my urine and dung are cleansing, are used to purify,
my oxen plow for men, I give them to be raised."
"Mother Sheep, you must go to the star obstructions," he said.
Mother Sheep said, "This is not my share, this is not my sacrifice,
my rams I will give at Barāh's post,
in place of man I will not go," she said.
"Mother Goat, you must go to the star obstructions," he said.
"My sacrifices I will give at the goddess's shrine,
I will go for important things,
I will not go for unimportant things," she said.
"This is important, you must go, Mother Goat."
"If man will eat my flesh, I will go,
otherwise I won't go," she said.
"One share we'll give to the Eastern Parts,
one share we'll give to the Northern Parts,
one share we'll give to the Western Parts,
one share we'll give to the Southern Parts,
the collected blood we'll give to the King of Death,
ears and hooves we'll give to the Extreme Obstruction,
the head and feet Tārātālī's Rammā Jumrātam will take,
half the body will be eaten by the master of the house,
half the body will be eaten by those who come and go,
the sin of your killing will not be on me,
it also won't be on my patient,
go to the star obstructions," he said.

(1.8)

If, however, the shaman's patron had previously arranged to sacrifice a chicken, not a goat, a different ending must be used (2.22). In this passage, we already see how a shaman represents himself as the arbiter of the world's order, capable of bartering with both catastrophic astrological situations and domestic animals, whose place in that order, along with those of shamans and their negotiations, is reaffirmed and circumscribed by the text.

By documenting the ways that phrases of ritual texts acquire specific references, how specialists and their clients establish contemporary meanings for the archaic details of ritual language, this work becomes a thoroughly anthropological test of Wittgensteinian semantics. I examine whether descriptions (as available in the memorized texts) can be successfully interpreted as "directions for use," and whether the meanings of phrases are most often found in their uses. The goal of my analysis at this level is a better understanding of discourse practices, of the connections between language and behavior. I investigate the ways that social realities integrate speech into practical actions. By studying these events in the context of extra-ordinary events in a traditional society, I attempt to uncover aspects of discourse that we as observers tend to ignore when looking at more "ordinary" events in more familiar settings. How is it that for many Nepalis something so striking as possession by spirits becomes an everyday activity? In a general sense, this is to ask how different societies differently draw the distinction between what is real and what is unreal. What we can talk about frames what we commonsensically regard as real: those distinctions our language allows us to draw. Therefore, by analyzing the language of these accounts, I reveal the ways that spirits participate as parts of a common real world of activities, both as discursive and as intersubjective entities.

Of more traditional anthropological interest, the texts also tell us of major traditional concerns in Nepalese society. They demonstrate the interrelatedness and everydayness of illness, death, witchcraft, sorcery, astrological impasses, childlessness, problems with in-laws, accidents—how all of these articulate with and are informed by worlds seen and unseen. They detail the symptoms of these concerns with a precision ordinarily absent in most accounts that local people offer of their problems. They document the seamlessness of the natural and the supernatural, the tangible and the intangible, the extravagant and the prosaic with an unparalleled richness. A passage that speaks of troublesome dreams and inauspicious omens weaves together worlds of very different ontological status, blending the political world of caste, the oneiric world of sleep, the everyday world of agriculture, and the supernatural world of troublesome ghosts. It begins with a complex set of embedded synecdoches, with honor standing for women in the community, who represent the community's caste hierarchy, which represents the entire society, all of which are implicated in the construction of inauspicious dreams:

> In the king's neighborhood, the king's women's honor,
> In the minister's neighborhood, the minister's women's honor,

in the Ṭhākurī's neighborhood, the Ṭhākurī's women's honor,
in the Bāhun's neighborhood, the Bāhun's women's honor . . .
(1.9)

The summons continues with honor of women in the neighborhood of Magars, blacksmiths, leather workers, minstrels, prostitutes, sweepers, and excrement collectors (6.23). The caste system of the dominant social order is acknowledged, but responsibility for it shifts into the shaman's own world. Suddenly, these women and these neighborhoods are collectively addressed:

Show respect, elder sisters, show respect, younger sisters.
Hey, sisters! Honorable neighborhoods, listen!
In your house, dreams may be broken, visions may be broken.
From the dream, a ladle breaks, a stirring stick breaks,
the drying rack falls, a wall sags, it dries up,
a rockslide falls, a landslide falls,
a mustache disintegrates, hair falls out from a topknot,
a tooth falls out, a leech sucks,
one person is pressed atop another, mushrooms are picked,
your house is filled with strife.
From a dream you may ride a black horse,
wearing black clothes, heading toward the south.
From a dream you may ride a red horse,
wearing red clothes, heading toward the east.
From a dream you may carry a load of salt,
you may carry a load of cooking oil, heading toward the north.
There may be inauspicious things at your house,
a chicken may have laid a shell-less egg, a chick may dry up,
a black dog may climb the roof beam and bark toward the east,
in [the month of] Māgh, a water buffalo calves,
in Cait a dog litters,
you may have met someone eaten by the heat of spring,
you may have met someone eaten by a tiger in fall,
you may have met a wheat sprout, a barley sprout,
a banana sprout, a cucumber sprout,
a taro sprout, a ginger sprout,
a blood leaf plant sprout;
strike it, command it!
Plow furrows may not be straight,
they may have struck a ridge grave,

the plow shear may have shorn a burrowed snake,
a buffalo in Māgh, a cow in Bhadau,
a dog in Cait may give birth,
strike it, command it!

(1.10)

Each omen mentioned is inauspicious, a list more extensive than any that my Nepalese friends would casually provide. Some entries seem to be determined mostly by wordplay that cannot be preserved in translation, such as the tmesis of *cyāpīyo: cyāu ṭipīyo* that produces the pair "people pressing/mushroom picking," but Karṇa Vīr assured me that both are images of the Time of Death, and other villagers confirmed this. Leaving aside connections that might be drawn between dreams, sexual intercourse, and puns, what is important here are the imperatives. A villager plagued by bad dreams must take control of her life, must take action through verbalized commands. She must emulate the orderliness of a shaman.

Ordinary villagers, talking of their problems, tend to provide informal and vague portraits of their troubles, telling anecdotes rather than enumerating precise symptoms or delineating exact causalities. Someone may privately report a bad dream or disconcerting incident to family or close friends, but to discuss abstractly the subject of inauspicious things not only is distasteful but may be irresponsibly provocative. Shaman texts, in contrast, enumerate specifics. For Nepalis, simply saying *sapanā bigriyo* (a dream has broken) or *boksī lāgyo* (a witch has attacked) sums up complex sets of experiences that are nearly impossible to untangle, or their disentangling may embarrassingly implicate close relatives or neighbors. Shamans, too, are reluctant to discuss some aspects of their profession in casual situations. Disinclined to expose themselves to possible ridicule, they deflect questions away from their personal experience and hesitate to voice claims of power, especially in situations where their abilities are not being actively demonstrated. By working with the same individuals for the past fifteen years, I have dispelled their fear of unexpected consequences if they answer my sometimes intrusive, obtuse, apparently meaningless, or seemingly deranged questions, but they still cite Nepal's traditional legal code as grounds for their caution. Every shaman is acutely aware that it contained severe punishments not only for acts of witchcraft and sorcery, but also for accusations of either that could not be vigorously proven, an issue I discuss further in the next chapter. In contrast to the scarcity of casual self-descriptive information, the texts, with poetically formal elegance, provide detailed accounts of these concerns, descriptions whose accuracy is attested to by the spellbinding effect they repeatedly have on their audiences, who affirm their mastery and relevance. To study these texts is to study precise, accurate accounts of the major concerns that individuals and communities continue to experience in western Nepal. Malinowski was scarcely exaggerating that "linguistic analysis inevitably leads us into the study of all the subjects covered by ethnographic field research" (1923:302).

The next chapter examines, from a shamanic point of view, the things that can go wrong with the world, and the ways those flaws may be repaired. I identify the types of affliction which clients regard intercessors as effective in curing, e.g., witchcraft, malevolent spirit possession, and astrological imbalance, and show how these specifically provide the rationale for shamanic intervention. That is, I organize the etiology of afflictions and describe their treatments. In describing rituals performed during treatment to confront and manipulate particular afflictions, I show how these actions, too, are grounded in the repertories of oral texts.

Chapter 3 shifts to a wider social perspective, introducing the different ritual practitioners of western Nepal and their cosmological context, to demonstrate how shaman texts anchor these practitioners as well as their universe. This also expands my systematic inquiry into shaman texts, by examining how the texts specifically describe jhāṅgarīs and their rituals, uncovering shamanic descriptions of "shamanizing" (local Nepali: *jhāṅgarī lāgnu*).

Chapter 4 undertakes to bridge the gap between text and performance uncovered in the preceding two chapters. In it, I concentrate on the directions that one text gives to a shaman and his assistants on how to perform the ceremony, and examine the ways that texts are directions for use, and how shamans interpret those directions during an actual ceremony. I also discursively analyze some of the most intense moments of shaman ceremonies, including the beginning, the end, and the spirits' arrivals. I place these, along with other relevant technical points of the recitals, such as transitions—shifts from introduction to the narrative proper, and from the narrative to the conclusion, along with ensuing shifts in the accompanying performance—into the overall framework of what shamans say and what they do.

Shamans justify their interventionary practices in their long public narratives, but the intervention itself, they insist, takes place with the incantations that they secretly whisper. Chapter 5 examines these private and secretive sides of their practice, analyzing various mantars. Shamans never publicly recite these texts, though they are required in every ceremony. In an emergency situation, the rituals are curtailed or even omitted, but the necessary mantars are never optional. I apply various ideas about speech acts and performatives to identify the ways that these mantars resemble the publicly recited texts. Texts that I examine include, for example, those for raising and subsequently quelling spirits of the dead at the cremation ground. I also consider the less sensational, but crucial, formulas for beginning and ending public ceremonies, and show how these closely relate to those ceremonies and to the recitals used within them.

Chapter 6 considers shamanic initiation and death ceremonies as metaritual templates for all other shaman rituals. I look at how the relevant texts and the rituals contribute to the continuity of shamanic practices, how these events embed shamans in wider social contexts. I contrast informal accounts that shamans offer of their early experiences with the polished formulations of the texts, to demonstrate ways that these texts transform shaman "selves."

My concluding chapter reflects on this project as it has unfolded and attempts to summarize the directions that it has taken. I reevaluate some of the philosophical and theoretical presuppositions that inform this inquiry, and address the issue of competence, of why anyone should accept my reflections as particularly valid or coherent ones.

Throughout, I explore the ways we discover and create meaning, how it is sustained and transmitted. I seek the various ways that what shamans say in their performances answer the questions of what shamans are, and what, exactly, they are doing. I have taken a set of speech events that initially seemed to me meaningless, and which members insisted were meaningless, and shown how relentlessly and absolutely meaningful those words are. Rather than using pure reflection (or philosophic "thought") to approach this problem, I have addressed it ethnographically, a pragmatic sidestepping of metaphysics. I do not claim a god's-eye view of my topic, capable of all angles, of eternal certainty, but I have learned to respect shamans who claim precisely such awe-filled authority. I have benefited from their precision and certainty, and sometimes attempt to imitate the clarity of their words. At the end, I reexamine the validity of having shuffled together such contrasting approaches. By then, I hope to have convincingly demonstrated not just a text that speaks of texts, but one that allows others' echoes to be heard, voices, not just mine, that quietly speak of poetics and healing, of sacrifice, ritual, and their languages, of how living on, and sometimes beyond, the edges of existence in lands behind mountains, behind time, carries conversations with us with words that create and sustain worlds of life.

2
How to Recast Affliction

Shamans everywhere concentrate on treating ontological conditions permeating affliction rather than focusing exclusively upon mundane, particular symptoms by which those conditions are physically expressed. This does not imply, however, that they fail to categorize those temporal symptoms. Nepali shamans reveal extensive efforts to relate symptoms as the effects of particular causes; they have effectively composed a comprehensive etiology of affliction. In this chapter, I demonstrate that etiology. Shamanic concentration on conditions of being does not lead to exclusively metaphysical explanations of the origin of afflictions. Instead of a strictly otherworldly locus of causality, we find a more balanced distribution of causes bounded within the extremes of the natural and supernatural worlds. Consequences, likewise, are not limited to purely existential states, but range throughout the possibilities of physical ills and metaphysical effects.

Second, I show that this comprehensive range of possibilities is articulately formulated by the shamans themselves, within their oral texts. Expressively incorporated into every ritual cure, the theories found in these texts become accessible to, and shared by, ordinary villagers. Although this etiology is most thoroughly developed within professionally acquired and controlled oral texts, because of the repeated public recitation of those texts, the public also possesses knowledge of these theories of causation. This public knowledge actively reinforces the continued acceptance of intervention by shamans as a valid and meaningful response to situations of adversity.

Shamans do not just interpret a particular situation for a particular patient, as Lévi-Strauss long ago realized (Lévi-Strauss 1963b). They have furthermore organized those particularities within coherent and comprehensive etiologies. These theories of affliction do not simply permit the continuation of shamanic practices, they absolutely require it. In contrast to the less extensive etiologies and less elaborate rituals of other interventionary specialists found in Nepal, shamanic etiologies and shamanic practice mutually confirm one another in every recitation of the ritual texts, in every performance. Although the excessive length of the material involved does not allow a full comparison to be drawn with the etiological theories of local spirit mediums, astrologers, or the minimally trained health post workers, none of these other practitioners formulate such extensive ranges of causes or effects. What is more important, none of the other practitioners expressly incorporate etiological theories into their healing practices. In contrast, as I will demonstrate here, shamans, using a poetic but accessible language, clearly articulate their concepts of causality. At every opportunity, they provide understandable explanations of what they do, and the reasons why they do it, to their patients and audiences.

I restrict my initial analysis of etiology to three repertories, those of Karṇa Vīr Kāmī and Abi Lal Kāmī of Churī Village, Jājarkoṭ, and Gumāne Kāmī of Syāulā, Jājarkoṭ. They are two brothers and their cousin, all blacksmiths. I have chosen these particular shamans not only for their excellent local reputations, but also because their texts are very similar, clearly sharing a single, probably recent, original source. Such a closure makes it easier to demonstrate the internal consistency of an existent system, relying less on my own theoretic conjuring out of diverse bits and pieces of texts. Nevertheless, the system analyzed here is generally true for each of the other eleven shamans with whom I worked, as well as for those studied by John T. Hitchcock in the Bhujī Valley (1974a,b, 1976), and even for the Magar shamans described by Anne de Sales (1991) and Michael Oppitz (1986, 1991). The recitations of other shamans mirror those discussed, though they sometimes change names or alter other details. By limiting my discussion to memorized texts, I present only material that is repeated over and over throughout a shaman's lifetime, and heard over and over by the same clients, thus excluding spontaneous explanations that may escape the attention of most members of the public. Impromptu explanations do occur, of course, but they must acknowledge the overarching context of the oral repertories, which represent relatively fixed points in the ongoing negotiation and reproduction of beliefs (Höfer 1981, 1985a,b). Those repertories are the fixed points that anchor my discussion.

There are, naturally, situations in which a single causative agent is identified as the source of a specific problem, so that some circumstances may be attributed to an entirely local event. Snakebites and scorpion stings are paradigmatic cases that rarely require further elaboration. Excessive consumption of intoxicants or natural poisons, such as the honey of certain wild bees, or the milk from cows that have grazed on hemlock blossoms, is also a comprehensively satisfactory explanation. Upsetting the body's humoral balance, by, for example, taking fish and milk at the same meal, is a third type of self-explanatory situation. Yet a possible response to each of these difficulties is to request a shaman's treatment. Shamans do treat scorpion stings, and treating snakebite is a major source of income for many shamans. Because of its profitability, their mantar for this is one they are perhaps most reluctant to teach. It taunts the snake, mocking its appearance and habits, and comparing its poison unfavorably to the shaman's own poison. It goes, in part:

Eating in reverse, writhing below,
tiny lentils your eyes, long your throat,
backward your teeth.
Your poison shall die,
my poison shall fly.
This poison, who knows it?
My Father Guru knows it!

(2.1)

To see why clients repeatedly regard shamans as effective even for such events as snakebite, we need to consider the entire range of a shaman's intervention. However, the effects end of this cause-and-effect paradigm is analytically trivial, since the range of afflictions that a shaman may be summoned to treat is so inclusive as to be nearly exhaustive. Other than broken bones, loss of limbs or eyes or teeth, trivial skin conditions, minor bruises, and other passing aches and pains, nearly anything unfortunate that may befall a villager, his or her family, or possessions, is potential reason for a shamanic intervention. The illness or death of domestic animals, the eroding away of land, and expensive court litigation are all common grounds for at least a preliminary consultation with a shaman. Given this all-embracing sense of effects, I concentrate, as do the shamans themselves, on causes. To focus the discussion more sharply, I concentrate on causes that ordinarily require a shaman's intervention, rather than situations in which it may be optionally appended. As elaborated below, archetypal cases include witchcraft, sorcery, curses, madness, uncontrolled spirit possession, soul loss, restless ancestors, reproductive disorders (including infertility, miscarriages, and stillbirths), severe, persistent aches, pains, and fevers, and astrological impasses.

As afflicted persons and their families exhaust simple methods and household cures without success, straightforward natural explanations become less applicable to the situation. Extended causalities become necessary, along with the services of a professional capable of diagnosing and treating them. Elaborated explanations commonly involve some combination of five sorts of causes, listed in order of declining tangibility:

1. curses and spells, especially acts of witchcraft or sorcery, traceable to particular, identifiable individuals;
2. misfortunate astrological configurations involving physical, but heavenly, bodies;
3. the intrusion of physical or quasi-physical substances into the body;
4. damage to the body's life forces or souls;
5. the activities of spirits.

What kinds of cases in each set require the intervention of a shaman? Beginning with curses and spells, the oral texts explicitly document examples of shamans themselves causing malicious disturbances, as in 1.5. Certainly, victims expect shamans to cure afflictions for which they or their colleagues are held responsible. This, however, makes up a negligible number of the cases for which they are consulted; at least, it rarely emerges in either public consultations or informal discussions. No one is eager to accuse someone openly of being the cause of one's problems and then pay that person to cure them. Shamans clearly have professional reasons not to accuse fellow practitioners too often: clients might conclude that shamans are too dangerous and might choose safer forms of alternate treatment. After all, various possibilities exist, such as undertaking a pilgrimage to an important oracular shrine or venturing into the health post, though each involves different risks, expenses, and uncertainties. Both shamans and clients face the possibility of ending up in court if they openly make accusations of sorcery and cannot prove them. The traditional sanctions were very harsh and remain well remembered. Nepal's first legal code, the *Muluki Ain* of 1853/54 (Höfer 1979; H.M.G. V.S. 2022), enforced for over a hundred years and still quoted in local discussions, states that after a bewitchment complaint has been lodged, "if after investigation the bewitchment is not proven, he who lodged the complaint must pay a fine" (Macdonald 1976:378). Failure to pay the fine resulted in imprisonment. Strict criteria determined acceptable proofs of bewitchment. Vicariously branding the sorcerer by directly branding the patient is a legally acceptable proof. So, too, is vicariously causing the sorcerer's head to be shaved by shaving the patient's head, or using a mantar to make the sorcerer dance in public. I have collected vivid reports of all three proofs, both in Jājarkoṭ and elsewhere (they seem particularly common in Nepal's capital, Kathmandu), but I have never witnessed any successful demonstration of them. Karṇa Vīr insisted that making a witch dance in public *(boksī nacāunu)* was still legally punishable. The fine levied on an accuser who could not prove the case with methods such as these was more than most villagers would spend in a year, a severe penalty strongly discouraging even private discussion of sorcery and witchcraft. Currently, possible fines remain significant and any litigation inevitably becomes very expensive; even so, accusations surface and lead to bitter disputes.

Shamans, therefore, hesitate to brag of their abilities as sorcerers. For years, none would discuss the issue with me, for curses are the final material that a shaman teaches a pupil, only when he determines that his student is "ready" to raise the dead and plague enemies. This silence had a serendipitous rupture, however, while I was discussing cures for madness with Gore Sārkī. My question was unclear, and he requested clarification: "Do you mean madness caused by deities *(deutā)*, or madness that we've caused ourselves?" This produced a detailed discussion, complete with texts of instructions, in which he explained techniques used to cause madness. Armed with this introduction, I was afterward able to elicit more material from other shamans, none of whom wanted to admit that some colleague possessed knowledge that they didn't. One basic technique uses mantars to send *vāṇ*, which has connotations of both "arrows," from Nepali *vān*, and "supernatural assistants," from Sanskrit *vāhana* (vehicle), to drive the victim crazy (5.33). A shaman may also command spirits, such as those of the recent dead (masān), ghosts *(bhut, pret)*, or even wild animals to attack an enemy, as the following suggests:

Om namāmo!
Rise up, dear masān! Rise up, dear āsān!
Rise up, bhut! Rise up, pret!
Hey, wake up!
Rise up, tigers! Rise up, bears!
Rise up, monkeys! Rise up, hundreds of thousands!
Rise up, bhut, pret of the lands!
Rise up, tigers, bears, monkeys!
Come, little brothers, take oaths!
Come, lick up the oaths!

[Directions to the shaman are embedded at this point in the text, and refer to another mantar in his collection.]

Bind the masān's hands with the *aṅgār* mantar,
send them to an enemy's house, their own share.
Hu! Hu! Hu!
Eat, masān, leave only bones at the enemy's house!

(2.2)

Other vāṇ that shamans command consist of natural phenomena such as fog, thunder, lightning, hail, rainbows, and locust swarms.

To avoid explicit and dangerous confrontations, cases of malicious "shamanizing" *(jhāṅgarī lāgnu)* ordinarily are subsumed within a larger category of disturbances, those of *gauḍā lāgnu.* This loosely means "to have a crisis, to reach an impasse," and more technically "to suffer a star obstruction." The most serious *gauḍā* is to reach the appointed time of death, a situation requiring deliberate interference with divinely fixed fate, exactly as fate must be tampered with to kill an enemy. Parallels between astrological crises and shamanic sorcery are further underscored by using the same text, the Recital of Tilīkarmā, to treat both situations. That text, telling of shamanic malice, significantly chooses to emphasize the shaman's skill at maintaining social order, rather than his abilities as a sorcerer, though it explicitly documents those malicious abilities as well (see 3.35):

He shamanized *[jhāṅgarī lāgyo]*
struck a blow, used his power,
played a secret trick on the king of Sijā.
The throne was cheerless,
the kingdom was cheerless,
the people were cheerless,
the offices and courts all closed.

He struck him with nasal blockage,
struck him with blocked ears,
struck him with a blocked stomach,
bit him with bone aches.
He went to Tilīkarmā, stayed there.

(2.3)

Tilīkarmā is the lowest underworld. Throughout their recitals, jhāṅgarīs ascend and descend the *mandāmī*, the seven levels of this world. They even heal otherworldly inhabitants. These episodes always demonstrate the shaman's superiority over other specialists, but most relevant to the discussion here, they also assert that a shaman can repair problems, like astrological fate, that originate in the heavens—precisely the application of this text, and a second category of causes shamans explicitly identify.

Treating cases of gauḍā requires various texts in addition to the Recital to Postpone the Star Obstructions, which together form a set of cosmological recitals. Different combinations are used depending on whether the patient is male or female, young or old, of high status or low. In every case, however, cosmological concerns find expression as social concerns. When the patient is male, the basic text used is the Recital of Tilīkarmā, also called the Recital to Cast Off Star Obstructions *(gauḍā phālne melā)*. Every shaman that I know has unequivocally stated that this is their most important recital. Not only used to treat cases of crises, and of shamanic sorcery, it also plays a prominent part in the initiation and death ceremonies of every shaman (Chapter 6). Every version of Tilīkarmā relates how the first shaman, called Jumrātam or Jhiṅgrātam in some versions, Purācan in others, acquires a wife whose sister marries the local ruler (whose identity also varies). The king and the shaman become enemies, and the shaman afflicts the king (or his son, the prince). In most cases, the vindictiveness of the shaman follows extreme provocation from the king, who is furious that his wife has stayed away scandalously long on a visit to Jumrātam's home. The king sends his attendants to bring back Jumrātam's heart (6.40):

"He has confused my queen, confounded my queen.
Go attendants,
bring me that longhair's warm heart, I'll eat it,
grind it in a grindstone, husk it in a rice husker,
leave it out to dry on a hill," he said.

(2.4)

Jumrātam tricks the messengers by coughing up an imitation of his own heart. The king orders it processed and, by eating it, becomes deathly ill. Given the antecedent provocations and seen as a dispute between social unequals, the text emphasizes the shaman's skill at maintaining social order, rather than his abilities as a sorcerer. Equally emphasized are his accessibility and impartiality, for at the end of the recital, when the king rewards him royally, Jumrātam's wife (the principal wife of a shaman is known as a *jhagrenī* or *jhaṅgerelnī*) makes him return most of the loot:

> Taking nine shares of grain, nine rolls of cloth,
> a payment of ninety thousand rupees,
> the jhāṅgarī came to his own home.
> The jhagrenī said,
> "Oh ho, these are a king's presents.
> You must consult in happy homes,
> you must consult in unhappy homes,
> You must consult in homes that have much,
> you must consult in homes that have nothing,
> the ordinary people cannot give that much,
> set a payment of one rupee, one hen,
> one share of grain, one share of sacred rice,
> one roll of cloth, give back everything else,
> the rulings of the day are the king's,
> the rulings of the night are yours, that's okay,
> you must make the rulings of the night,
> the king can make the rulings of the day."
> All of this the jhagrenī said.
> This is still true today.
>
> (2.5)

Thus the text also sets modest limits for paying a shaman, and establishes the principle that he must go when and wherever called, guidelines of which every shaman is aware, even to the extent of insisting that they would have to pay a fine if they were summoned sincerely but failed to go.

When a woman suffers from gauḍā, the appropriate text, the Dowry Recital *(daijo melā)*, continues the story of the world's creation, introducing women into the world. These episodes stress the divine ancestry of females, as opposed to the grossly material origin of men, but also relegate women to subordinate places in contemporary social order. The first man, Andhāserā, formed from sandalwood ash and chicken dung, requires a wife, and later, after the birth of a son, a daughter-in-law. Twice Indra sends one of his own descendants down to "the world of death":

> Andhāserā was old, he tore at his chest, he tore at the earth,
> he wailed and wept, was in tears.
> It was night at night, it was night at day.
> He was heard at Indra's house. "Go now, attendants, go,
> in the world of death, who is there,
> what's this, why this weeping?"
> The attendants came to the world of death.
> "Who's there, what's this, why this weeping?"
> "My eyes are blind, my ears are deaf,
> it's night at night, it's night at day,
> there's no one with me, no companion,
> no elder sister, no younger sister, at whose face can I look?"
> He wailed and wept, he tore at his chest, he tore at the earth.
> The attendants went to Indra's house. "Why does Andhāserā cry?"
> "'There's no one else, no companion,
> it's night at night, it's night at day,
> at whose face can I look?' he says,
> he tears at his chest, he tears at the earth, he wails and weeps."
> He gave him Maitācelī.
> "Go now, Maitācelī, to the world of death,
> that is your kingdom," he said.
> Maitācelī descended to the world of death,
> was given to Andhāserā.
> Six months, a full year passed, a son was born.
> "There's no one with me, no companion,
> no elder sister, no younger sister,
> it's night at night, it's night at day, at whose face can I look?"
> she tears at his chest, she wails.
> "Get a daughter-in-law, go now, Maitācelī,
> call one from your parents' home," he said.
> Maitācelī wailed and wept.
> "How can I go to my parents' house?" she said.
> She was heard at Indra's house. "Why does Maitācelī cry?
> Go now, attendants, to the world of death."
>
> (2.6)

Again the attendants descend to this world. They discover that Maitācelī needs a companion, a daughter-in-law. They report this to Indra, who sends them another of his relatives:

> He gave them Candravatī.
> "Wonderful daughter Candra, go now, Candra,
> below to the world of death,
> that is your kingdom," he said, gave her to the world of death.
> Candravatī descended seven levels of the world.
> Andhāserā was the father-in-law,
> Maitācelī was the mother-in-law.
>
> (2.7)

Since this world remains "dark at night, dark at day," the parents-in-law soon send their new daughter-in-law home to demand a dowry of nine suns and nine moons. Indra refuses and she commits suicide, becoming the first creature to die. He restores her to life, using the same techniques—waving yak tails, striking with a staff—that animated the first male (6.32). She returns to life fully human, and he reluctantly gives her the demanded dowry. It provides too much light and heat, however. Not only is it "day at day, day at night," the suns and moons dry up the earth and set it aflame:

> With nine moons, with nine suns,
> the night was day, the day was day,
> there was hissing, there was trembling.
> Dry trees were torched, green trees were scorched,
> wet season springs dried up, dry season springs fried up,
> the sixty great rivers were struck down.
> Proper rivers were drying,
> the stupid race of man sat in the shade of a lentil bush.
> The land began to burn, the soil began to burn.
>
> (2.8)

To remove the superfluous heavenly bodies, the father-in-law orders the daughter-in-law to do inauspicious things. The first is to address him with abuse, using the special abusive verb conjugation found in Nepali, usually reserved for animals, very small children, wives, and daughters-in-law. After eight inauspicious actions, one sun and one moon remain.

> "Do something, daughter-in-law,
> do something inauspicious!" he said.

"What inauspicious thing, father-in-law?" she said.
"Address your elders abusively!" he said.
"How can I address my elders abusively?" she said.
"Say it!" he said, one moon, one sun departed.
"To a guest arriving at dusk,
say that there's no place to stay!" he said,
one moon, one sun departed.
"Hit a dog sitting in a doorway with a stick, daughter-in-law!"
one moon, one sun departed.
"With uncombed hair go in and out of the house!" he said,
one moon, one sun departed.
"Comb your hair backward with a wooden comb,
daughter-in-law!"
one moon, one sun departed.
"Beat together two pots!" he said,
one moon, one sun departed.
"Rub your right foot with your left foot, daughter-in-law!"
one moon, one sun departed.
"Spit atop the drying shelf ["doorstep" in another version],
daughter-in-law!"
one moon, one sun departed.
Eight moons departed, eight suns departed,
one moon remained, one sun remained,
they rose in the east, they set in the west.
There was nightfall, dawn was born,
the land was chilled, the soil was chilled,
wet season springs bubbled, dry season springs trickled,
the Sattivatī Gaṅgā began to flow with force.

(2.9)

Indra resuscitates the dying race of man, repeating for a third time the life-giving techniques that earlier created man and revived his own descendant. The shaman mimics precisely these actions over his own patient. Finally, he (Indra in the recital, the shaman in the present) transfers away the star obstructions stage by stage, from the house top to its feet, to the door step, to the courtyard, and out to the crossroads. The star obstructions complain: "What will we eat when we go, what will we take as we go?" Indra negotiates with different animals to ransom man. Mother Goat finally agrees to sacrifice her son, so long as his flesh is eaten, half of it going to the householder, the other half to the shaman (1.8). The star obstructions are satisfied and retreat. As the recital emphasizes, since even heaven-dwelling beings are not immune to the touch of death, the mortality of humans is inevitable. Unable to cure death, shamans claim only to delay it. At best, their rituals may force it to retreat a few steps, though no permanent postponement is possible.

Within the narrative, this recital gives step-by-step directions for restoring the dead to life, for escorting the star obstructions away from the patient's house, and for selecting appropriate animals for sacrifice. It vividly reminds women to behave properly or else expect cosmological catastrophe. These directions and injunctions continue in the Recital of Kadum and Padum, and the Drongo Recital, texts applied to young mothers and children, whose star obstructions are called *khaḍgā*. These texts warn parents-in-law not to be too harsh to their daughters-in-law. The in-laws of the recital demand impossible tasks, such as fetching water in a sieve and chopping firewood without an axe. The poor daughter-in-law, whose husband is away on a trading trip, has no time to nurse her infant son. She keeps asking it to wait, her "pak, pak" ("wait, wait") sounding like a mother hen. The starving baby undergoes metamorphosis into a drongo bird *(nyāulo)*, whose cry, *nyāu, nyāu,* resembles that of a hungry baby. Various trees nourish the baby bird with their milky or bloody sap. It matures and flies away. He later causes his father's death, luring him higher and higher into a tree with his plaintive cries until the father falls, becoming a spirit who captures the souls of small children (4.28).

After the child in the recital has tried different reincarnations but finally returns to its mother, the force of the narrative abruptly shifts into a paraenetic section (4.23). The shaman directly addresses the child (whether present or unborn) of his patient, using language very similar to the Mongolian text reported by Bawden (1962).

> Where would you go, son?
> You will find no path, you will find no alms,
> keep your heartmind [*mancit*] in a bronze plate, a bronze cup,
> stay in your mother's lap, stay in your father's lap,
> don't let your heartmind wander,
> don't take them elsewhere,
> don't leave home, don't leave your own house.
>
> (2.10)

She prophesies the child's fate if it chooses to be born to a horse, buffalo, cow, sheep, goat, pig, or chicken. The child nevertheless tries each, but dies violently every time. Her curse concludes:

> "you will find no path to take, you will find no alms to take,
> you will come to be born in my lap.
> If you rise into the sky, Indra will stop you,
> if you sink into hell, Vāsu Deu will stop you,
> if you go east, Bhairabnāth will stop you,
> if you go south, Gorakhnāth will stop you,
> if you go west, Ratannāth will stop you,
> if you go north, Candannāth will stop you,
> if you rise into the sky, a hand will hold your foot,
> if you sink into the underworld,
> a hand will hold your topknot,"
> the mother delivered a prophecy, delivered a curse.
>
> (2.11)

The shaman speaks this directly to a dying infant, or, in the case of a woman unable to bear children properly, or whose children all die at an early age, to the still-unborn children, and to recently deceased children whose presence troubles their family. The recital instructs the child's spirit that it can find no other home, and should return to its parents, repeating the sentiments of the overworked mother. This recital is also useful in conjunction with others to treat cases of a child's soul loss, a third source of affliction commonly diagnosed and treated by shamans.

Each text used to treat star obstructions translates what allegedly originate as astrological disturbances into local problems of social order, teaching listeners the correct forms of that order. The one to treat males warns kings to be just, and shamans not to be greedy; the Dowry Recital, for females, warns women of the dangers of unseemly behavior; the Drongo Recital, for children's crises, teaches parents-in-law to moderate their demands of a daughter-in-law and tells the souls of children that they are better off in human form than in any other rebirth, so they should remain home and be dutiful. All three explicitly connect cosmology with ordered social relations, translating those relations into clear, moralistic injunctions complete with heuristic examples of the consequences when they are violated.

There are many specifically unfortunate astrological configurations, though most are not severe enough to constitute a crisis. Another severe star obstruction is the astrological disturbance of *mūl.* Mūl occurs when certain planets of both a newly born child and either of its parents occupy the *mūl nakṣatra,* one of twenty-seven subdivisions of the lunar elliptic based on fixed stars, superimposed on the twelve houses of the zodiac. Mūl is a crisis that lasts for a finite, calculable length, sometimes a lifetime, sometimes for just a few moments. The parent who shares the configuration is fated to die quickly if it sees the child within mūl's duration. A shaman sometimes intervenes in these cases, as will be detailed below. Since the spirit Maṣṭā was himself a mūl birth, his mediums (*dhāmīs*, discussed in the next chapter) show considerable effectiveness in dealing with this problem. But as for other problems, Maṣṭā, through his medium, simply promises his protection to the affected individual, remaining silent on issues of cause and effect. This is the generic solution applied to all problems for which dhāmic spirits are consulted. Astrologers *(jaiśī)* can diagnose mūl, but do not treat it. Shamans rarely meddle with less serious astrological configurations, though some supply amulets *(jantar)* to ward off their negative influences (Fig. 3.1), a service more commonly performed by local astrologers.

Astrologically determined fate often compounds other causes, however, both nonphysical and quasi-physical, as in the cases of women's reproductive problems, another set of problems that requires a shaman's intervention. This category includes not only miscarriages and stillbirths, but also infertility, the recurrent deaths of children at an early age, and the failure to bear male offspring. A wife's karma, rather than a husband's, is usually responsible for these problems, though some may be diagnosed as a child's crisis. Possible contributory causes for these problems include:

1. offending spirits, particularly the patrilineal family gods *(kūl deutā, pitār);*
2. careless acts of ritual pollution, such as accidentally touching or stepping over droppings of another woman's menstrual blood;
3. having once had an abortion performed, in this or in a previous life.

Three sets of agents—the Nine Nāgs, *moc,* and *rāh*—administer these afflictions. All three are related classes of entities that can find their way into a woman's womb, and must be extracted by the shaman. He sucks on the patient's stomach after making ritual cuts above it with a blade while reciting a mantar:

> Of iron shape, of iron form, knife made of iron,
> cause this knife to fall on the heads of the Nine Nāgs.
>
> (2.12)

This symbolic operation is done in the middle of the Recital of Kadum and Padum, a story that vaguely recalls the episode of Vinatā and Kadrū found in the *Mahābhārata* 1.5, a rare, severely transformed appearance of classic mythology in the shamans' material. The recital relates the impious behavior of the younger of two sisters. It was because of her sinful actions that God (Bhagavān) introduced these forces into the world. She herself was their first victim. The elder sister performs austerities for twelve years to obtain the blessing of sons, while the younger sister lives luxuriously instead:

> I eat richly, dress richly, wrap up richly,
> I have a wealth of blankets, a wealth of bedding,
> I have everything, I will not meditate,
> I will not request the blessing of sons.
>
> (2.13)

When the time comes for the elder sister to collect her blessing, however, the younger sister deceives God and receives it instead. Learning of his mistake, he turns the nine sons that he promised her into the Nine Nāgs, moc, and rāh. Nāgs parallel Kadrū's sons, the Nine Nāgās, serpent kings of the underworld, who are closely associated with fertility. However, with the exception of Vāsuki Nāg (who was the rope when the gods and demons churned the ocean), all names listed in the recital differ from the classical ones. Shamans identified them strictly as causes of infertility, premature births, stillbirths, and drying up of a mother's milk. They could report no positive aspects to their characters or to their interventions.

Moc simply fall out of the sky. When a woman is unfortunate enough to step over one, it may enter her womb and cause her to be infertile by drying up her menstruation. Witches may collect them and deliberately insert them into their victims. Moc resemble bird embryos, an image perhaps derived from the appearance of a two- or three-months'-old human embryo, a time when miscarriages are particularly common. There are several different forms which moc can take; Abi Lal sketched four possibilities (see Fig. 2.1).

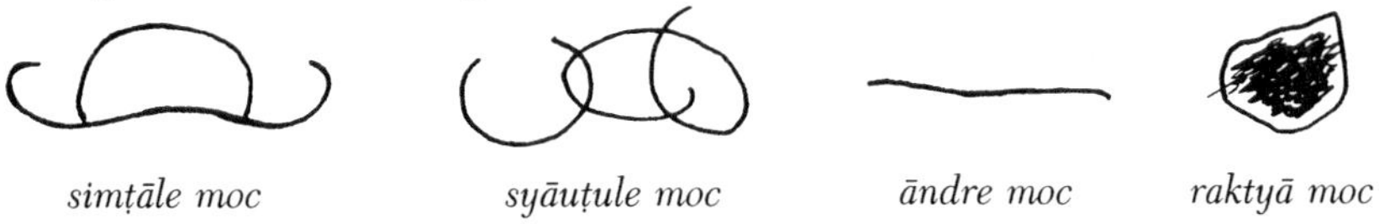

Figure 2.1. Varieties of *moc*

Rāh are spirits of deceased children, including stillbirths, who wander around trying to participate in the family, or who reenter the womb in a futile attempt to be reborn. Once in the womb, rāh obtain a quasi-physical existence and closely resemble moc. When drawing moc, Abi Lal included a picture of one (see Fig. 2.2).

Figure 2.2. *Rāh moc*

When neither can be extracted, rāh may be causing adverse effects from a distance, possibly along with the myriad spirits of the forest. In such cases, the appropriate supplemental recital is that of Satī Barbā, a mythical hero who was the first being strong enough to subdue those spirits (6.28). As a result, many shamans now worship him as one of their lineage gods (kūl deutā). His recital helps to retrieve lost wits, a condition known as *sāto gāyo*. Losing one's wits is a common problem that results from falling or from fright. Ordinarily it is not serious, and can be simply treated by a household mantar. Occasionally the victim's senses fail to return, having been captured by Hiyā Rāj. Another forest-dwelling spirit, he originated when Satī Barbā slew an evil king, and has joined the many other malicious forces explicitly named in the recital. These others include the father killed by the drongo child and the descendants of the Kubaṁs Lāmā (the lāmā of "bad lineage"). He is the only lāmā mentioned in the public repertories, suggesting that these shaman texts are relatively independent of Buddhist influences (see next chapter). Satī Barbā announces his intentions to protect the world, protect the days, to kill evil forces, and goes off into the forest:

> Turning around backward-flowing rivers,
> killing Forest Rāh, killing Hiyā Rāj,
> killing spells and charms,
> grinding the cliffs to make the plains.
>
> (2.14)

Other agents subdued belong to much larger classes of minor spirits, many of whom cause uncontrolled and disruptive states of possession along with numerous other symptoms, including many varieties of madness. Sometimes, a diagnostic session conclusively identifies one specific spirit responsible for the situation. This most often happens when that spirit speaks through its possessed victim and announces the offense that incurred its wrath, such as polluting a sacred spot, or failing to make a promised offering. In such cases, that spirit will be personally appeased, with an offering at its shrine. Likely spirits include the Burmā and Bajyū (the haunting spirits of, respectively, male and female suicides), the eighteen brothers Barāh (whose story of origin appears in the recital to treat such possessions), Deurālī (the spirit of springs), and all the local spirits who inhabit particular hilltops, trees, waterfalls, and rivers.

Sometimes, the diagnostic session does not isolate a single spirit, or those involved are related to the shaman. These situations require a more general appeasement of untamed agents. This begins with the Recital of Gorāpā. Gorāpā and his sons collectively represent the autochthonous threats that originate in the uncultivated, wild parts of the earth, from the forests, streams, lakes, and ridges found outside the boundaries of human settlement (Lecomte-Tilouine 1987). This group includes not only various ghosts and demons, but also physical curses like wasps, wild bees, and vipers. The recital tells of the competitions and conflicts of two brothers, Gorāpā and Serāpā, born one day apart from trees on the high ridges. They play various games, bumping together like competitive males of different species and trying different feats of strength. Serāpā wins every contest, usually leaving Gorāpā injured or humiliated. As a result, they divide the earth between themselves.

"So, older brother,
let's cross the rainy season flooded river ford," he said,
they went to cross the rainy season flooded river ford.
Serāpā Ranja stayed dry crossing over,
Gorāpā Ranja was swept off down stream.
"So, older brother, until now you've won,
I've lost, our promise is fulfilled,
I've lost, you've won, lift me out," he said.
He made him promise three times, lifted him out.
"You have seven sons, I have eight sons,
dropping a rope line, let's cross the flooded river,
let's allot the furrows, let's allot the landmarks,
Serāpā Ranja, older brother, or later they'll argue,
your sons and my sons," he said.

(2.15)

Gorāpā tricks his older brother Serāpā out of ownership of the fertile lands, by choosing more permanent boundary markers and then delaying for a year their examination of them. Later, Gorāpā's sons murder Serāpā by setting out hunting traps in the forest to which he and his sons have retreated: he falls into one of their pits and dies impaled on sharp stakes. His sons come to claim vengeance, but Gorāpā appeases them by surrendering all the fertile land to them. He and his own sons go into hiding:

They went to stay in the middle of Budo Lake,
went to stay in the middle of rivers,
went to stay as wasp stingers in trees,
went to stay as wild bee stingers on cliffs,
went to stay as short-tailed star vipers in Śilā Khāgar,
went to stay as young wild goats on Rātā Pahar,
went to stay as pheasant wings in Chārkābhoṭ,
went to stay as honeybee stingers in hives,
went to stay as hornet stingers in leaves,
went to stay as bears and she-bears,
tigers and she-tigers in Śilā Khāgar,
went to stay as young red deer in Khairyān groves,
went to stay as wild sows and wild boars in Bāṛejatāka.
Gorāpā's sons said,
"What would we eat, father, what would we wear?"
Those sons that stayed in the water were Jal Barāh,

those that stayed on hilltops were Iṇyāl Thiṇyāl,
those that stayed in trees on jhāṅgarī tombs were jhāṅgarīs,
those that stayed in waterfalls were ghosts,
those that stayed in springs were Deurālī,
those that stayed in rivers were *vāi*,
those that stayed in bodies were *rāi*.

(2.16)

"What happened to the descendants of Serāpā?" I asked Karṇa Vīr. "That's us!" he replied. The greater local spirits, such as Maṣṭā or Mahākāl, are not included among the threatening forces descended from Gorāpā. Shamans insist that they can control these major spirits as well, by using the Recital of Tilīkarmā and adding the spirit's personal history. Also excluded here are some spirits who specialize in driving victims mad. These include the female divinities collectively known as the Mālā, most especially Ālaṅg Mālaṅg, along with their male counterparts, the Eighteen Brothers Barāh. There is a particular recital devoted to the histories of each of these collectivities. Each such recital reminds the spirits that they are subsidiary to the shaman. Each exhorts them to return to the wilderness where they belong, orders them to leave humans alone, and reminds them of previous negotiations in which they relinquished all rights to the better, more productive, lands (see 2.27, below).

Summarizing the variety of spirits that can cause problems into a loosely structured hierarchy:

1. the chief local gods (deutā), particularly Maṣṭā;
2. minor deities of nonhuman origin, such as the Barāh and the Mālā;
3. avenging spirits of high-caste suicides, the Burmā (males) and the Bajyū (females);
4. unpacified ancestors (pitār, bāyu);
5. villagers who died by suicide or by accident (siyo, pret);
6. ghosts of human origin (e.g., Hiyā Rāj), the spirits of recent dead (masān), those of dead shamans, of dead witches (*ḍaṁkī,* vāi);
7. ghosts and demons of nonhuman origin (Iṇyāl Ṭhiṇyāl, bhut, *rākṣas*);
8. quasi-sprits (Nāg, moc, rāh);
9. shaman accessorial spirits, including those of living or dead nonhuman creatures *(dhām, dhuwā, bīr),* of plants and inanimate natural forces *(barāṅg, māphī, sawā)*, and those of their tutelary spirits *(piṭṭṛ, gel).*

The examples with which I illustrate each category are not exhaustive—hundreds of entries can be individually named; for partial listings of some of these categories, see Oppitz (1986), Lecomte-Tilouine (1987), Greve (1981/82), and Macdonald (1962). When I asked Abi Lal to name important spirits that he might summon, he recited a list of more than 250, each indexed by the location of its shrine. Every spirit in that listing belongs only to the first three categories above, while every other category can be similarly expanded with precisely identified entities. However, this general classification adequately shows that shamans recognize many distinct types of spirit-entities as well as nonspiritual entities that may trouble their clients.

This ordering of spirits is my own. I have discussed it with the shamans, who offered neither objections nor alternatives to it, but their own accounts of unseen forces are less hierarchical and less structured. This is probably one reason shamans' theories of causation have sometimes been described, in varying degrees, as vague or ambiguous (Allen 1976; Gaenszle 1992; Holmberg 1989). But a lack of hierarchy need not imply ambiguity. Rather, it suggests that every potential threat is a serious one and becomes foremost while being treated, reflecting the South Asian tendency toward what Max Müller called "henotheism," the belief in gods alternately regarded as the highest, each treated in turn as though absolutely independent and supreme. At the other extreme, a mantar describing the subduing of evil influences by a kānphaṭa yogin illustrates how the various agents of affliction can sometimes be lumped together:

> He did "aum," he did "aum,"
> *māi masān* of the Dead,
> Gods and Goddesses [*deva* and *devī*],
> Witches and Minor Witches [*kapṭī* and boksī],
> Ghosts and Ghouls [bhut and pret],
> he thrusts into hell.
>
> (2.17)

To hear "gods and goddesses" alongside "ghosts, ghouls, and witches" as malicious forces to be thrust into hell is surprising, but it does not necessarily imply a vague conception of supernatural beings. Shamans commonly speak of multiple worlds with differing ontological statuses, but it is always for some particular purpose, such as curing those who suffer from multiple causes, that the boundaries of worlds are equivocally drawn. Blurring boundaries is a deliberate technique practiced by shamans, not some fuzzy state from which their thinking suffers.

All the problems so far discussed are good reasons to consult a shaman. However, the most common reason to summon a shaman is for cases of suspected witchcraft. Ever since the battles between the first shaman and the first witches, the two groups have been celebrated antagonists. Everyone recognizes cases of witchcraft as the special domain of shamans, even other ritual specialists. Technically, the protection of a dhāmic spirit should also cure a sufferer from the effects of witches, but victims of witchcraft rarely consult the mediums of those spirits. That is, witchcraft is rarely mentioned in such consultations. In Jājarkoṭ District, the most important dhāmic spirit is Maṣṭā of Saru. Of over a hundred consultations with his medium that I've taped, only three involved witchcraft accusations. In none of those cases were the accusations, suggested by supplicants themselves, developed by the medium. I would not want to argue from a statistical point of view, however, since dhāmic spirits are expected to protect anyone who offers them blood sacrifices, from any manner of affliction. Treating every case the same, mediums have no interest in exploring the details of causes and effects: the spirit either promises or declines to help. There is no need to identify specific causes of afflictions, no specifically dhāmic etiology.

Witches cause many maladies less extreme than death. When the Nine Little Sisters were subdued by the first shaman, they danced. Speaking directly to the witches, Karṇa Vīr's recital relates this dance:

> Go down or I'll put you down,
> be put down or else go down,
> at this point you began to dance.
> You danced with a hold on your heads,
> became the vāi of aching heads;
> you danced with a hold on your hair,
> became the vāi of oozing blisters;
> you danced with a hold on your torsos,
> became the vāi of sharp pains;
> you danced with a hold on your flesh,
> became the vāi of white skin splotches;
> you danced with a hold on your bones,
> became the vāi of burning joints;

you danced with a hold on your waists,
became the vãi of stomach cramps;
you danced moving your whole bodies,
became the vãi of bloody blisters;
you danced with a hold on your teeth,
became the vãi of loose teeth;
you danced with a hold on your lips,
became the vãi of blistered lips;
you danced with a hold on your eyes,
became the vãi of failing sight;
you danced with a hold on your noses,
became the vãi of blocked noses;
you danced with a hold on your ears,
became the vãi of infected ears;
you became the curse of cramps,
the curse of shifting pains,
the vãi of deformities,
you became the eighty-four vãi.

(2.18)

Having resulted from the death agonies of the original witches, vãi have characters quasi-independent from the witches themselves. Contemporary witches now command them, sending them out to cause havoc exactly as shamans dispatch vān or masān. They resemble *bāyu*, the spirits of those who died by accident or suicide, or whose corpses were polluted. Widely known throughout Nepal (Höfer and Shrestha 1973; Sharma 1970; Gaborieau 1975a; Messerschmidt 1976; and Stone 1988), bāyu result, however, from the deaths of particular, identifiable, members of one's own family, while the vãi survive anonymously on the edges of villages. The eighty-four vãi all cause different localized aches, pains, and other specific physical problems of the body. These, significantly, are the only afflictions that shaman texts attribute to witches. Popularly attributed problems like loss of breath in the night (for which there is a specific term: *aitḥan lāgnu*), mysterious bites, nonphysical catastrophes to property or person are absent from the texts. Shamans laughed when I questioned them about popularly held beliefs. They would not categorically deny these extremely generalized symptoms, but drew careful distinctions between superstition and reality when it came to witches, upholding the texts' versions as accurate. In this case, as for other categories of affliction, shaman texts form a precisely identified subset within a total set of possibilities more ambiguously held by nonspecialists. From the shaman's point of view, witches, when unable to cause outright death, produce very solidly physical afflictions, consistent with their own physical state as humans. Gumāne's somewhat different version of this recital further supports this conclusion. In it, the original shaman drowns each of the older eight witches at different river fords along the lower Bherī River. Again, each becomes a different *vāi:*

1. *aulo āgan vāi*—causer of malarial and other periodically recurring fevers;
2. *hādyā vāi*—causer of bone aches;
3. *ḍhaḍe vāi*—causer of diseases in children's stomachs;
4. *lāṭā aulo vāi*—causer of the severest malarial fevers and of deafness;
5. *Kārtik maināmā lāgne āgan vāi*—causer of fevers that come in the month of Kārtik (October/November);
6. *nakṣaro vāi*—causer of diseases of the nose, and of blocked noses;
7. *hāḍ khānyā, muṭu khānyā, salkyā vāi*—consumer of bones; of the heart;
8. *cālne vāi*—causer of aches throughout the body; if they reach the heart, they cause death.

While the details differ, the afflictions have a very physical reality, just as do those of Karṇa Vīr's version, and these afflictions, too, have a physical locus in the bodies of those who suffer them.

I will next discuss methods used to treat these various afflictions, but, so far, what can be concluded about shamanic theories of afflictions? Throughout the texts, sources of ailments and crises are explicitly postulated. These spectrums of causality provide the rationale for the intervention by spirit possession and spirit manipulation in an equally wide range of cases, ranging from snakebite to the approach of death's messenger. Each of these diverse continua demonstrates the unreasonableness of considering the practice of shamans as comparable to secular systems of medicine, of evaluating their activities by the rationale of such systems, or attempting to create hybrids between them, a point well argued by Caspar Miller (1979:187), who cautions against attempts to incorporate shamans (and other autonomous indigenous health care systems) into some "appropriate" modern hybrid.

Neither, however, is a shaman's practice exclusively religious in orientation. Shamans deal specifically with both ontic and physic dimensions of everyday problems of illness, affliction, and death, satisfying human predicaments no purely epistemic medical system is able to treat. They endeavor to reorder and refashion both seen and unseen worlds, and recognize well-defined ranges of forces in each. At the end of the Tilīkarmā recital, a shaman's powers are summarized in a speech the King of Sijā makes to Jumrātam:

> "Older brother, the rulings of the day are mine,
> the rulings of the night are yours.
> When someone is attacked by a spirit of the dead [masān],
> when someone is attacked by a ghost [bhut],
> when someone is attacked by a god [deutā],
> those rulings you will make at night.
> When the people have problems,
> when someone is worried,
> when someone has a dispute over land,
> when someone has a dispute over a divorce,
> those rulings I will make," said the king.
> "You are the older brother,
> I am the younger brother,
> the rulings of the night are yours,
> the rulings of the day are mine," he said.
>
> (2.19)

Shamans, those who make the rulings of the night, claim no authority in problems of divorce or land tenure (unless, of course, these issues are complicated by sorcery, witchcraft, or astrological conditions), separating the political from the medical. This limits shamans from converting their abilities into tangible social influence. But through a refined etiology, spirits, ghosts, and gods are delineated not only from one another but from other specific, clearly conceived causes of affliction. Shamans, through the texts they memorize, learn to identify these multiplicities of causes. Patients and public also learn to recognize these relations of specific causes to specific conditions, as the shamans repeatedly recite their texts. By actively maintaining this shared knowledge, these shared meanings, and these shared explanations, shamanic practices sustain their contemporary relevance. "The rulings of the night" continue to be required, rulings that other interventionary specialists and other interventionary systems cannot deliver. By featuring oral texts in every ceremony that they perform, shamans effectively reproduce worlds that require shamanic interventions.

Each intervention involves a distinctive ritual. To examine these helps to develop a more thorough understanding of what a shaman is. While the variety of ritual activity is no less limited than is either the diversity of possible afflictions or the selection of texts used to treat them, the acts are more flexible than are the texts. That is, there are few specific techniques uniquely used to treat only a particular affliction or to accompany only a particular recital. Instead, many of the activities are repeated in different performances even when distinct texts are used and distinct afflictions are being treated. Although elaborately constructed, the rituals can be broken up into smaller constituent units, different sequences of which are used in different cases.

Again, following the practice of the shamans themselves, I privilege the descriptions found within their texts. Inevitably when I discussed ritual techniques *(vidhī)* with shamans, they would resort to quoting from the appropriate text that describes what should be done, rather than try to elaborate extemporaneously an account of that activity. The reverse, using a ritual activity to clarify a text, was extremely rare. The usual response that I got when trying to clarify an obscure passage of text was for the shaman to repeat it carefully a few times, so that I could "understand" it clearly—the test of my understanding was to repeat it back accurately. For the shamans, words and what they designate have a much closer connection than they do for, say, someone familiar with modern language philosophy: theirs is a constitutive theory of language, with direct identities between words and objects (see Chapter 5).

Sometimes, sections of the recitals that describe ritual activity are so indexically tied to what should be done as they are recited (e.g., "he made one motion," 2.25 below) that I required additional explanations and gestures from the shamans to clarify them. Such explanations were often not very satisfactory, being nearly as vague as the passages themselves. Just attending ceremonies in which they are performed is little help, for it is often too dark to see much. However, the audience is equally unable to penetrate this opacity, so as long as we focus on the public side of what shamans do, this obscurity is less a problem than it might initially seem. It is experienced as much by patients and audiences as by an ethnographer. Occasionally irremediable deixis can therefore be marginalized, again supporting my argument that the shaman texts are themselves the best possible basis from which to understand shamanic ritual activity. Listening to the texts that accompany each performance reveals the structure of the ritual activities as well as their rationale and significance. Here, I show how the texts not only refer to, but also help clarify, both the details and the meaning of the rituals which shamans perform.

Consider an account of the very first shaman performance, found in Karṇa Vīr's Recital for Postponing the Star Obstructions. This is what Jumrātam says and does when summoned to Indra's heaven to evaluate his abilities as an intercessor:

> He assembled his equipment, beat a copper plate,
> "Begin a transfer with the right foot,
> a good period of sunlight will result,
> begin a transfer with the left foot,
> a good period of twenty-four hours will result," he said.
> Chirenāth, Ciplai Gaurī, Cāyāneṭī he crossed,
> he went to Indra's house.
> He danced and drummed out to the crossroads,
> he danced and drummed back from the crossroads
> [alternate reading: played the spirits Ālaṅg and Mālaṅg],
> searched from the top of a ceremonial pole
> [alternate reading: assembled his *suwā*],
> "Listen, everyone! The seven times of natural death,
> I will make into one time,
> the fourteen times of unnatural death,
> I will make into one time,
> I will postpone the planets,
> will postpone the star obstructions,
> will postpone the crises,
> will postpone the planetary threats,
> barren cows, lame oxen,
> I will make into valuable property," he said.
>
> (2.20)

This passage refers to all the chief features of a shaman's performance: his need for paraphernalia, including the costume and drum; the making of cryptic pronouncements, the part of a seance known as "speaking" *(baknu)*, when the audience asks questions and the shaman gives advice; magical travel, here, instantaneously crossing the difficult mountain passes and valleys on the path souls take at death; dancing and drumming to and from the crossroads while possessed by specific, identifiable spirits; and making a diagnosis. The passage also explicitly announces his deliberate intervention to postpone fate. Finally, the ceremonial pole refers to the rites of initiation and their yearly reenactment, when the shaman climbs a pine tree trunk erected in the center of the village to deliver prophecies while physically poised on the boundary of heaven and earth (Chapter 6). The lines that refer to drumming and dancing and searching from the pole top do so metonymically, using the particular spirits involved. Only the most basic requirements, such as mustard seeds and a fire, are not explicitly referenced, subsumed under "he assembled his equipment."

The "star obstructions" mentioned in this passage are, of course, gauḍā. As has been shown, they are one of the most significant shamanic concerns, calling for several of the most important and most cosmological texts. Correspondingly, they call for a greater variety of ritual activity than do other situations. The crucial part of the treatment, though, like the treatment of nearly all other afflictions, is an animal sacrifice. The passage quoted above (1.8) continues with Jumrātam's attempts to find an animal willing to be the substituted victim in place of man.

> "Mother Goat, you must go to the star obstructions."
> "This is not my share of sacrifice,
> my sacrifices I will give at the goddess's shrine,
> I will go for important things,
> I will not go for unimportant things," she said.
> "Mother Pig, you must go to the star obstructions."
> "This is not my share, this is not my sacrifice,
> my piglets I will give to be killed by jhāṅgarīs."
> "Go now, attendants, in Maraṅ Land, Rāvaṇ's house,
> there's an old cock, and old hen, bring them here," he said.
> (2.21)

After negotiations, first with the queen of the underworld, Rāvaṇ's wife, and then with the chickens themselves, the cock and hen agree to satisfy the star obstructions as man's proxy. In return they obtain special privileges, such as being allowed to scratch for food and defecate even inside kitchens:

> They went to Maraṅ Land, Rāvaṇ's house.
> "You must give the old cock, the old hen,

Rāvaṇ Mother," they said.
"You cannot buy my hen,
diamond, pearls, a thousand rupees is the price," she said.
From the cage, "Open up my cage,
I will change my price myself," said the old hen.
They opened the cage, the old hen spoke,
"Full pots I will upset, clean pots I will dirty,"
she trembled lightly, trembled more heavily,
"That is my price,
I will go for happy deaths, I will go for unhappy deaths,
will increase what's around, will increase what's found."

(2.22)

When I asked Karṇa Vīr what else he needed for such a ceremony besides the animal, he hesitantly attempted to recall the requirements, paused, then quoted directly from the Recital for Offering to the Nine Planets, which relates the creation and cursing of man. He "fast-forwarded" to the list of things that were first demanded by Mahādev himself when he descended to earth to perform a *pūjā* (ritual sacrifice) and accept the fate of man as an offering:

He got nine grains, got nine mustard seeds,
got nine flowers, got nine cloths,
got black goats, got black cloth,
made an offering of grain, made an offering of wealth,
made an offering of gold, silver, copper,
made nine shares of garlands,
got nine trees, the fruit of nine trees,
the leaves of nine trees,
nine little sacks, nine little packs,
to the Time of Death, the Messenger of Death,
he gave their share.
Mahādev took his pair of begging bowls to the road,
put main man in the begging bowls, gave away main man,
Mahādev took the black goats, took them to the crossroads,
gave away nine shares,
gave away nine little sacks, nine little packs,
gave away at the Barmā Crossroads, cut the black goats,
gave away a load of blood.

(2.23)

Nine, the number of planets, of Viṣṇu's incarnations so far, of the Bhawānī sisters, and of the original witches, has been a crucial number in Himalayan rituals for millennia, having settled into unquestioned tradition. Mahādev created the nine planets from his own discarded, leprous body after taking a new *avatār* (reincarnation) (3.9). These planets do not quite correspond to those of Western astronomy. They are the Sun, Moon, Mercury, Venus, Mars, Saturn, Jupiter, and the nodal points of the moon, Rāhu and Ketu. Since these latter are the only points at which an eclipse can take place, and since due to parallax an eclipse sometimes occurs when both the sun and moon are above the horizon, they are regarded as genuinely physical, but invisible, bodies, responsible for eclipses. I could not engage the shamans in any interesting speculation as to the importance of the number nine—"That's just how it is" *(tyestai cha)*, or "Whatever the guru taught us, that's it" *(jo jo gurule sikāyo, tyai ho)*, typify the inevitable responses to such lines of inquiry. Only Mahādev himself would demand nine goats, though—contemporary shamans are keenly aware of their clients' more limited resources. In any case, nine is an ideal number for any of the things mentioned, and ordinarily a dishful of each item suffices—only when the offering is for witches or nāgs is it crucial that nine dishes of offerings (balls of ash mixed with blood, with chicken feathers stuck into them) be set at the crossroads.

As noted above, gauḍā require different texts depending on whether the patient is a man, a woman, or a child. In each case, the ritual possibilities that accompany these recitals are fairly similar, though a chicken rather than a goat is always adequate when a very young child is the patient. Instead of distinct rituals for different cases, the shaman has for any given case a variety of options. Each of these differently illustrates the activities of repairing and postponing adverse fate and setting up barriers to protect the patient from its return. The different possibilities are not exclusive; a shaman may perform several of them for the same patient and even in the same session, depending on how close death seems and how extensive the patient's family offerings are (or how closely related the patient is, since shamans in this area frequently treat members of their own family). Karṇa Vīr, for example, explicitly stated that the more important the patient, the more elaborate the ritual. Shamans may also save some possibilities for a sequel if the patient has shown no signs of improvement after the first try.

Many rituals differently illustrate the activities of repairing and postponing adverse fate and setting up barriers to protect the patient from its return. Two of these incorporate explicit acts of raising the patient heavenward, where the crossed stars need repair. In the first, the shaman moves the patient's foot step by step up a small model of a pole ladder, in which he has cut nine notches; in the second, nine relatives and neighbors lift the patient as she crouches atop nine winnowing trays. To reinforce the sense that the patient is being conveyed into the heavens, the shaman sometimes suspends models of the sun and moon from the main roofbeam of the central room of the house along with a plant shoot (sometimes just a bunch of cinnamon or guava leaves). The patient is lifted up to them. While elevated, the patient should bite the plant shoot. Upon return, the recital takes the form of a dialogue between the shaman and the patient, with the shaman speaking both parts:

> Did you eat the green grass, the fresh water?
> Yes, did you see the nine suns, the nine moons?
> Yes, did you cross the seven star obstructions,
> the seven heavenly barriers?
> Yes, if you ascend to the sky,
> I'll pull you pack by your feet.
> If you descend to hell,
> I'll pull you back by your topknot.
>
> (2.24)

When a shoot has been tied to the roofbeam for this ritual and the patient "tastes it" when lifted, her family plants it the next day. Its life course will mirror that of the patient; if it catches and sprouts, the patient will recover, otherwise not. Another prediction is calculated by filling the tray under the patient with grain (ideally, nine measures of it), usually corn kernels. The patient grasps some of these with her toes. Upon her return from the heavens, the shaman counts the number of kernels grasped in the toes to decide whether the ritual has succeeded. However, no shared system seems to exist for this calculation—some said that an even number of kernels was auspicious, others said an odd number indicated success. Hitchcock notes a similar lack of system in the Bhujī Valley, where the same rituals are performed. There, following the ceremony, the nine measures of grain raised in the winnowing along with the patient are later brewed into beer, which is shared by the shaman and the patient (Hitchcock 1974b).

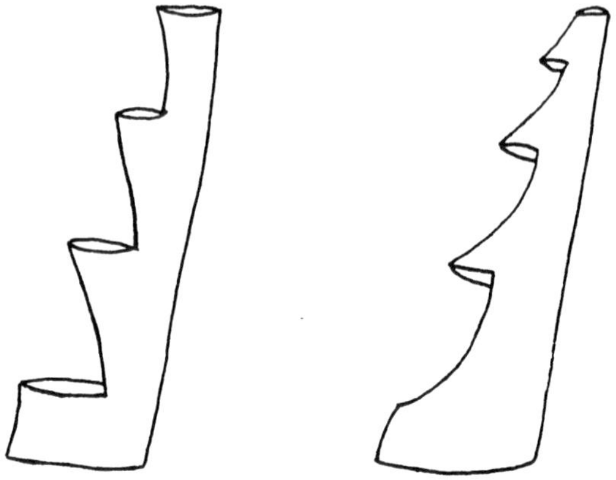

Figure 2.3. Pole ladders

When a ladder is used and the foot has been assisted to the top and back down again, the ladder itself is buried upside down at a crossroads, to prevent the star obstructions from retracing the steps back to the patient. A variation is to cut a "backward" ladder, one on which the notches are cut in reverse so that it cannot be used. (It is identical to an upside down ladder, except that the base, the wider part of each pole, is at the bottom, Fig. 2.3.) This backward ladder stands in front of the shaman's fire throughout the ritual, sometimes with a powdered clay or turmeric powder maṇḍala drawn around it. It, too, is buried at a crossroads toward the end of the session (or the next morning, since no one, not even a shaman, wants to spend much time at crossroads at night: one of the most frequently cited criteria of a better shaman is that he goes to more distant crossroads, and stays longer, than do others). In the Bhujī Valley, Deo Rām Kāmī reported using a single model of a ladder, with nine steps cut upward on one side, and seven downward on the other, nine for the planets, seven for the levels of the earth. The patient's big toe is first moved down the seven steps, then the ladder is turned over and the toe is moved up nine steps. Afterward, the ladder is buried, not at a crossroads, but under the place where the patient's head rests when sleeping (the *sirañ*).

Often, at the conclusion of the nighttime ceremony, the shaman weaves together a small barrier resembling a funeral pyre in front of the patient's house. This helps keep away the gaudā, and especially placates the Time of Death, Jama (Sanskrit: Yama) Kāl, and his ambassador, Jama Dūt, who also rule the second asterism. The conclusion of the Tilīkarmā text describes its construction by the first shaman when treating his brother-in-law the king:

> He danced and drummed out to the crossroads,
> he danced and drummed back from the crossroads
> [was possessed by Ālaṅg, was possessed by Mālaṅg],
> he began to sacrifice the blood of the offerings.
> He made one motion, collected one strip,
> made two motions, collected two strips
> [through nine],
> he made one pass, wove one line,
> made two passes, wove two lines
> [through nine].
> He wove a protective net, wove a selective net,
> wove the warp, wove the woof,
> wove a solid weave, wove a net-like weave,
> charmed the planets, charmed the star obstructions,
> freed the spirits, freed the powers,
> charmed the planets, charmed the star obstructions.
>
> (2.25)

This is a passage of considerable indexicality; the words for "motion," "strip," "pass," and "line" are all extremely vague, and required repeated discussion with the shamans before I arrived at these translations. But the interpretation provided by Jājarkoṭ shamans finds support in a passage from the Bhujī Valley. It describes how the chief divinities weave a barrier to reduce the original dowry of nine suns, nine moons, and nine *lākh* (nine hundred thousand) stars, a procedure they do instead of the daughter-in-law's inauspicious actions (2.9) above:

> Good Parameśvara, Good Mahādeu, Good Goronāth,
> [made] four oaths, going.
> They were very embarrassed, were very worried.
> "What was desolated, let's make productive."
> From Manṭā Lok, descending to Cinṭā Lok,
> they went to the Western House, ha!
> They buried an iron *liṅga* [phallic emblem], they buried an iron pillar.
> They came to the Southern House,
> they buried a brass liṅga, they buried a brass pillar.

They came to the Northern Direction,
they buried a copper liṅga, they buried a copper pillar.
They went to the Eastern House,
they buried a bronze liṅga, they buried a bronze pillar.
"Black Spider, weave a web," so saying,
Black Spider began to weave a web, began to spread a web.
From east to west, from north to south,
he finished weaving a web, finished spreading a web.
Black Termite finished carrying dirt, finished drying dirt.
Good Parameśvara, Good Mahādeu,
began to transfer the suns, began to transfer the moons.
Sealing one barricade, completing one barricade,
transferring one thread of the warp, smearing it with white clay,
they prepared the transfer.
Of the nine suns, a first sun was transferred.
Of the nine moons, a first moon was transferred.
Of the nine lākh of stars, one lākh was transferred.
Sealing one barricade, completing one barricade,
smearing it with white clay, they prepared the transfer.
Transferring one thread of the warp,
a second sun was transferred
[and so forth, through eight of each].

(2.26)

This describes the same ritual that Karṇa Vīr does, splitting strips of cane and weaving them back and forth, though his texts no longer include this episode. As the text says, the result resembles as much a net as a pyre. This allusion is certainly deliberate, since nets as well as pyres play a major part in shaman ceremonies. For example, when a *siyo* (a lost part of the soul) is being pacified, the relevant text instructs that the entire family of the patient should be wrapped up in a fishing net while the siyo is trapped in a gourd (4.31). It is aroused by whistling and then lured inside by chicken's blood and small pieces of bread. A small net is sometimes hung over the doorway of a house troubled by ghosts, to ward them off—any spirit who wishes to enter must first pass through all the openings and gets thoroughly confused in the attempt.

Besides resembling a pyre or net, the object constructed at the end of a *gauḍā phālne* (crisis postponing) ceremony also looks like a section of the split cane fences put around vegetable gardens or temporary animal pens. This comparison, too, is textually supported. As Gorāpā and

Serāpā's sons divide the earth between them, the passage describes this kind of fence being constructed to separate them:

> As far as a hand can reach is ours,
> as far as a stick can reach is yours,
> may you and we not see each other,
> may these sons not meet,
> between us and you there is a fence,
> there is a woven fence, there is a wooden fence,
> from today you and we will be as the sun and the moon,
> may we not meet, may we not see each other.
>
> (2.27)

The pyre explicitly reappears in a final ritual attempt to postpone the most stubborn star obstructions, after every other technique has been tried without success. The shaman lies at a crossroads at night, wrapped in a shroud. He sets splinters of wood crisscross on his chest, and lights them, offering himself as a ransom to the star obstructions (he concludes this sacrifice before the flames scorch his chest). In doing this, he performs a neat double inversion of normal order by placing a living body beneath a pyre, rather than a dead one on top of one. Several villagers pointed out this structural reversal to me in case I had missed it, though no one offered any insight into the particular significance of this inversion or into its play on the borders involved. Perhaps, this self-sacrifice shows the influence (or was itself the source for?) the Tibetan *chöd* ceremony (Nakazawa 1986), though conclusive evidence is probably impossible to uncover.

A more elaborate version of this ceremony also exists, when the patient's family is willing to invest in an extra goat. The shaman's assistants bring this goat to the crossroads, where the shaman lies down in a shroud. He lights a small fire in a bowl on his chest. The assistants behead the goat beside him. Immediately, as the head falls, the shaman leaps up and scatters the fire around the crossroads with his feet. The goat must be beheaded in one blow, or the shaman is in danger of being dragged off (*latārdai laijāncha,* which also means to "gobble up in a greedy fashion") by the masān who have assembled to drink its blood. Kamāro Kāmī added that this was one of the most difficult moments in any ceremony. Once the fire is lit, "it's just like watching a dream. You can hear what is said, but you can't open your eyes. You see gold on a woman's ear, a cow, a water buffalo. It's a struggle to come back." The assistants meanwhile disembowel the goat so that the shaman can examine its liver and spleen. If the signs show the relatives coming to a funeral, indicating that the patient is in grave danger, the nine-level pyre is next lit on the shaman's chest. He is possessed with māphī at his head and "Monkey Dhuwā" at his feet. He calls out to the Time of Death and the Messenger of Death, filling in the blanks with his client's name and social position:

> The cremation of so-and-so,
> the cremation of such and such a man has begun!
> Come now! The pyre is lit.
> Any which way, wandering here and there, now depart!
>
> (2.28)

Patients and shamans realize that the best possible outcome is only to postpone the time of death, sometimes only for minutes, and that everyone will die when the appointed life span has expired. Fatalistic realism tempers the hope for miracles, even within shaman texts. In Karṇa Vīr's Historical Recital, a more modern and less elegant text than the rest of his repertoire, telling of more or less historic ancestors of his, the king of Nepal (Kathmandu) summons two shaman brothers to his palace, where the queen is experiencing a difficult childbirth. Passing every test the king poses for them, they finally conduct a successful ritual and sacrifice, and a son is born. The king remains unsatisfied:

> "One son is no security, can you give another son or not?"
> "Majesty, we need two black goats."

They repeat their ritual, and a twin son is born, but the king wants yet another. The brothers agree, but they observe:

> "Five days after birth,
> it won't be able to survive," they said.
> Five days after birth it was in distress.
> "So, what can be done to save it, do something, quick."
> "Majesty, we need one black goat."
> The black goat was sacrificed as before.
> One drop of hail fell, was fed [to the child].
> "Mahārāj, having obeyed your command,
> it will survive two hours only."
> From then, in two hours, it departed.
>
> (2.29)

Despite the death of his third son, the king rewards them generously with a land grant, acknowledging, as do villagers, that to diagnose correctly some cases as hopeless adds to the shaman's reputation. Both shamans and villagers cite such diagnoses as proof of an ability to discern, not as evidence of powerlessness. The universal laws of fate can only be bent a little, on some occasions.

As part of every treatment of star obstructions, the shaman waves a yak tail at the head and feet of his patient, blows into the ears, sprinkles the body with water, and strikes it with an iron staff, gestures used by major deities throughout the recitals. They also appear ironically in a passage where a clearly brāhmanical deity, Four-Faced Barmā, performs with only trivial success on the race of man. He tries to use his book knowledge *(veda)* as a shaman uses his cane *(veta),* striking patients with them and using them to draw patterns in the dust. The seven times of death just climb a nearby tree and laugh:

> "Who may be learned, who may have listened?
> Knowledge is dying," thus they began to speak.
> "Go to the Northern Parts, going to the Northern Parts,
> Four-Faced Barmā, he's read the Four Veda,
> he's really learned, he has really listened, summon him here."
> Four-Faces, going, brought the White Veda, brought the Black Veda,
> having brought the Garul Veda, having brought a black yak tail,
> having brought a white yak tail, the Gaṅgā, the Jamunā,
> immortal water, he came spattering, he came scattering.
> Oh, Four-Faces, going.
> "He's come, Four-Faces, now, he may consume us," saying,
> the nine planets, going, the seven times of death, going,
> from the race of man, having left off,
> climbed a tree to watch.
>
> (2.30)

As soon as Four-Faced Barmā returns home, the causes of death return to plague mankind, until a similar ritual is finally performed by the first shaman, who causes them to retreat much further.

Second only to the variety of rituals called for by cases of star obstructions are those required for treating witchcraft. Again, a blood sacrifice is essential, usually a cock. There was some confusion about this, since a few shamans claimed that while a cock satisfies the witches, vāi require at the same time a goat, but in practice they did not insist on this.

In either case, shamans mix the animal's blood with ashes taken from under a three-footed iron cooking ring, knead the paste into little balls, and set them into dishes made from green leaves stitched together with twigs. The recital tells the witches how tasty this and other revolting offerings are while providing further details on what else to include:

> With rice grains of sand, fish of *tusārā* leaves,
> tobacco of *dhāturā,* cooked rice kneaded with blood,
> chili peppers of ashes, half-cooked flatbreads,
> he filled nine open leaf dishes, nine closed leaf dishes,
> the *rammā* [shaman] set out a snack for the witches.
> The rammā set out sweet flaky cakes,
> milk solid sweets, rice flour cakes.

The Nine Little Witch Sisters find this treat on their way to attack the first shaman. They consume it with relish, though it is not enough to satisfy them.

> Now the nine great witch sisters arrived.
> "We'll leave no breath, we'll leave no life," they said,
> they ate the nine dishes, took the nine shares, . . .
> They ate the rice grains of sand, the tobacco of dhāturā,
> the rice kneaded with blood, the chilies of ashes,
> the half cooked flatbreads.
> "The rammā's snack is so tasty,
> how tasty will be the rammā's flesh,
> let's eat the rammā," they said.
>
> (2.31)

This begins the battle between the witches and the shaman. Although he wins it in the recital, it continues to this day and is reenacted whenever a shaman is called upon to treat a witchcraft victim.

As discussed above (2.18), vāi are quasi-independent manifestations of the first witches, and their symptoms are often identical to those of witches. No shaman could abstractly clarify how to tell when a patient was suffering from one rather than the other, except to suggest relying on a patient's dreams. A diagnosis of vāi affliction is well suited to cases in which no one wants to take responsibility for identifying a witch. Sometimes, though, vāi appear in oppressively sexual dreams, particularly in those that trouble adolescent girls. To pacify these dreams, vāi receive a set of miniature household equipment, a metonymic representation of the domestic world, which some villagers explicitly likened to a dowry. The set should include a broom, cooking stand, sickle, axe, bowl, plate, winnowing tray, basket, head strap, water jug, shoulder bag, hair comb, delousing comb, rice pot, sauce pot, tongs, and pincers. The patient's family places them at the edge of the village along with scraps of the patient's clothing and bits of camphor. They sacrifice a goat over the offerings. Families may do this ceremony without a shaman's assistance, as, for example, when a particular vāi has identified himself (they are all male) in a dream, but this is rare. When a shaman is in charge, some recite a simple dialogue (taking, of course, both parts):

> "From where have you come, assistant?"
> "I've come from the east."
> "Cast off your load, cast off everything!"
> This will reduce dreams, will reduce fantasies.
> In a hole in the ground, the earth, presented atop leaves!
> (2.32)

When I asked Śiva Bahādur about placating vāi, he first insisted that he didn't know how to do it. When I then prompted him by describing the models that you need, he exclaimed, "But that's just ritual [pūjā]!" Not having a specific text for the occasion meant that there was "nothing to know." However, when I compared lists of offerings with him, he added grains of rice colored red and black, and suddenly remembered a few lines to recite over the grains, addressing the vāi with the second-person familiar pronoun:

> With these red and black grains,
> today we worship you *[āja timīlāi manāyāū̃]*.
> Today, quit your effect,
> release those whose dreams you infect,
> Blow, mantar! Śrī Mahādev's oath!
> (2.33)

Both witches and shamans use a technique known as "cutting a circle" (or pentagram) *(cakra katāunu)*. This involves the drawing of diagrams at a crossroads and then burying personal artifacts inside the charmed space. Such diagrams are not elaborate maṇḍalas; often, they consist only of a simple circle or cross-hatching made with flour or turmeric powder. Inside the demarcated space, a shaman digs a hole and buries personal relics of the witch—hair, nail clippings, bits of used clothing (usually tie-strap tips from a blouse or headbands), earth on which she has stepped barefoot, and ashes from her main hearth. The family whom she is troubling must supply all this, shifting on to them the burden of identifying the witch. The shaman blows two mantars into the hole:

> Death at the head, protect the head.
> Cutting the obstructions, the guru's promise!
> Bind the immodest mouth,
> bind the immodest Magar woman.
> Bind the immodest Khas woman,
> bind the immodest Ṭhākurī woman.
> Bind the immodest damned Bāhun woman.
> Your curse is reversed, my curse is straightforward!
> Blow, mantar! Śrī Mahādev's oath!
>
> (2.34)

Using abusive language, the shaman may cite witches belonging to each caste, or may include only those specific to the occasion. Then, without a pause:

> These witches, you witches' acts be trapped.
> Killing you witches, transferring you witches into a deep hole,
> die, you witches! Blow, mantar! Śrī Mahādev's oath!
>
> (2.35)

Before filling in the hole, shamans may add a small model of a plow, made from *kharsu* wood, the iron-clad tip pointing upward to prevent the witch from returning. Alternatively, a gourd with a nail pounded into it may be buried, for the same reason.

Shamans also practice "returning the effects" *(lāgu pharkāune)* against witches. In this, they use a different set of mantars (5.28) to deflect back upon the witch all the ill effects that she has caused. They sometimes also inscribe jantars on slate tablets and set them out on hillsides overlooking the patient's home, marking them with bamboo poles visible from the house. Shamans may add these details when cutting a circle, or after sucking foreign debris, called *putlā,* out of the patient, like the Eskimo shamans of Lévi-Strauss's brilliant article (1963a). Some shamans spit this debris into a bowl and bury it at a crossroads. Putlā are not necessarily corporeal objects, however, and were described by some shamans as definitely noncorporeal. One even called them "younger brothers" of *sāto,* equivalent to siyo (Chapter 4), except that they afflict persons when directed to do so by a witch.

While the actual rituals used to treat witchcraft are not so distinctive as those for star obstructions, every shaman had a surprisingly extensive repertoire of mantars to use against witches. While for most other situations, shamans had one or perhaps two mantars, every shaman knew at least a half dozen to use against witches (Chapter 5).

Sucking not only removes items that witches have inserted into victims; it is also an important technique in cases of women who have moc or nāgs lodged in their wombs. Shamans first symbolically cut loose the foreign intrusions stuck inside the body (2.12). This technique better conforms with the traditional laws concerning shamans, which specifically forbid them to apply their lips directly to women. Despite the law, however, direct sucking is still done in Jājarkoṭ, though in Rukum and the Bhujī Valley (Hitchcock 1974b), shamans interpose their drumsticks between their mouth and the woman's body. Moc and nāgs have only a one-dimensional, quasi-physical existence. Therefore, a shaman often prepares a tray of seductive forms to lure them away. Using dough, he may mold a set of nine serpents, plus a lizard, frog, turtle, cat, mouse, dog, and scorpion, all overseen by a pair of eagles. Once the nāgs occupy the serpents and the moc occupy the forms of their choice, the eagles keep them from escaping, and the whole ensemble is then buried at a crossroads. The models, perhaps, assist the patient's disidentification with the recital's analogies (Oppitz 1993), offering a severance from affliction as real as the knife blade that is waved (2.12).

Shamans also suck on patients to dislodge the invisible arrows (vāṇ) that forest spirits shoot into those who defile their sanctuaries. As I noted, "vāṇ" has several meanings. While it denotes "arrows" of forest spirits in this context, shamans themselves send auxiliary spirits of a deity, also called vāṇ, at their enemies. What is sucked out does not much resemble either. When discussing this technique, Kamāro Kāmī drew a distinction between removing blood, mucus, or small stones from a patient, which he himself has done, and reports of removing balls of hair or small animals such as lizards or toads, which he dismissed as pure superstition *(andhaviśwās),* another example of theoretical distinctions between the possible and the impossible which shamans themselves make. What I have most often seen resembles a stone or soft lump, along with blood. No one seems impressed by any of this. Villagers commonly dismissed it all as sleights of hand, comparing it to the tricks of a magician *(jādu)*, done purely to dramatically enhance the shaman's performance. Significantly, this skepticism never extended to the potential power of mantars, which everyone acknowledges. Again, texts take precedence over the performance.

Other than cases of star obstructions and witchcraft, the next most elaborate shaman ritual is that of binding a house. They do this when a family suffers a series of inexplicable misfortunes. The ceremony attempts to protect the family, their house, animals, and property from all possible threats and problems *(lāgu)*. Depending on the symptoms that family members report, different texts can be used, but the most common set is Tilīkarmā followed by either the Recital of Satī Barbā or the Ban Bhampā, or both. This set of recitals serves the purpose very well, for it treats big cosmological issues, like star obstructions, first, and then covers smaller mundane ones, like all various threats that arise from the forest [2.16].

"Binding a house" is not just a metaphorical title of the ritual. The shaman takes a long cord, roughly woven out of strong vines *(kukur ḍāṅgu)*, and wraps it around the house. It remains behind as a visible sign of the protection that he conveys, reminding spirits of the boundary between human settlements and the uncultivated wilderness, their rightful domain. To reinforce that boundary, the shaman also pounds stakes of wood cut from a wild plum tree into the four corners of the house plot and sets up a leafy branch at each. He implants a long iron rod in front of the entrance. A goat is sacrificed amid the usual ritual preparations of leaf dishes containing various offerings, such as vermilion powder and betel nuts. Sometimes, to send back any lāgu and prevent them from returning, a small model of a plow, or a cowry shell, is buried at a crossroads. Again, the appropriate recital supplies the details:

> They went to Tārātālī,
> brought back the great rammā Jumrātam.
> He danced and drummed out to the crossroads,
> he danced and drummed back from the crossroads,
> began to bind the house.
> Raising the foundation stone [or, setting down the challenge],
> he firmly fixed the foundation stone.
> Breaking up the pentagrams, he released the pentagrams.
> He bound the shares of grain, he bound the shares of wealth,

> he bound the shares of land.
> He killed forest rāh, killed the descendants of Kaṁsa,
> killed the ghosts and goblins, killed the major spirits of the dead,
> killed the spells, charms, tricks of witches,
> began to bind the house . . .
> He bound the four corner pegs, cut with four gestures . . .
> bound the four directions, bound the four quarters,
> drove in a four-cornered iron peg, drove in a thunderbolt staff.
> He struck it for all time, killed the effects for all time,
> buried a cowry, wrapped everything into a ball.
>
> (2.36)

This passage also illustrates the generic nature of this ritual. It covers a very wide variety of sources of supernatural trouble and sweeps the house and property clean of both major and minor threats to its security.

Shamans also bind individual patients by tying a string around the neck or wrist to offer general protection. A recital gives a somewhat hyperbolic account of this technique, using the vocabulary of tethering a domestic animal:

> Having gone to heaven, you're brought back by the feet.
> Having gone to hell, you're brought back by the hair.
> [With] cotton thread, going, with nine strands,
> I've bridled the mouth, bound the feet,
> bound the hands, bound the neck.
>
> (2.37)

Sometimes, as the text suggests, strings are tied around all the various limbs, but a single one around the wrist or neck is, I've observed, far more common.

Another, uncommon, ritual also involving the crossroads is that of burying for a moment a child born under the mūl configuration (described above), when it has been calculated that the mūl period will be very short. This is rare, and neither I nor any villager that I know has ever seen this done. The affected child is buried up to its neck at the crossroads for the duration of the mūl period, and then uncovered and declared reborn as an orphan under a new configuration. While the child is buried, scraps of old cloth taken from nine houses are burned. The parents come to the crossroads along with neighbors and friends, and, if available, a Brāhman. They claim the child, exclaiming: "Look what I've found at the crossroads, who could have put this here! We should keep it!" The father presents the mother with a small gift of money. Assistants cut a goat and drench the child in its blood. Next they wash it with water from "one hundred" springs, sprinkled through a copper sieve and coursed down a banana stalk spout. The water and blood is left behind at the crossroads. Juice from the leaves and roots of "one hundred" trees is fed to the child daily for nine days, with the remainder thrown out at the crossroads on the ninth day. After this, the mūl is said to have departed. Karṇa Vīr, who described this technique to me, made it clear that you don't need knowledge to do this *(gyān cāen)*, a sharp contrast with the Brāhmanical treatment that Raheja reports from north India (1988:102–18). Both Karṇa Vīr and his brother spoke dismissively of all this when I tried to pursue it with them, disclaiming: "That's just technique [vidhī]." For them, as for Śiva Bahādur in the example concerning vāi, the decisive factor was that they had no mantar to say, though there are a few lines to tell the mūl to go away. Other shamans said that if an astrologer could do nothing about mūl, nothing could be done about it.

Finally, shamans also employ diverse techniques not directly connected with any recital as diagnostic or evaluative divinations. These are used either at the beginning of treatment to identify the source of affliction, or afterward to determine if the ceremony has been efficacious. Precisely because they are unaccompanied by any text, they vary from shaman to shaman much more than do any of the other rituals.

The simplest of these diagnostic techniques, though, is done in similar ways by all shamans. After a goat has been beheaded, the man who cuts it puts the head into the shaman's drum. The shaman, possessed, picks up the head in his teeth, shakes it back and forth, and tosses it back toward the body, checking to see if it aligns properly with the neck, which is a good sign. The heart is then put in the drum, and the shaman tosses it with his teeth toward the body. It should land against the stomach between the legs.

More complicated techniques vary widely. Often, in place of the test just described, after an animal has been sacrificed, the shaman carefully examines the liver of a goat or the gallbladder, spleen, or liver of a chicken to decide whether the patient will benefit from the offering. I discussed this with a dozen different shamans, and learned a dozen different ways to evaluate the viscera. The simplest was Karṇa Vīr's: "If their color is good, then the result is good; if their color is bad, then the

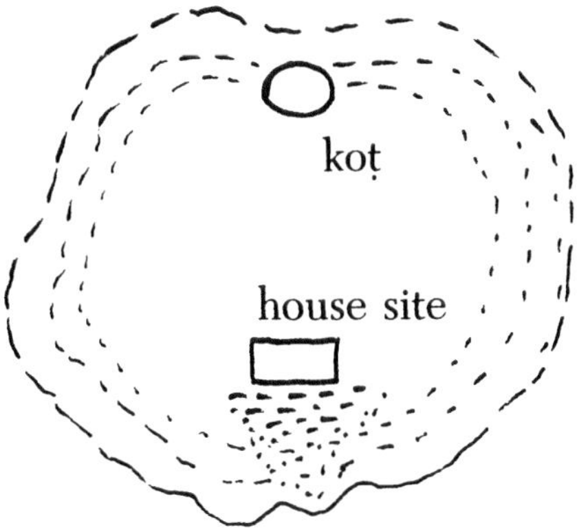

Figure 2.4. Kamāro Kāmī's diagram for reading a spleen

result is bad." Pressed for further details, he said that the half of the goat's liver toward the gallbladder is the patient's half, the other side represents the village, and if you could see "funeral goers" *(malāmi)* arriving in the patient's half, or a grave (a deep cleft) at the top, then the patient would die. He added that if a chicken's gallbladder is clear, then the ritual must be repeated, or the patient would suffer. Other shamans, including Man Dev Kumaĩ of the Bhujī Valley, felt that the amount of grayish membrane around the liver was the critical factor. Others divided it into quadrants rather than halves, one for the patient, one for his house, one for the house's god, and one for the village. Sibe Damāi divided the liver into three parallel bands from top to bottom, and said that there was nothing to worry about if any two of them were firm. Others examined the depth and direction of creases in the liver. Still others practiced classic haruspication, counting the bumps on the intestines, with different ways of calculating success and failure.

Kamāro Kāmī provided the diagram in Figure 2.4. He would check the spleen for little bumps. If they were clustered below the house site, the patient's trouble originated in the village. If they surrounded the entire organ, including both the house site and the "*koṭ*" (fort), then the patient's problems came from further away, either the untamed wilds outside the village, or a different village.

The "standard" technique for deciding at a distance whether a potential patient would respond positively to treatment, called "looking at dirt" *(māilo herne)*, shows a similarly wide range of variation. Most shamans require small pieces of cloth cut off the patient's clothing, but what they do with them varies from practitioner to practitioner. Some shamans put these on the skin of their drum, beat it lightly, and see if the pieces come together or go separate ways. Karṇa Vīr would request a scrap of clothing from the patient's mother and father as well as from the patient. If the two others come to join the patient's scrap, the patient can be cured, otherwise not. Other shamans put the pieces in a bowl of water and see if they float or sink, others put them in alcohol and watch if they move to the left or right, still others just feel them to see if they are warm or not.

I found the contradictory diversity of these techniques frustrating, and drew it to the attention of both shamans and villagers. They failed to find it remarkable or provocative. This recalls Evans-Pritchard's remark that "A witch-doctor divines successfully because he says what his listener wishes him to say, and because he uses tact" (1937:170). Perhaps, too, these aleatory exercises allow a shaman to tap "tacit realms of knowledge," as Desjarlais speculates (1992b:24), comparing them to the divinatory exercise of ethnography. However, I find them more noteworthy as further examples of how knowing and reciting memorized texts produce very exact standards of activity. In the absence of such texts, the alternate is a wide divergence of practice.

I find it tempting to summarize the variety of ritual activities in which shamans engage, whether textually grounded or improvised, as being either propitiatory or magical. Shamans themselves declined to suggest any such classification, and were puzzled by my attempts to solicit one. Propitiatory rituals include sacrifices and offerings, while "magical" acts include rituals of binding and burying, sucking or blowing, raising the patient toward the heavens, and all the acts of divination. Clearly, the two categories are not genuinely exclusive, and all activities fall into a more general one: "acts of intervention," probably the only precise summary with which the shamans themselves might agree. However described, the loci of both shamanic actions and shamanic prescriptions—what they do and what they advise clients to do—run along parallel continua, ranging from the personal and invasive to the social and ethical, spectrums that parallel the etiology I have described here.

This chapter has provided a rationale for shamans based on their therapeutic abilities and their relations to individual clients, but this does not exhaust the reasons why shamans continue to be necessary and effective. I next shift to a wider social setting for these issues. For, as Roberte Hamayon (1990) has persuasively shown, however important shamanic healing is to particular individuals, it must not be taken as the interpretive principle of their social roles. She has suggested that although a shaman apparently intervenes to repair some disorder only on someone's request, "on analyzing the cases, sickness or other disorders appear as being often merely pretexts for shamanic intervention; shamanic intervention is considered necessary *per se*, and is carried out on any opportunity when too much time has elapsed since the previous ritual" (Hamayon 1993:204). Having pursued an overt "medicalization" of shamans in this chapter, in the next I explore their social and cosmological contexts.

3
Worlds Requiring Shamans

The hills and valleys of western Nepal offer a harsh, rugged setting in which inhabitants continually struggle to survive. Agriculture and animal husbandry are the only significant economic activity, yet harvests and incomes rarely exceed subsistence, and are frequently much less, leading to chronic malnutrition and periodic famine. Inequitable land distribution and an exploitive local aristocracy compound natural problems. In this materially impoverished setting I was surprised to find two competing forms of systematic intercession that each manipulate partially overlapping sets of "spirits" (deutā, dhām, bāyu burmā), manipulation supported at considerable cost by the local population. My surprise intensified when I saw that both traditions exist outside the mainstream of the Hindu religion and social system, which I had expected to dominate local society. Both forms of intercessor must compete not only with each other for clients, but also with Brāhman priests, traveling mendicants, and Jaiśī astrologers of popular Hinduism, and further compete with the recently introduced, government-sponsored practitioners of Western-style allopathic medicine. Nevertheless, throughout Jājarkoṭ and adjacent areas, we find flourishing two distinct types of practitioners of spirit intercession, dhāmīs, whom I will identify as oracles or mediums, and jhāṅgarīs, who are shamans in the most precise meanings of that term.

Shaman texts themselves echo this diversity of practitioners, as the continuation of 1.1 explicitly demonstrates. Having cursed the race of man, Mahādev relents and creates intercessors. Speaking of humans, he predicts:

"They can die when old, let them live when young," he said.
Old men died, babies died, there were miscarriages.
There were seven times of natural death,
fourteen times of unnatural death.
"For the race of man, how will time pass,
how will there be a world? Now I will play a trick," he said.
"For the race of man, the seven times of natural death,
the fourteen times of unnatural death, I will postpone," he said.
"I will make Maitu Dhāmī,
I will make Sato Gyānī, Bharṣā Paṇḍit," he said.
At Chārkābhoṭ, he made Bharṣā Paṇḍit, Sato Gyānī, Prajā Prakil.
At Tāgāserā he made Ratan Pārkī, at Bāchigāū̃ he made Kālu Jaiśī,
at Tārābhoṭ he made Maitu Dhāmī,
at Tārātālī he made Rammā Jumrātam.

(3.1)

In this chapter, I will examine these alternate specialists, including oracles (dhāmī), Brāhman priests (paṇḍit), astrologers (jaiśī), seers *(gyānī, herneharu),* counselors *(prakil),* pulse readers/fortunetellers *(pārkī),* Tibetan priests *(lāmā)* and wandering holy men (*kānphaṭa* yogins), along with one extratextual addition, the local health post workers (called "doctors"). My purpose is not, however, to provide a comparative summary of all varieties of specialists, even less to synthesize them into a single "system" that I can then analyze as a complete "structure." Initially, I admit, I tried to do so, to follow a recent trend in interpretive anthropology of the kind best associated with Clifford Geertz (1973). The material itself has firmly resisted this. I have had to conclude that the co-presence of multiple forms of ritual activity is only that, an accidental co-presence, not a system of balance, nor a system of contradiction, nor a system of paradox—simply, not a system. Convenience and convention, not some division that satisfies different social "functions" or psychological "needs," influence choices between alternatives when choices exist, and often, for reasons of habit, availability, cost, and custom, choices are not really present. Decisions as to whom to consult do not really have to be made. I will look at some of these issues later in this chapter, when I further develop the contrast between jhāṅgarīs and dhāmīs. I do so to clarify a semantic confusion that exists about them, and as a device for bounding the sphere of shamanic activities, but not to propose some system of beliefs, or activities, or whatever, that embraces both of them. I relate details to other details at diverse levels, from

Illustration 3.1. Jhāṅgarī Gumāne Kāmī

semantic structures to practical ontologies, but I no longer try to shift to so general a frame that I could produce some total "interpretation." Moments of harmony, of grace, and of truth can all be heard within a "shamanocentric" universe. They do not require interpretive processes of "contextualization" or of "guessing at meanings" to recognize their stunning coherence. I am unwilling to force these details into a single unifying structure, and insist that interconnected but divergent explorations are the way in which they are best approached.

As an alternative to positing a "totality" of ritual activity in western Nepal, I conduct a thorough, detailed study of one type of specialist, the shamans. I do so without endorsing the unfortunately prevalent neologism of "shaman-ism," with its "sinister ending" (Hatto 1970:1) misleadingly connoting a complete, coherent system of eschatological beliefs and religious practices. Nor do I find any improvement in "shaman-ship," with its fashionable emphasis on performance and its rejection of shamans as a "self-contained problem" in favor of a breathtakingly prodigious attempt to understand them as "historically situated and culturally mediated social practice" (Atkinson 1989, 1992). If a culture is a particular way of conceiving what really is, of what is genuinely good, true, and beautiful, then I do not exaggerate to suggest that shaman texts produce for those who know them a distinct culture, often at odds with the surrounding dominant culture(s) of western Nepal. These texts do not just express an antihegemonic discourse of moments of critical awareness, but form an autonomous system of conditioned actors participating in a fully conceived reality. Those same actors, admittedly, sometimes find themselves mediated by other cultures, other realities, some of which intersect or refract each other, some of which are fundamentally unconnected with their ordinary ones. My sense of culture is neither a stratographic one, underlying the actors, nor a holistic one, embracing all of their widely disparate phenomena. Instead, I see it as momentary coherencies of point events in space and time, intentional worlds that flare intensely and slowly fade. Yet, following precedents as disparate as Malinowski (1965), Held (1935), Stein (1959), Jackson (1979), and Favret-Saada (1980), all of whom have verified that significant anthropological discoveries can be found within universes of texts, this work is an ethnographic study. Each has also helped to confirm my opinion that good translation and good ethnography are practically indistinguishable.

Instead of limiting myself to the detailed study of a single village, as

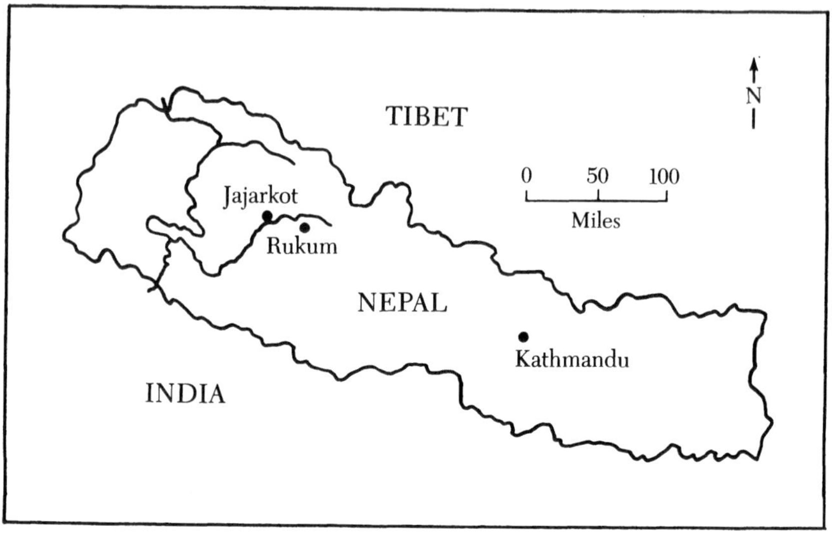

Map 3.1. Nepal, showing field sites, in relation to Kathmandu

is most typical of anthropology, I analyze material that I have collected over the past fifteen years throughout a hundred square miles of western Nepal, overlapping Jājarkoṭ and Rukum Districts. My sites of concentrated effort include more than a dozen different villages, ranging from hamlets of less than twenty houses whose inhabitants are of a single caste to growing towns of hundreds of diverse families where there are now post offices, schools, and shops. Shamans that I know represent several different castes, though blacksmiths (*kāmīs*) predominate, as apparently they do throughout the Himalayas. The remarkable similarity of many texts that I collected from different shamans clearly demonstrates their relative stability. That stability makes them central to my study. I have concluded that such texts are the most invariant, the least indexical or reflexive, of all possible personal, cultural, social, or performative variables from which shamans might be approached. Though the words gain additional relevance from external referents such as gesture, they are themselves sufficient to generate sense. They are clearly the most suitable material from which to begin any analysis amid a streaming flow of individual beliefs that are often changing, contradictory, inarticulately expressed, or artfully concealed. While I sometimes make generalizations concerning what people do or "believe," I endeavor to keep such reflections to a minimum, and limit my focus to what the texts themselves say. Only with a collection of such sharply focused, not too quickly "interpretive" studies, I believe, can real justice be done to the incredible complexities of ritual activity in Nepal. However, to highlight more quickly some of the distinctive features of the shamans, I will introduce some of the other specialists found in western Nepal, concentrating on how the shaman recitals themselves characterize them.

"Shamans" are, of course, not only shamans. Each with whom I have worked is Nepalese, male, adult, husband, father. They do not just perform heroic feats like searching heaven and hell for lost souls; much of the time they farm, they herd, go on trading trips, dig ore, and forge iron. Most of them are blacksmiths, ranked among the lowest, "untouchable" castes, from whose hand a sip of water would pollute and degrade a higher caste member. As such, they are losers in local power distributions. Each suffers economic and political marginality within a generally impoverished setting. Throughout Nepal, members of the lowest castes struggle, often unsuccessfully, to feed their families. The dominant ideologies and practices of local society tightly constrain the possibilities of their social being. They live in a world of (to anticipate characterizations found in the shaman texts themselves) powerful royal politicians, exploitative landholders, manipulative Brāhman priests, sly mediums of oracular divinities, usurious tradesmen, evil Buddhist lāmās, and, obviously, neighbors and families, including wives, in-laws, and children. But those individuals who, through ambition, initiative, aptitude, and persistence, have succeeded in becoming shamans, fashion and have crafted for themselves an identity detached from these powerful constraints. Neighbors become clients. Tradesmen become patrons, sons become disciples, kings even become brothers-in-law. All participants in local hierarchies, including foreign anthropologists, become respectful and solicitous. Identity as a shaman comprehensively encompasses all other partial identities of the individual who succeeds in realizing it. An ordinary blacksmith is socially powerless. One who becomes a shaman dislodges hegemonic constraints to connect social webs and personal relations in new, advantageous ways that others are forced to acknowledge. At the same time, a shamanic identity reshapes personal experiences and memories to conform to professional role. More than anything else in the complexities of their self, they are shamans. Learning the recitals' models of their ideal relations to kings, priests, and ordinary villagers enables them to improve those relations. As I will show in later chapters, this new powerfulness is maintained by threats of supernatural retribution, for which the recitals also provide prototypes.

Each of my shaman informants actively defined himself to me as a shaman rather than as a Kāmī, or an indentured laborer, or family member, or whatever else he happened to be. That is, the topic of this work is not only a research finding, it defined the limits of my research with these individuals. They encouraged me to attend ceremonies, but never invited me into their homes. This is not only because they were untouchables, but also because they were shamans: "One does not go to a shaman's house," states the Tilīkarmā Recital (6.39). They taught me secret mantars more readily than they would recite family genealogies. They never spontaneously discussed nor introduced relatives. Unlike just about everyone else in Nepal, they never asked that I take family portraits. The result is that I know much more about their identity as shamans than about their other identities. That is how they identify themselves and want to be known, not just by me or my readers, but by everyone. It is how they conceive of themselves.

Any discussion relating other ritual experts to shamans needs to begin with witches, which, as the preceding chapter demonstrated, are their great adversaries. Both shamans and villagers tended to identify the practices of witches as closely paralleling shamanic ones. Most important, they state that witches must learn texts, especially secret mantars, to practice. Witches also have helping spirits, including bīr and māphī, and they perform various rituals similar to those of shamans, such as "cutting a circle" (2.34). However, since I never found anyone who would freely admit being a witch, and most specific identifications made to me were of women already dead, all these claims must remain speculative.

Shaman texts have much to tell us about them. The first witches are known by the collective term "The Nine Skillful Little Sisters," an antonomastic designation of all witches. The recital used to treat their afflictions reports their origin:

> At first the world was filled with demons,
> no respect was shown to holy men,
> no respect was shown to kings by subjects,
> no alms were given, no respect was shown to anyone at all.

Bhagavān said, "I'll play a trick," . . .
he took on the appearance of a yogi,
he descended Hā̃gābāṅg, went to Pāṭan Melā.
There was an eighty-year-old childless bent old woman,
he went to her house.
"Give me a place to stay, aunt, it's twilight," he said.
"Come in and stay, yogi, it's twilight," she said.
She gave him a cane mat to lie on,
gave Bhagavān three flatbreads to eat.
He put one bread under the bedding,
placed one bread atop the drying rack,
put one bread in the folds of her clothing,
Nārānjī got up and left. . . .

[The shift from "Bhagavān" to "Nārānjī" is apparently without significance. In another text, he is called "Mahādev." The recitals treat names borrowed from Hindu stories very casually.]

She lifted up the bedding, found a thick disk of gold,
felt above the drying rack, found a thick disk of silver,
felt in the folds of her clothing,
found a delicious fruit, found a grapefruit's orb.
"Ai, that was Bhagavān,
I must eat the fruit that Bhagavān has given," she said,
she gobbled up the grapefruit's seed,
the Nine Skillful Little Sisters were conceived.
From the short section,
Lāṭā Pārān Gyāpā Rañjan was conceived.

(3.2)

Thanks to the advice of the original astrologer, Kālu Jaiśī, they become the great enemy of shamans:

The Nine Little Sisters originated at Tāgāserā,
in the villages of Bāchīgāũ, Rāḍīgāũ, Māḍīgāũ.
Afterward they said,
"In this country we've left no flies, we've left no fleas,
we've consumed the newborn babies,
consumed the newborn animals,
dried up the young trees,
shifted the unmovable stones,
turned back the downward-flowing rivers.
Who is more skillful than we are?"

The villagers replied,
"Kālu Jaiśī is more skillful than you are.
Can you consume Kālu Jaiśī or not?"
With waving hands and lilting heads,
the Nine Little Sisters arrived at Kālu's room.
Kālu Jaiśī said to them:
"Why consume me, sisters?
We have no quarrel, no cause to fight.
I look at men's planets and at their configurations,
I choose auspicious days, calculate the correct time,
draw up horoscopes, I have no quarrel with you.
The person that's a match for you is at Tārātālī Tilīgramā,
Rammā Purācan, Jhāṅgarī Jhiṅgrātam.
Go there, eat him, I can't match you," said the astrologer.
(3.3)

Although belief in witchcraft is pervasive throughout Nepal, precise information on its nature and practices, like most of the forces that jhāṅgarī recitals treat, is rare. Informants are extremely reluctant to discuss most of these issues in detail, commonly citing their fear that their comments may provoke retribution from those forces, whether witches, ghosts, or divine spirits.

Few villagers expressed any ideas on how this world came to have witches. Some said, however, that the original witches were created because their assistance was required by the gods in their primordial battle against the demons who originally controlled the earth. The witches' mantar is called Indra Jāl (Indra's Net) because Indra taught it to them at that time. Dazzled by their new power, the witches soon turned to evil meddling in the affairs of men, and have been causing problems ever since. In Kathmandu, the Indra Jāl is even said to exist in manuscript, though no one seems to know the whereabouts of any copy. If witches learned their knowledge when the nectar of immortality was churned from the primordial ocean, there may be parallels between the first witches and the Nau Durgā Bhawānī, nine goddesses who are worshiped throughout Nepal, most prominently in the Kathmandu Valley (detailed in Levy 1987, 1991, and in Toffin 1984). Villagers to whom I made such a suggestion found it abhorrent: they vehemently rejected any association whatsoever between goddesses, even tantric ones, and witches, and found my speculations offensive. However, the extensive blood sacrifices that the Nau Durgā Bhawānī annually receive also offend more orthodox Hindus. At the culmination of the Dasaĩ festival each fall, representatives of the king slaughter a male buffalo for the Nine Goddesses at a permanent post in front of their shrine, as Mother Buffalo noted in the sacrifice negotiations (1.8), suggesting another possible link between them and witches.

In Jājarkoṭ, witches are ordinarily female. Stories of a single male witch in the last generation circulate, vaguely. Both jhāṅgarī texts and popular belief distinguish three classes of witches: *ḍaṁkī, boksī,* and *kapṭī,* each often expressed by its diminutive, *ḍaṁkinī, boksinī,* and *kapṭinī.* Ḍaṁkī—sometimes identified as spirits of dead witches—are the most powerful: they may cause sudden death with just a glance, even, the standard example, of a bird passing overhead in flight. Kapṭī, at the other extreme, are capable only of minor mischief, such as tense stomachs, facial blemishes, or swelling, usually in children. Throughout Nepal, witches are commonly called boksī, and this term is also most often used in Jājarkoṭ, both by shamans and by ordinary villagers. Sometimes, boksī cause the death of their victims, but they are often responsible for many less extreme but always physically experienced difficulties, as were discussed in the preceding chapter.

What are the chief characteristics of witches? A hatred of males (of all species) is seminal. In their natal village(s) of "Rāḍīgāũ/Māḍīgāũ," soon after birth, the first witches began their attacks:

> They went to the elephant sheds,
> consumed the tusked bull elephants.
> They went to the horse stables,
> consumed the white-hoofed stallions.
> They went to the buffalo sheds,
> consumed the good stud buffalos.
> They went to the cow sheds;
> consumed the good bulls.
> They went to the homes of men,
> consumed the virile men.
> They left behind no male seed, . . .
> "Now let's wander in the world of death,
> let's eat all the males there, older sister,
> let's eat them, younger sister," they said.
>
> (3.4)

They attack the first shaman, Jumrātam, but he outwits them by donning a costume that confuses them, carefully replicated by the contemporary shaman (3.30). "In this strange form, in this strange norm, what animal have we met?" they ask, unable to consume him because of his protective disguise, designed by the jhagrenī. He leads the witch sisters on a tiring journey throughout the world, leaving them so exhausted that he can eliminate them.

Witches do not only attack men. The recital even tells of them consuming their own mother, having found her head lice so tasty that they couldn't resist eating her flesh as well. Witches attack close relatives more often than they do other villagers, and they attack children and women as often as they do men.

Highlighting problems of gender relations, the texts set up a dichotomy between the deviousness of the witches and the virtuousness of Jumrātam's first wife, who devises his marvelous costume. Just before addressing the witch sisters by their personal names, he elaborately praises their beauty, an episode called the "seduction" *(phakāunu)* of the witches. Śiva Bahādur insisted that this passage must be included at the beginning of every ceremony; otherwise the witches would pick a fight with you:

> Such sisters, lithe bamboo stalks,
> look at your heads, polished walking stick knobs,
> look at your foreheads, straight furrows,
> look at your ears, delicate *kacur* leaves,
> look at your eyes, the eyes of does,
> look at your noses, the blades of axes,
> look at your lips, coral colored lips,
> look at your tongues, darting little snakes,
> look at your teeth, the seeds of pomegranates,
> look at your necks, the necks of cranes . . .
>
> (3.5)

He continues with these strikingly rustic metaphors for the rest of their anatomy, from throat to heel. When it comes time to destroy them, it appears that Jumrātam is sexually attracted to the youngest witch, whom he allows to survive (1.4). (In Chapter 5, I will argue that this is just a devious deception.) However, he refuses to let her enter his house.

"O Uncle Rammācan, in your storeroom,
give me a place, Uncle, give me a space, Uncle,"
the youngest Little Sister, Pirai Mālā, going, [said].
"In my storeroom, there may be my Ancestral Gods,
there may be my Family Gods.
My spirits won't permit it, my powers won't permit it,
my Ancestral Gods won't permit it.
O my little girl,
you can't have a place, you can't have a space."

(3.6)

Similarly, he refuses her a place in the entrance way, where her evil eye would affect the food that his wife prepares; on the balcony, where she would scare the pigeons and doves; in the basement, where she would spook the cattle; not even in the drainage ditch or the courtyard:

"In my courtyard, Kansyāl blacksmiths come,
wandering mendicants come, guests, supplicants come,
maternal in-laws come, sons-in-law, their children come,
friends, relatives come.
Your evil eye may have effect, girl,
your influences may have effect, girl.
You can't have a place, you can't have a space.
My spirits won't permit it, my powers won't permit it."

(3.7)

The text is silent on whether they marry or have sexual relations. Shamans inconclusively debated the issue. Some were convinced that he did, others equally convinced that he didn't. Still others had no opinion on the matter, pointing out that the texts don't tell us, so it is pointless to speculate. Gumāne was horrified by the topic. "She was his sister, how could he marry her?" No one else, however, agreed that the polite address "little sister," so common throughout Nepal, implied that the witches were true sisters of the shaman, though Magars in Tākā relate an imaginative genealogy connecting witches with many of the first ritual specialists (Oppitz 1991:259). Whatever the exact kinship status assigned witches, they are the specialists with whom shamans most commonly interact.

An important phrase in the story of the origin of witches (3.2) describes Bhagavān as deciding to play a trick on the race of man and taking on "the appearance of a yogi." Expanding this to a fuller version,

> Bhagavān said, "I'll play a trick,"
> he put on his head a tiger's skin,
> put on his forehead sandalwood ashes,
> put on his ear a large pendant,
> put around his neck a *rudrākṣa* necklace,
> slung over his shoulder a pair of begging bowls,
> held in his hand a thunderbolt staff,
> slung in his waist a double-edged knife,
> put on his ankles heavy anklets,
> dressed in frayed saffron cloth,
> took on the appearance of a yogi,
> he descended Hā̃gābāṅg, went to Pāṭan Melā.
>
> (3.8)

This unmistakably describes a kānphaṭa yogin (Briggs 1989; Unbescheid 1986). Kānphaṭas have established centers in both Jumlā Khalaṅgā and at Swargadwārā in Sallyān, traveling between the two through Jājarkoṭ, a route that was used in the past by pilgrims to Mount Kailās (Adhikari 1988). These wandering mendicants are, and have long been, a religious presence in Jājarkoṭ. I could not find any evidence of their interacting with any of the shamans that I know, but textual references to them are very common, in both recitals and mantars. These references connect the treatment of witches with the cosmological texts that include the creation of the world, the planets, and the race of man. In each the creator, Mahādev, takes on the appearance of a kānphaṭa. The nine planets result from his meditation in a cave where he develops leprosy.

> "For man the nine planets have begun to originate," he said.
> Mahādev went to bathe, from bathing,
> Mahādev went to stay in a cave.
> Staying in the cave six months, Pārvatā waited in the kitchen,
> Mahādev's rice was cooked.
> "Where can I throw Mahādev's rice?" she said.
> Thrown on the snowy mountains,
> the snowy mountains had a downy fleece.
> Mahādev, after six months, a full year, emerged from the cave,
> Pārvatā wrapped him in sweet-smelling musk.

The sweet-smelling musk opened up his wounds.
Mahādev's twenty-two lumps of filth emerged.
"Where can I throw Mahādev's filth?
If I throw it on the trash heap, a piglet may eat it,
Mahādev would go to hell," she said.
"If I throw it at Barmā Crossroads,
lepers, cripples, beggars, mendicants,
yogis, or holy men may touch it,
Mahādev would go to hell. Where can I throw it?" she said.
"Go now, Pārvatau,
you must throw it into Rakta Pokhārī [Blood Lake]," he said.
She threw it into Rakta Pokhārī.
The nine planets originated,
the nine star obstructions originated,
having finished off Rakta Pokhārī they arose.
Mahādev was able to get up, a blade in his hand,
he cut eight planets, cut eight star obstructions.
The eldest planet is Ketu, the eldest star obstruction is Kālcakra.
He cut the first, there were two, cut the second, there were three,
cut the third, there were four, cut the fourth, there were five,
cut the fifth, there were six, cut the sixth, there were seven,
cut the seventh, there were eight, cut the eighth, there were nine,
cutting he increased them.
Mahādev left off cutting the nine planets,
the nine star obstructions.

(3.9)

The sequence of time represented here is enigmatic, since these events both precede and follow the creation of the earth and its inhabitants. The primordial cosmos, the "Blood Lake," has no origin in these stories, though it is sometimes identified as a star obstruction. The earth, though, has a separate genesis, with roots in Hindu stories. Mahādev slays a primordial demon, Madhu Kaiṭi, who himself originated from Viṣṇu's earwax:

He finished meditating, he finished contemplating,
twelve divine years, eighteen ages,
Good Parameśvara, Good Mahādeu.
going to Jalathala [one of the nine levels of this world],
he became awake.
Of Madhu Kaiṭe, going, oh, of his great blood,

rivers and streams formed,
the sources of lakes settled.
Of Madhu Kaiṭe, going, of his great fat, going,
the frost settled, the snowy regions formed,
the mountain regions formed.
Of his great flesh, also, of Madhu Kaiṭe, going,
having formed the clay, settled.
His bones, also, formed all the hills,
went to form the hills.
Of Madhu Kaiṭe, going, oh, his great flesh,
having formed the clay, settled.
Oh, his bones, went to form the hills.
The earth was created, the earth was formed.
Good Parameśvara, Good Mahādeu,
Viṣṇu Rājā, going,
what was desolated, they made productive.

(3.10)

These events are often telescoped into a few lines, simply reporting that "Mahādev designed the solid and liquid world." This is how the decision that the world requires men is reported:

Self-created Mahādev designed the solid and liquid world.
The world was just a disorderly place.
"Be," he said, there were no men.
"Speak," he said, there were no men.
"How will time pass, how will there be a world?
I shall make the race of man," he said.

(3.11)

Mahādev reflects that without the race of man, the world will not survive. He tries, as I initially noted, a variety of materials, including gold, silver, copper, nickel, brass, and iron, none of which function properly. Then Mahādev orders a funeral pyre of the best sandalwood to be built and burned. He sends messengers below to the realm of the Kaṁsa Rānī to negotiate the release of an aged cock and hen. From the ash of the pyre and the dung of the chickens,

He joined hands, joined feet, joined a head, joined legs.
"Well, put in a full breath," so saying,
he put in a full breath, left it a bloodline.
"Well, now on the sixth night, look man, your share,"

so saying, Bhābi wrote, "The day of birth yields fate."
Mahādev brushed a white yak tail at the head,
brushed a black yak tail at the feet,
with a powerbolt staff delivering seven blows,
"Speak, man" he said, "Hā̃ hā̃, hũ hũ," it went.
"Go and die," said Mahādev, he gave a curse.

(3.12)

This passage is from Gumāne's recital. Karṇa Vīr's version is less dramatic, with man cursed only after the population increases so greatly as to threaten the survival of the world.

The race of man didn't die,
became so many they didn't fit, didn't diminish.
"The soft unstable earth is finished.
I will trick the race of man."

(3.13)

The curse involves another organic metaphor of growing and of agricultural cycles of time, but instead of the earth-piercing growth of mustard seeds, human fate hangs with a cucumber vine. In Karṇa Vīr's version, Mahādev tricks Pārvatā, who persuaded him to create man, into administering the curse herself, so that she sees its justice. He requests that she go and pick cucumbers to satisfy his thirst, and she picks them at different stages of ripeness. Mahādev then interprets the cucumbers, a plant of little value which sprouts in dung heaps, whose flowers frequently fall off without setting, and whose fruit rots quickly, as an allegory for man:

Flowers that you picked and put on your head,
they are miscarriages;
tiny ones you picked and put in your mouth,
they are infants' deaths;
half ripe cucumbers you picked,
they are three- and two-year-olds' deaths;
those the size of sickle handles you picked,
they are adolescents' deaths;
those with a yellow shadow you picked,
they are thirty-six-, thirty-two-year-olds' deaths;
those that were completely yellow you picked,
they are middle-aged deaths;
split open ones you picked, they are old ones' deaths.

(3.14)

Sitā weeps, and Mahādev agrees to create different intercessors who can attempt to postpone man's fate, including paṇḍits, jaiśīs, dhāmīs, *jyānīs*, prakils, and pārkīs, and, of course, most important, jhāṅgarīs.

"Why do you weep, Sitau, I'll put up a fence for man,
I'll postpone the effects of the planets," declared Mahādev.
"I'll put there Kālu Jaiśī, he'll calculate auspicious moments,
will calculate the correct time,
will calculate the foundations of planets,
will calculate the signs of planets.
I'll put there Hunyā Bāhun, he will read the stories,
will read the seven-day ritual, will do the Rudrī lesson,
will diminish the effects of man's planets.
Don't cry, Sitau, I'll put there Rammā Purācan, Jhāṅgarī Jhiṅgrātam.
For man, the Messenger of Death,
the Time of Death he will postpone,
untimely deaths, untimely crises he will postpone,
secretly at the Dhuwā crossroads,
causing the masān to be with him,
having sat in the underworld,
untimely deaths, untimely obstructions he will postpone,
he will save man," he said.

(3.15)

This passage mentions three popular specialists, astrologers, Brāhmans, and shamans, and sketches their key activities. The sequel follows in the Recital to Postpone the Star Obstructions, which begins with a quick summary of the recital just quoted. Then Indra, lord of the heaven that is nearest our earth, tests each of the newly created experts. Each is summoned to "Indra's house, Nārāyaṇ's city, Śiva's palace," where

Daughter Kṛṣṇa Mother Padmā
was pierced by death, bowed her forehead to the ground.
Her throat had gone dry, it was sealed with a block,
she was one moment pierced, one moment dying.

(3.16)

The second line has a double meaning of both tilting her head in respect, and of bumping it on the ground in pain. The text sounds as if two individuals are meant, Daughter Kṛṣṇa and Mother Padmā (names, but rarely other details, are sometimes shared with Hindu myths), but shamans always heard this as a single entity, and the text uses singular conjugations for her.

First the original Brāhman paṇḍit, named Hunyā Bāhun in some recitals, Bharṣā Paṇḍit in others, is summoned. He reads standard printed texts in Sanskrit, such as the Rudrī lesson or the *Śrīsvastānī Bratakathā* (Purājulī V.S. 2036), over periods of seven or twelve days. There are very few paṇḍits in Jājarkoṭ. As locally used, the term means any Brāhman who performs canonical Hindu ceremonies, that is, any that include Sanskrit texts. One local paṇḍit, for example, does ceremonies for the royal family, another for the family from which the prime ministers traditionally came, the Kārkis. Neither has much command of Sanskrit. They struggle to pronounce it and cannot translate it into Nepali. At Indra's house, the original paṇḍit was not successful:

> Bharṣā Paṇḍit did knowledge [*jyān*], did meditation [*dhyān*],
> read the stories, read the seven day ritual,
> worshiped Satya Nārāyaṇ.
> "I don't know this illness, don't know its cause," he said.
>
> (3.17)

Next summoned are a series of minor specialists, the seers, councilors, and palmists. They

> do knowledge, do meditation,
> make oblations, measure pulses,
> . . . examine and discriminate.
>
> (3.18)

This broadly sums up the things that everyone does when problems are first encountered. All villagers know at least a few mantars, some read palms, others check pulses, and nearly everyone knows a variety of herbal treatments. These skills are too common for those who know these things to be considered specialists, however. Possibly, the texts refer to individuals who know significantly more than average, but the three terms are not in common usage in Jājarkoṭ, other than a loose application of gyānī, "knowledgeable," to any display of cleverness, especially by children. Karṇa Vīr defined a prakil as someone who makes a diagnosis on the basis of reading the nine pulses of the body, and a pārkī as someone who knows the hearts of others. Another villager suggested that the terms might refer to lawyers and government officials, that prakil is possibly a corruption of *vakil,* lawyer, a profession whose members can be accurately described as examining and discriminating. This would, however, rely on an unusual distortion of a word recently borrowed through Hindi from Persian, and such loan words are very rare in any of the shaman texts, except in the Historical Recital. In the recital, none of these minor specialists are successful. Each concludes: "I don't know this illness, it's cause."

Indra next summons the original astrologer, Kālu Jaiśī, whom we have already met in the story of the Nine Little Sisters.

> "Go now, attendants, Kālu Jaiśī is in Bāchigāũ,
> bring back Kālu Jaiśī." They brought back Kālu Jaiśī.
> He checked the horoscopes, checked the auspicious days,
> checked figures on a chalkboard,
> calculated times to travel to bazaars, to Tibet,
> to fight and dispute, the time to marry,
> gave the time to begin a house,
> "I don't know this illness, its cause."
>
> (3.19)

Of all these activities, which astrologers still commonly perform throughout Nepal, most important are the charts that they draw up at a birth. All parents have an astrological prediction made when a child is born to them. They take the forecast very seriously, as the example of mūl has shown. Villagers also consult astrologers on many other occasions than just births, as the text indicates. Their intercession is, however, limited to giving advice, and to preparing jantars, amulets worn around the neck that contain a drawing of auspicious astrological configurations copied out of a book. Astrologers do not otherwise actively intercede to try to correct unfortunate conditions, in the way shamans do, nor do they diagnose ills other than those that originate astrologically. Such amulets are not exclusively made by astrologers; anyone who has access to such books and who can read enough to copy letters can prepare one, including some shamans.

Karṇa Vīr provided the example in Figure 3.1. He painstakingly copied it from a book of birch paper bound in tiger skin that has belonged to his family for generations. This jantar undertakes to remap relations between the sun and moon (*ravī* and *candra*) at the top of the picture to achieve an alignment more favorable to the patient.

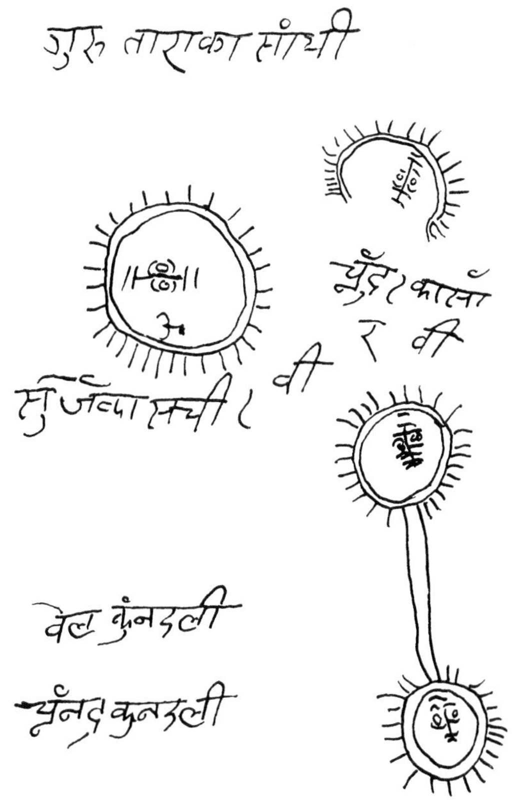

Figure 3.1. *Jantar* to treat astrological disturbances

Before we return to the narrative of the recital, two conspicuous absences in the texts deserve note. First, Buddhist lāmās fail to share even the small respect shown other ritual specialists. This is significant, for while none practice in Jājarkoṭ proper, there are important ones in the adjacent areas of Jumlā and Ḍolpā, where most of the characters have their mythical origin, including both the original dhāmīs and jhāṅgarīs. In the public recitals, lāmās play minor, entirely negative roles. Their use in mantars is even worse, providing nefarious assistance when raising spirits of the dead, an activity for which they hold the most extreme reputations. In the recitals, they appear only as another source of problems. The history of Satī Barbā, the lineage god of many jhāṅgarīs, describes his battles with the Kubaṁs Lāmā, the lāmā of "bad lineage," who tries to have him assassinated as soon as he is born:

> "Go now, attendants, in the east, on the western slope,
> what strength is awakened, what talent is awakened?
> My seat has been tilted.
> Go now, attendants, seven attendants, go and
> pull him here by the nose, pull him here by the ears,
> leave no breath, leave no life" . . .
> "Go now, attendants, what strength comes, what talent,
> set up a sixty-hand-high tree trunk, go as a group, go to one side,
> sharpen an axe blade, cause it to fall, from above,
> Satī Barbā will come,
> from below, cause it to fall,
> it will strike his body, Satī Barbā's,
> then he will die," he said.
>
> (3.20)

That other local specialists all earn less unfavorable mention, and only lāmās are represented so badly, may indicate otherwise forgotten affinities between Nepali shamans and practitioners of *bon* (the supposedly indigenous religion of the inner Himalayas). Since Jājarkoṭ was once part of the Malla kingdom (Naraharī Nāth V.S. 2012; Tucci 1956), this speculation has a historic plausibility. Shaman texts, however, offer no further evidence. Lāmās are not prominent in dhāmic stories either, even though the dhāmic spirits migrated from the north. The history of the dhāmic spirit Mahā̃kāl relates that once, an eighty-four-avatār lāmā used his own wisdom to dry up the ponds where Mahā̃kāl (a thirsty, demonic sort of spirit) was living. But Mahā̃kāl took the form of a wasp and stung the lāmā in his eyes, blinding him. He could no longer read his books, and all his power evaporated. A similar story from Jājarkoṭ Khalaṅgā concerned the royal family's dhāmic spirit, who also blinded a lāmā who tried to perform in front of the palace. None of the many other stories that the dhāmīs tell include antagonistic references to other classes of intercessors, only to other spirits who have their own dhāmīs. Jhā̃garīs and dhāmīs share this reciprocated animosity toward lāmās not only with each other, but with diverse specialists elsewhere in the Himalayas, many of whom also distinguish between the power of a text and the power of speech (Das 1881; Holmberg 1989; Mumford 1989; Paul 1976; Pignède 1966).

The second "absence" among the ritual specialists summoned to be tested, probably because too recently introduced to find any place in the shaman texts, is the village health worker. As may be expected from the marginal level of subsistence in Jājarkoṭ, the quality of individual health, as defined in Western terms, is low. My own observations during the six years that I lived there and the family histories that I collected suggest that child mortality may exceed 40 percent. Western Nepal has very high incidence rates of leprosy and tuberculosis; cholera, typhoid, and rabies epidemics occur, and other severe diseases like encephalitis, meningitis, and hepatitis are common. The Dutch built an expensive hospital at the district center, completing it in 1983. It is the only building in the district to have glass windowpanes and furnishings imported from India. Through 1993, it has remained inoperative and has begun to fall apart, due to a dispute with the government in Kathmandu over staffing it. Temporary collections of staff and patients were rounded up for a royal visit in 1989, but this was more of a photo opportunity for the Kathmandu royalty than anything relevant to health care.

There is also a four-room government health center in Jājarkoṭ Khalaṅgā and four one-room health posts in outlying villages. After an initial period of considerable experimentation, most villagers accurately concluded that these are best avoided, except in cases that are probably hopeless anyway and after all other options have failed. Mismanagement, corruption, and medical incompetence have all contributed to this conclusion. A single M.B.B.S (an Indian degree of bachelor in medical science) is assigned to cover the entire district, and, like many other officials, he is frequently away on official or casual leave. One that was assigned to Jājarkoṭ for much of the time that I lived there was a chronic alcoholic, more in need of treatment than capable of dispensing it. Drug consignments are limited and are often long past their expiration dates. They are consistently blackmarketed, either sold to middlemen who hoard them or else sold at exorbitant prices directly to the patients, who are supposed to receive them at nominal cost. Generous "gifts" are often made to the "doctor" just to be seen by him. Several cases of penicillin reaction resulting in death have occurred, for the powerful antibiotics that do become available are used indiscriminately, with drug therapy almost inevitably mismanaged. Nevertheless, as throughout the world, injections and capsules have rapidly acquired a nearly magical status, so that most villagers who do consult a "modern" medical practitioner expect these medicines to have an immediate curative effect on all ailments. They are thoroughly disappointed if their treatment doesn't include these techniques, regardless of their symptoms. The health post officials, whose three-month training course beyond their high school education earns them locally the title of "doctor," actively encourage this attitude toward drugs, since a major portion of their income is derived from charging for services that are supposed to be either free or minimally priced. Even so, a visit to the health post can be much less costly than consulting a spirit intercessor, so we must look beyond economics to understand the continuing success of the spirit intercessors. The most important reasons are local theories of disease causality, discussed in Chapter 2. Spirit intercession is also more familiar, less frightening, and less intrusive than is Western-style medicine, its practitioners less condescending and far easier to understand, and its success rate is no worse than that of its competitors.

Finally, we return to the last two ritual specialists summoned for testing to Indra's house, dhāmīs and jhāṅgarīs. Of the many distinct types of ritual practitioners found in Jājarkoṭ, these are the two who rely on systematic spirit possession as a definitive part of their practices, in clear contrast to other religious specialists, such as Brāhman paṇḍits and Jaiśī astrologers, who make no use of spirits.

Why not call both dhāmīs and jhāṅgarīs "shamans"? The same confusion after all exists in "standard" Nepali. Nepali speakers from elsewhere in the country often treat the two words as synonyms (Śarmā V.S. 2019). The compound *dhāmījhā̃krī* refers, usually disparagingly, to any ritual practitioner who calls spirits. This connotation exists in Jājarkoṭ, and shaman texts even parody it. In one case, a Kathmandu king abusively taunts ancestors of the present jhāṅgarī with the term.

> "Dhāmījhā̃krīs, jaiśīs, they are all thieves,
> they are all tricksters."
> So saying, the king had them seized and destroyed.
>
> (3.21)

Because of this persistent confusion, I will carefully examine the differences between these two specialists. Thoroughly developing this contrast serves two purposes beyond clarifying a problem of definition. First, it again demonstrates the potential that these texts have for clarifying problems of cultural meanings. Second, it explores key aspects of how these specialists regard their professional capacities. In this way emerges another answer to the question "What does a jhāṅgarī do?"

When Indra needed a cure, he sent his messengers to fetch the original dhāmī:

> They went to Tārābhoṭ, brought back Maitu Dhāmī.
> He slaughtered a goat at the goat pole,
> tossed out sixteen patterns of sacred rice,
> gave one handful to Indrajyū,
> gave one handful to Vāsudeu,
> postponed the crises,
> postponed the star positions.
>
> (3.22)

Remarkably, the dhāmī has some effect in postponing the problems. Shamans never consult dhāmīs, but they show respect for the spirits who possess them. However, as I argued in the previous chapter, only shamans are concerned with exploring causes and effects. Immediately, Maitu Dhāmī concludes, as did the astrologer and other specialists before him:

> "I don't know this illness,
> I don't know its cause."
>
> (3.23)

Elsewhere in the Bherī/Karnālī area dhāmīs are the exclusive vehicles for spirits (Sharma 1972, 1974; Śreṣṭha V.S. 2028; Jośī 2028, 2032). They are the most common form of spirit intercessor found in Jājarkoṭ, outnumbering jhāṅgarīs by more than ten to one. In a population of around a hundred thousand, there are some forty practicing shamans, while there are more than five hundred mediums. Dhāmīs come from all castes, including those who wear a sacred thread, while all jhāṅgarīs are either Dums (the local term for all untouchables) or Magars. Most, as I have already noted, are blacksmiths. All currently practicing jhāṅgarīs and most dhāmīs are male, although it is possible for a woman to practice either calling. For both dhāmīs and jhāṅgarīs, the transition over generations tends to remain within the patrilineage of a single family, passing to son or nephew, so males are favored, though there is no rule demanding this and exceptions are fairly common. In particular, it is not unusual for a dhāmī's wife to succeed him, especially when they have no son or until an infant son matures. There are also minor dhāmic spirits always represented by women. In most cases, these are the spirits of female suicides. The best known is Pritini in Paĩk Village, who has now been active for four generations. The wife of a Maṣṭā dhāmī, she ruined his departure on a trading trip by not revealing that her menstruation had begun. When her mother-in-law discovered this and severely abused her for ritually polluting the occasion, she hanged herself in the animal shed behind the house. Her spirit returned to plague the family until they provided a *dhāminī* who is regularly possessed by her. So far, she has always been a wife or daughter-in-law of the current Maṣṭā dhāmī, replicating the original suicide's position in the family.

Villages home to a particularly powerful dhāmī, such as Paĩk, forbid jhāṅgarīs to perform, or even to enter the village. Certain households elsewhere in the area that have a particularly strong relation with a dhāmic god also never summon shamans. For example, the Kārkis of Jājarkoṭ Khalaṅgā intermarry with the Rokāyas of Paĩk, from whom the Maṣṭā dhāmī traditionally comes, so none of them ever summon a jhāṅgarī to their houses. Maṣṭā is exceptional, however, respected by everyone in the area as the most powerful god of western Nepal. While other dhāmīs aspire to imitate his exclusiveness, most are less successful. Although the royal family of Jājarkoṭ Khalaṅgā has its own dhāmic spirit, an assassinated ancestor who returns to demand regular sacrifices, they regularly consult both other dhāmīs and local jhāṅgarīs, often consecutively for the same cases. According to their recitals, jhāṅgarīs sometimes send their clients to appease dhāmic gods, but I have never heard even rumors of a case in which a dhāmī recommended going to a jhāṅgarī. Supplicants travel for weeks to consult a particular dhāmī, but would never consider such a trip just to see a jhāṅgarī. Nevertheless, jhāṅgarīs manage in several recitals to assert their supremacy over dhāmīs and all other ritual specialists, even if there are few other opportunities to express these sentiments.

Sometimes, shaman recitals emphasize similarities between shamans and oracles, for jhāṅgarīs are very sensitive to the claims of important dhāmīs and attempt to claim equal status with them. Gumāne's version of how an ancestor of his was summoned to Nepal (Kathmandu) emphasizes this. The shaman successfully treated the queen, who was unable to give birth. He diagnosed Maṣṭā as responsible for her prolonged labor and ordered the king to appease the god in Saru. In return, the dhāmī honors the shaman for extending his fame:

"Where is this god? How should we worship Maṣṭā?
What must be done?" [said the king.]
They said, "Maṣṭā is at Kawā Kā̃ḍā, at Bijulī Ḍā̃ḍā.
Give him the rice field at Saro,
give him a brass bell for his temple,
order that all the people worship him."
The king ordered that all of this be done.
The Mahārānī's body was lightened, a son was born.
Later the jhā̇ṅgarī went to Bijulī Ḍā̃ḍā,
and was welcomed by Maṣṭā.
"You have made my arrangements for me,
I give you thanks."
Then he patted the jhāṅgarī on the back.
"May all that you do as a jhāṅgarī be good," he said,
gave him a blessing, sent him away.

(3.24)

The present dhāmīs of Bijulī Ḍā̃ḍā and those of Paīk, who now control the rice field in question, dismiss this story as complete fabrication. They tell a different version of how they came to possess that land (3.36).

That the word *shaman* comes from Siberia is a major reason ethnologists inevitably draw comparisons between "shamanic" phenomena elsewhere and those of Central Asia, for those were the first to attract scholarly interest, a history detailed in Flaherty (1992). Unfortunately, in trying to classify manifestations of so-called "primitive" religion throughout the world, observers have drawn such comparisons so widely, involving such a great variety of phenomena, that the word has become extremely ambiguous (hopelessly ambiguous, an "insipid category," suggests Geertz 1966:39). Even for Central Asia, there is disagreement over what really constitutes an "essence" or necessary features of a shaman. The word reached the West from Tungus, for whom it is also apparently a loan word: Mironov and Shirokogoroff (1924) convincingly argue that the Tungus word *shaman* derives from Sanskrit *śramaṇa* (Buddhist monk, or, more generally, any religious adept), by way of its intermediary Pāli form *samaṇa*. This etymology is, however, contested, and the word may also stem from the root *sam-*, found throughout the Altaic languages, which "contains the idea of dance and leap on the one hand, and trouble and agitation on the other" (Lok-Falck 1977:9). Both etymologies are suggestive, and inconclusive. In either case, popularized out of a wide set of possible choices used by diverse populations (Hultkrantz 1973:26–27), "shaman" entered English through Russian seventeenth-century travelers who first described Siberian peoples and their customs.

Shirokogoroff provides an excellent definition in his discussion of Tungus: "In all Tungus languages the term refers to *persons of both sexes who have mastered spirits, who at their will can introduce these spirits into themselves and use their power over the spirits in their own interests, particularly helping other people, who suffer from the spirits . . .*" (1935:269, italics in original). He further clarifies this definition with the remark that "the most important and characteristic condition which makes of an ordinary man a shaman is that he is a *master of spirits*, at least of a group of spirits" (1935:271). Shirokogoroff mentions the undertaking of "soul-journeys" to the underworld as an infrequent and relatively unimportant characteristic (1935:310). Yet it is precisely supernatural travel that Eliade, often considered the foremost expert in the field of shaman studies, insists to be its central feature, in conjunction with "ecstasy." He argues that historically, "the shaman specializes in a trance during which his soul is believed to leave his body and ascend to the sky or descend to the underworld" (1964:5). Eliade explicitly excludes spirit possession as a necessary element of a shaman, insisting that it is a historically derivative feature, whereas a soul journey is not a necessary characteristic in the ceremonies of Tungus shamans. One could combine these two definitions, to avoid arguing about hypothetical chronologies and "classic" versus "degenerate" forms. Johan Reinhard has done exactly this for the specific context of Nepal: "A shaman is a person who at his will can enter into a non-ordinary psychic state (in which he either has his soul undertake a journey to the spirit world or he becomes possessed by a spirit) in order to make contact with the spirit world on behalf of members of his community" (1976:16). Reinhard commendably tried to find a way around much of the debate, particularly by shifting the focus away from the extremely subjective, theologically charged concept of "ecstasy." However, using his definition, or ones similar to it, leads to calling both dhāmīs and jhāṅgarīs "shamans," creating a false sense of equivalence between the two practices (3.21). Jhāṅgarīs may themselves have goals of professional enhancement for suggesting just such an equivalence, since there is higher status attached to dhāmīs, but the two practices are remarkably distinctive.

Both dhāmīs and jhāṅgarīs of Jājarkoṭ enter apparently "ecstatic" states, in which they consider themselves and are considered by their clients to be possessed by one (or more) spirits. They also undertake forms of supernatural travel through this and other worlds—soul journeys—while so possessed. Self-descriptive passages of oral texts explicitly illustrate these conditions for both forms of spirit intercession. When the first jhāṅgarī, Rammā Jumrātam, prepares to match his strength against that of the first witches, the Nine Little Sisters, the account states:

> He began to tremble lightly,
> began to tremble heavily,
> with twelve familiar spirits [bīr],
> with twenty-two bloodthirsting spirits [māphī],
> the fields shook, the forests shook,
> the land shook, the ground shook,
> Rammā Jumrātam began to be possessed.
>
> (3.25)

Along with bīr and māphī, other classes of spirits that possess shamans include deutā, dhām, dhuwā, and barāṅg. Jhāṅgārīs commonly summon all of these different classes, frequently in multiple combinations.

We find an excellent example of dhāmīs becoming possessed in an account provided by the Maṣṭā dhāmī of Paīk. He describes the first visit of Mahādev Śāhī, an early king of Jājarkoṭ, who came to consult the dhāmī at Khaphallā:

> the god arrived.
> The god leapt from one person's shoulders to another's,
> causing everyone to tremble,
> until it finally settled on the dhāmī,
> who grabbed the king and dragged him onto the throne.
>
> (3.26)

For examples of soul travel, jhāṅgarī texts have more eloquent illustrations. They travel through the world's many levels, ranging from the heaven of Indra Lok, where Jumrātam finally cures Daughter Kṛṣṇa Mother Padmā, down to the lowest underworld, Tilīkarmā, where Jumrātam learns to be a blacksmith:

> He lowered a loosely spun thread, from this thread
> he descended the seven levels of the world,
> descended to Tilīkarmā.
>
> (3.27)

There are different paths to Tilīkarmā, including one used by jhāṅgarīs and one used by witches. Jumrātam describes them to his wife in the form of a riddle that becomes important during the death rites. The name "Tilīkarmā" (often pronounced Tīlīgramā) probably means "Ironwork," the karma of blacksmithing. The first shaman learns to be a smith there. Shamans to whom I suggested this definition thought it likely, but found such speculation pointless, since there is no textual authority for etymological guesses. Between us and Tilīkarmā are several other levels of the world, including those of decaying vegetable matter, soil, and rocks, where, as will be seen in the next chapter, jhāṅgarīs sometimes search for lost souls.

I have been unable to collect such cosmic examples of soul travel for dhāmīs, but there are stories of instantaneous bodily transmigrations over great distances, and incredible leaps into the air. When the Mahādev dhāmī of Aulrijā, the Mukhiyā, agreed to intercede in a dispute that others had with the Sundārgāũ dhāmī in Jumlā, he sent the others on ahead.

> They traveled for three days to reach Sundārgāũ.
> Since the Mukhiyā had not accompanied them,
> the Sundārgāũ dhāmī ignored the supplicants and went to bathe.
> At the time he went to bathe,
> the Mukhiyā finally left his home in Aulrijā.
> By the time the Sundārgāũ dhāmī returned from his bath,
> the Mukhiyā sat beside his throne, smoking tobacco.
>
> (3.28)

The activities of dhāmic spirits are more firmly part of this world, or, at least, of a slightly enlarged version of it, one that has room for such spirits. Those spirits travel on, and belong to, this earth's surface and its adjacent air space, which are only two levels of seven for jhāṅgarīs. Maṣṭā's story of origin begins in Indralok, though, from which he was expelled due to the mūl catastrophe of his birth. That story also reports the dhāmī releasing tigers from his hair to scare villagers that had teased his wife, a variation on the theme of "soul travel."

So far, these examples loosely illustrate the apparent appropriateness of calling both jhāṅgarīs and dhāmīs "shamans." The key phenomenal attributes defining the term shaman, possession by spirits and supernatural travel, characterize both kinds of intercessors. One key difference remains: whether or not the intercessors regard themselves as possessed "at will." While seemingly a minor point, intentionality, more than anything else, distinguishes how they characterize their states of possession. Reinhard clarifies his definition by calling our attention to the way the phrase "at will" differentiates a shaman from a medium, or any other "who may become possessed in various situations but who does not have the ability to do this whenever he so desires, or who requires the assistance of others in order to become possessed" (1976:16).

A dhāmī is spontaneously selected by a single tutelary god, nearly always a deutā. That god alone regularly possesses his dhāmī. The possession too, is spontaneous, a consequence of the god's will, not the dhāmī's, as shown in the example involving Mahādev Śāhi above. If the dhāmī offends the deutā, it chooses someone else.

Dhāmic possessions take place on a fixed schedule based on the lunar calendar. These possessions take place either in small shrines set outside the villages or in special throne rooms within the dhāmī's house. They take place whether or not supplicants are in attendance.

Each of these points contrasts to a jhāṅgarī's practice. Jhāṅgarīs compel, through their recital of memorized texts, many different spirits to come, at the former's convenience:

> "Come when I say come,
> go when I say go"
>
> (3.29)

as one line of a summons puts it. Such spirits may be deutā, or they may be māphī, bīr, barāṅg, dhām, or dhuwā. To a jhāṅgarī these are distinct classes of spirits, to be summoned for distinct purposes. Some are protective, solicitous, benign, and undemanding; others are malicious, oppressive, and threatening (1.5).

A jhāṅgarī performs at the house of his patient. He will summon spirits on any night of the month, regardless of the phase of the moon, excepting days of an eclipse. Certain performances even take place in the daytime. That is, a jhāṅgarī's possession is fixed neither in time nor in space, while that of a dhāmī is fixed in both. A single, identifiable, god chooses and regularly possesses a dhāmī, while a jhāṅgarī induces possession by a multitude of spirits, not all of whom are identified during the possession. The god "rides" the dhāmī, who carries it as its "horse," terms not used for a jhāṅgarī. The dhāmī's possession is usually described intransitively, the jhāṅgarī's, transitively (*kamnu,* locally *karnu,* versus *kamāunu*).

When someone needs a jhāṅgarī, a member of the patient's household must personally invite him. The patient's family must arrange for someone to carry the basket of the jhāṅgarī's paraphernalia, or perhaps pay a regular assistant, called a *curmi,* to do so; in no circumstances does the jhāṅgarī carry this basket himself, though he may find someone to do it. Typically, he arrives in the early evening, but does not eat before the ritual, which begins after sunset, when at least three stars can be seen in the sky. The seance often continues until dawn, culminating in a blood sacrifice. The hosts prepare a small space for a fire on the ground outside the patient's house. The jhāṅgarī sits on a circular mat or flat stool in front of this fire, facing east. Besides his drum and elaborate costume, he may require numerous things, which the patient's family must supply. Requirements vary from ceremony to ceremony, but the minimal requirements include firewood for the fire; some handfuls of rice; a deposit of one to twenty-five rupees; at least a chicken to sacrifice, if not a goat, sheep, or pig; mustard seeds; cotton wicks to burn clarified butter or oil in small leaf dishes; a bunch of fresh leaves, preferably cinnamon, oak, or guava. When not planning an animal sacrifice to their māphī (personal bloodthirsting spirits), a shaman beats a copper plate, rather than a skin drum. The plate is ritually pure *(choko),* unlike a drum for which blood has been shed, which is impure *(juṭho).*

The jhāṅgarī arranges the necessary items around the fire. He begins by crushing mustard seeds under his heel, protects himself with a mantar (5.17), and then prays publicly to the gods that he may succeed. Next he unpacks his drum, recites another mantar as he warms it over the fire (5.20), and starts to tap it lightly, praying out loud to his ancestral spirits, especially that of his own guru. He then dresses in his costume, which receives the protection of yet another mantar. Every costume varies somewhat, but the Recital of the Nine Little Sisters thoroughly describes an idealized version. When the witches threaten to attack her husband, the jhāṅgarī's wife assembles it for the first time, to protect him:

> From a *syālī* tree, she brought matted locks of hair,
> from Chārkābhoṭ, she brought pheasant feathers,
> from Kālā Pāṭan, she brought fragrant leaves,
> put these on his head.

From a *kacur* garden, she brought a piece of kacur root,
put it in his mouth.
From a merchant's store, she brought cowry shells,
from a *puwā* grove, she brought a tie string,
put these around his neck.
From the best Malāyāgirī sandalwood,
she brought charcoal ashes, put them on his forehead.
From the tree over an ancestral jhāṅgarī's tomb,
she brought the *sādan* wood hoop for a drum,
from Rātā Pahar, she brought a wild goat's skin,
from Sudār Pānī, she brought a drum's inner handles,
made a complete drum.
From a *gharī* vine, she brought a *gharī* wood drumstick.
From a brass worker's store,
she brought a pair of clanging bells.
From a *khair* grove, she brought a leather belt.
From a wild edible fig tree,
she brought a pair of bells and a pair of bell strikers.
From Chārkābhoṭ, she brought a swirl of yak's tail.
From newborn animals,
she brought the long teeth of wild sows and wild boars.
"Elder Brother Tikhu Kāmī, Elder Brother Ghāro Kāmī,
make for me a cowbell, a perforated bell, a solid bell,
a ringing bell," she said, brought them when they were made.
From a tailor's shop,
she brought two kinds of women's outer wraps,
brought stitched pajamas.
From a *śīśa* tree, she brought a wild boar's skin.
She assembled all the equipment for a jhāṅgarī.

(3.30)

This description closely matches all the costumes that I have seen, though the places of origin for the various items vary widely, and additional items, such as various animal skins and miscellaneous metal trinkets, are not uncommon. One major variation in Rukum and the Bhujī Valley is the wearing of an archer's wristguard *(bhoṭo),* which I have never seen worn in Jājarkoṭ. Magar shamans often wear emblems of the sun and moon forged of iron (Oppitz 1991:27), though most blacksmiths that I knew didn't wear these.

All jhāṅgarī drums are one-sided. The preferred hoop wood is sādan, whose thick red sap coagulates like human blood when the tree is cut.

The drum skin comes from a wild goat, the handles are of cane and mounted in a narrow X inside, loosely attached by iron loops, all points covered in a special recital for constructing a drum. That text reports, for example, on the hunt for the goat that will supply the drum skin:

> From the Eastern House, the Nine Hunters,
> [with] mouse-like dogs, mongoose-like dogs,
> the Nine Hunters went, shouting "ho ho," shouting "shu shu."
> On White Mountain, they raised it up, the spoor of a wild goat.
> Forcing it to the river, the dog [named] Bhārkī,
> clawed at it, snapped at it.
> The Nine Hunters, [with] a poisoned arrow tip,
> shot a dazzling arrow.
> Its hooves pointed to heaven, its back to hell.
> They burned incense, offered the ears and tongue,
> stripped off the skin, for my drum skin.
>
> (3.31)

For major ceremonies, the jhāṅgarī decorates the drum with simple line drawings of white clay. Karṇa Vīr sketched one such pattern (Fig. 3.2). Every jhāṅgarī also wears two kinds of women's outer wraps and men's pajamas, wears the mentioned leaves and feathers on his head, has a leather vest with bells and other iron trinkets attached, wears various necklaces, and places in his mouth a piece of kacur (a bitter root resembling turmeric). All of this provides protection against malevolent attacks.

Having put on his costume, the jhāṅgarī again sits and resumes drumming. The beat becomes more insistent and suddenly his possession begins. He trembles violently, his head, eyes, and tongue roll. His body twitches, thrashes, convulses. He shudders, shouts, sobs, pants, sniffs, and gestures wildly. Soon, he calms down and resumes his seat. His drumming becomes more restrained and rhythmic. Finally he begins to recite the text appropriate to the occasion. The intensity of his performance is not uniform throughout the remainder of the evening. It ranges from hebetude to frantic leaping and shouting in the six directions. His speech delivery spans inaudible muttering and rigorous, insistent singing. At times the jhāṅgarī will pause and rearrange things, smoke, and, still apparently entranced, listen to questions of the spectators, whom he advises.

A dhāmī's performance is quite distinct. Each god has a small shrine dedicated to it, usually located on the outskirts of a village, in forest

Figure 3.2. Drum decorations

clearings, or on hilltops. These shrines contain a small stone and mud platform raised about a foot off the ground, the dhāmī's throne. They are often cluttered, inside and out, with tridents, iron lamp stands, and strips of cloth, all offerings from supplicants.

A dhāmī wears no special costume, though he observes certain restrictions of dress that indicate his subservience to his god. He always dresses in homespun cloth and never wears either shoes or other footwear or hats and caps. Many do wear turbans, to wrap up their long hair, never cut. Usually, the dhāmī unwraps his hair, which may reach the ground, before a possession, but sometimes retains the turban throughout the ceremony. The dhāmī makes no special preparations for the ceremony, other than fasting and bathing on the days for which a possession is scheduled. A *dhaṅgrī* (the dhāmī's assistant, also called a *pujārī*) attends to technical details, such as cleaning the throne, lighting small oil lamps, and unpacking supplicants' *akṣeta* (whole grains of pure uncooked rice used for sacred purposes) to form a small mound at the front of the throne. The dhāmī rests, seated, beside the throne. If drumming is involved, as at all major full moons, *damāis* (the tailor caste, who are the traditional drummers) assemble outside. In the felicitous terms of Gilbert Rouget, a dhāmī is "musicated," while jhāṅgarīs are "musicants"

(1985:132). This contrast is underscored in the most important dhāmic sessions, when a group of village women sing *māṅgals*, auspicious hymns to the god. Rarely, when a literate Brāhman comes to consult, he may even recite Sanskrit texts to honor the god. Suddenly the dhāmī shakes. He leaps trembling onto the throne. His shaking diminishes as the dhaṅgrī places a *rudrākṣa* seed necklace on him. He may, rarely, recite the god's *parelī* (its personal history), but more often he says nothing, simply distributing *ṭikā* (forehead dots) and "three grains" of akṣeta to the supplicants as they begin to consult him.

Sometimes other dhāmīs are also present, both inside and outside the shrine, and their spirits also possess them. The most important of these occasions occurs yearly, at Bhadau *pūrṇimā* (the full moon in the lunar month of Bhadau, which usually falls in September or October) in Paīk. A frenzy of over forty dhāmīs and dhāminīs simultaneously become possessed at this event, dancing together in front of Maṣṭā's shrine. Those possessed by spirits subdued by Maṣṭā (his servants) carry his dhāmī on their shoulders around the shrine. Most often, though, dancing has no part in a dhāmī's ceremony and the dhāmī rarely leaves his throne until the god departs. For bloodthirsty gods such as Maṣṭā, many goats are sacrificed, but this takes place after the possession ceremony proper, and the dhāmī is simply an onlooker, doing no more than distributing the quarters of the animal to the supplicants and the villagers. This and the distribution of any *prasād* (blessed food prepared from offerings, such as rice pudding) concludes the event.

In contrast to jhāṅgarīs, who use oral texts as part of every ceremony, dhāmīs may or may not begin a ceremony with their parelī, the formal recital of the god's personal history. Dhāmic parelīs are much more public than are shaman texts, known and elaborated in casual retellings by many villagers. The māṅgal sung at major ceremonies are also dhāmic texts, although they differ in purpose from parelī. They invite and supplicate the god, whereas the parelī authenticates its presence. These hymns, too, are public, known and freely taught by the women associated with that god, either through kinship with the dhāmī or simply by identifying themselves as followers of that god.

> Our god who is always hidden inside,
> today our god is out in the sunlight.
> Come servants, come servants,

come bring the five-spouted pitcher.
Come servants, come Mahādev,
bring the five-spouted pitcher.
Come servants, come, bring the staff and mace.
Above the staff and mace sits Mahādev.
Put your shadow, Indra Nārāyaṇ, victor of Uchī Dungī,
above the five-spouted pitcher.
Come sit, Twelve Brothers Maṣṭā.
Above the staff and mace come sit, Indra Nārāyaṇ,
you, victor who conquered Uchī Dungī,
who now offers this five-spouted pitcher,
who offers sweet *dubo* grass to this staff and mace,
who offers fresh leaves, the five-spouted pitcher,
who offers rice and curd, the staff and mace,
who offers all, the staff and mace.
Above the golden globe come sit, Mahādev.
Spread your shadow, Indra Nārāyaṇ.
Here sit Twelve Brothers Maṣṭā.
Above the copper globe come sit, Indra Nārāyaṇ.

(3.32)

This example strives to place Maṣṭā, for whom it is sung, at the head of a divine assemblage. The women sing it when the dhāmī leaves his house for the forest temple.

Dhāmīs receive no training and so never formally memorize texts. The stories of the dhāmic gods, however, are common knowledge, even if no "canonical" version exists (as it does for a jhāṅgarī text, since the jhāṅgarī corrects his pupil's recitation repeatedly throughout the years of apprenticeship). Despite the importance of parelīs, they are, as I noted, rarely performed. Jājarkoṭ's most important dhāmī, Anarup Rokāya, Maṣṭā dhāmī of Paĩk (Illus. 3.2), reports that in twenty-seven years as a dhāmī, he has recited Maṣṭā's parelī only three times. The first time was when the god first came to him, at the full moon of Bhadau, V.S. 2013 (1957), during a fierce dispute between the then reigning Maṣṭā dhāmī and that dhāmī's younger brother, who insisted on being recognized as the Mahā̃kāl dhāmī and receiving rights to a share of the god's land, which is the most productive rice field in the area (3.24). He grabbed the necklace of his older brother and threw it out of the shrine. Anarup put it on, became possessed, recited Maṣṭā's parelī, and continued the ceremony. The second time he recited it was three years later, as the dispute over who was the authentic dhāmī continued, having reached such a violent level that the military intervened and placed all three disputants and their supporters under arrest. Anarup traveled to Kauwā, in Mugu, whose own Maṣṭā dhāmī is senior to that in Paīk and receives a goat every five years from him. There the dhāmī challenged him:

> When the god had come to the Kauwā dhāmī,
> he turned to Anarup and shouted:
> "You say that you are Bijulī Maṣṭā.
> There are twelve brothers, each has his own path.
> Among those twelve paths, tell me now yours.
> What is older brother's Ḍaḍār's path?
> What is Tharpā's path?
> Now, what is your path? If you know, come on, tell it.
> If you don't, I'll beat you over the head with a stick
> until you crawl away from here,
> with blood dripping from your feet."
> When the Kauwā dhāmī had said this,
> the god came to Anarup.
> He jumped onto the throne,
> and he chanted the entire history.
> "I am satisfied," announced the Kauwā dhāmī.
> "You are my brother Bijulī," and he said to everyone,
> "This is the true dhāmī."
>
> (3.33)

The third time Anarup recited the parelī was some twenty years later, after I had approached a dozen times as a supplicant to request it.

Other dhāmīs report having performed the parelī only once in their lives, though a few, such as the pair of Suwākotī dhāmīs in Caurātā include at least selections from theirs in every ceremony. Clearly, parelīs do not have the same relation to dhāmic ceremonies as do the *melās* (recitals) in jhāṅgarī ceremonies. The importance of jhāṅgarī texts is evident in every ceremony. When a jhāṅgarī is in trance, dressed in full costume, beating his drum and dancing excitedly, his recital is regarded by the audience, and glossed by jhāṅgarīs themselves, as direct communications with the spirit(s) possessing him. Despite this, jhāṅgarīs do not deny that they have had to learn these texts laboriously in hundreds of hours of rote drill throughout years of apprenticeship. These texts belong to jhāṅgarīs, who regard them as their private specialized knowledge. (I have found, however, a few individuals who know and use some of the recitals and mantars, even though they are definitely not, and do not claim to be, jhāṅgarīs.) Dhāmic texts bind the dhāmī to a particular vision of the world, but they lack the instrumental quality of jhāṅgarī melās; their recital provides no particular means of controlling events in the world, only a general framework for the involvement of a single god in those events.

Since dhāmic texts have much less importance attached to their exact reproduction, and there is no formal teacher who could correct them, their meanings have a problematic, unanchored quality to them. Many dhāmic ceremonies include no text, other than the consultations between intercessor and supplicant. Nevertheless, the ability to produce the parelī spontaneously is the crucial criterion in the selection of a new dhāmī, so in this sense texts are just as important to dhāmīs as they are to jhāṅgarīs.

In both traditions, texts provide the basis for authenticating the spirit's intercessor. For dhāmīs, however, the god determines every aspect of the possession, its agent, schedule, location, duration, every circumstance. The god legitimates his chosen vehicle with a text. This is always the "same" text, telling the origin story of the particular spirit who controls the entire event. However, the words, names, and incidents themselves may vary. That is, using Frege's (1970) distinction, a parelī always has the same referent (*Bedeutung*—that aspect of experience about which it says something), but is distinct in terms of its sense (*Sinn*—what it expresses about that which it designates). The spatiotemporal event too is the same, always held in the same locations and following a rigidly prescribed calendar.

On the other hand, each jhāṅgarī text treats a particular set of ailments. They mediate or aggravate particular crises. The jhāṅgarī himself claims control over the event of possession, compelling a spirit to come, using different texts to compel different spirits. These texts, then, are the same in terms of the sense, the words that are carefully reproduced in each performance, but distinct in their referents. Three poles of the dialectics of discourse suggested by Paul Ricoeur (1976) event, sense, and reference, provide convenient contrasts between the two practitioners. Ricoeur's fourth pole, "meaning," is less usefully contrastive. The texts of both kinds of intercessors define a space of social meanings. This is minimally true as a consequence of their being oral, so that the persons who recite them participate in at least this way with their content. Some familiarity is crucial, for I maintain that certain meanings contained in the texts give charter to certain social actions. Consequently, to examine those meanings is to examine how actors make sensible their behavior. Any social world is made operational by meaning, by meanings that its participants have selected as significant to them, not by concepts imposed by an observing subject. What we are looking at here is how certain meanings have been construed within the oral texts used by both dhāmīs and jhāṅgarīs, and how those meanings make intelligible the social practices that such ceremonies constitute. Examining texts provides a rather simple solution to the problems of intentionality, since, as Ricoeur (1976:30) put it, "the text's career escapes the finite horizon lived by its author," whose possibly subjective original intentions become coincident with the meaning of the text, open to public exploration. My study, however, dissolves Ricoeur's restrictive separation of speech from writing, since the characteristics of these formal oral texts are exactly the same as those of any written ones.

Not only do dhāmic texts vary with each performance, but different jhāṅgarīs recite different versions of the same texts. This in itself is not remarkable, and would be expected for an orally transmitted tradition. More noteworthy, different versions of the stories are equally coherent. It is not only a process of deterioration that has produced new versions, but also a process of re-creation, of meaning being reinvented. This shows that jhāṅgarīs do not simply memorize texts as if they were meaningless chants, nor is the sound so important that meaning is submerged within it. Rather, semantic intervention must at least occasionally take place, in which jhāṅgarīs thoroughly participate in the meanings that the texts contain, reestablishing a foundation of sense when the text is excessively threatened by ambiguity. Not every jhāṅgarī need do this, but meaning is periodically recreated, demonstrating the periodic intervention in their texts by jhāṅgarīs.

While dhāmīs repeat the same ceremony again and again, jhāṅgarīs perform a variety of different ceremonies, as can be documented by examples from their texts. One of these that most surprised me is to cause, rather than to cure, problems—performing deliberate acts of sorcery. For example, in the next selection, the jhāṅgarī raises spirits from the dead, performs a secret ritual, and sends those masān to plague his enemies. Not only does the text describe acts of sorcery, but in doing so it provides explicit directions for conducting them:

He assembled his equipment.
Having put on the *riṭhā* [black seed] necklace,
having put on the snakebone necklace,
having put on the Gurai necklace,
having put on the kacur necklace,
late in the evening, in the deepest time of night,
in the darkest time of night,
dancing with straight steps, dancing with backward steps,
he descended to the sixth crossroads,
descended to the Masān Ghāṭ.
Of the Bhampā kacur, going,
biting out one bit, he spat it toward the north.
Biting out one bit, he spat it toward the south.
Biting out one bit, he spat it toward the west.
Biting out one bit, he spat it toward the east.
Biting out one bit, he spat it toward heaven.
Biting out one bit, he spat it toward hell.
Going to the sixth crossroads, going to the Masān Ghāṭ,
he dances with reversed steps,
he dances with upside-down steps.
Of the Nine Little Sisters, Acam Sera's daughters,
their sides throbbed with pain,
they convulsed with pain, their lives were convulsed.
"O Eldest Sister, our sister,
Paternal Uncle Kabare, Paternal Uncle Masān,
has become threatening, has become challenging.
What secret knowledge [*bhed*] has been done,
what secret action [*ched*] has been done?"
thus they began to speak.
"O Eldest Sister, our sister, our lives have been convulsed,"
thus they began to speak.
Oh, Paternal Uncle Rammācan,
from the sixth crossroads, from the Masān Ghāṭ,
dancing with backward steps, biting the Bhampā kacur,
then came to there.

(3.34)

Here, the jhāṅgarī's victims are witches, so perhaps they deserve this treatment. However, another curse occurs in Tilīkarmā, when the angered jhāṅgarī makes the king's innocent son deathly ill before fleeing and hiding (see 2.3 for a different version, in which the king is directly cursed):

"You can't identify witches, you can't identify bewitchers,
you can't identify bāyu, you can't identify batās.
What kind of a jhāṅgarī are you, what kind of a dhāmī are you?"
He was sarcastic, he was sardonic.
Syāulā Rammā, going,
having been frantically possessed [*ranga bhanga*],
to Rājai Rautyālā [the king's son],
taking a straw from the roof, poked him in the eyes.
Ai, taking off his great wristguard, Rājai Rautyālā,
he poked in his right side, poked in left side.
With a twig of the Tāre tree, with a twig of the Māre tree,
he poked in the ears Rājai Rautyālā.
His ears couldn't hear, his eyes couldn't see,
his sides ached, his heart ached.
Ai, oh Rājai Rautyālā was a complete wreck.
He was half alive, half dead, felt fevers, chills.
Oh, Syāulā Rammā, going, fled, ran away.

(3.35)

Dhāmic gods also cause afflictions, but this does not ordinarily involve any active intervention of the dhāmī. The best-known case comes from Paĩk and concerns the same rice field whose ownership was recently disputed. Maṣṭā's parelī tells the story in the first person:

I declared this my home, I had nothing at all,
what else could I do, I chose a small field,
there at a resting place, I made him dance on his hands,
the *nāyak*'s [chief's] son, Pasāṅgro, Nātā Rāj the nāyak,
Pasāṅgro who had no sons, I seized him and held on.
Oh, my brothers, this was done,
for twelve years I held him.
This is what I had to do,
this solved my big problem . . .

(3.36)

For twelve years Pasāṅgro neither died nor recovered; insects hatched from his body, so many that every morning his mother filled up a bowl with them. This persisted until his father turned over the land in question, the most productive irrigated field in Saru, to the Maṣṭā dhāmī. Even when Maṣṭā promises a cure, often his curse is lifted only after twelve years, a tenet that certainly must test supplicants' patience. It did the nāyak's. He attacked the dhāmī's brother with a knife and nearly killed him. The dhāmī does not, however, play an active part in causing the afflictions, the agency being entirely attributed to Maṣṭā himself. Similarly, any cure is left to Maṣṭā as well.

The rest of this book will examine other aspects of what jhāṅgarīs do, but the passages already offered show how distinct a jhāṅgarī's activities are from those of a dhāmī. Returning to Shirokogoroff's discussion of Tungus shamans, we have documented every major aspect that he attributes to them for the jhāṅgarīs of western Nepal as well. He lists the essential formal characteristics of a shaman as (1) the shaman is a master of spirits; (2) he has mastered a group of spirits; (3) there is a complex of methods and paraphernalia recognized and transmitted; (4) there is a theoretical justification of the practice; (5) the shaman assumes a special social position (1935:274). Each point applies to jhāṅgarīs as well. As has been seen, a jhāṅgarī is "a *master of spirits,* at least of a group of spirits." He controls different spirits who possess different qualities. Jhāṅgarīs do possess a complex of special methods for dealing with the spirits, and they use and transmit an elaborate array of paraphernalia, chief of which is, as for the Tungus, the drum. Their "special social position" eloquently emerges in their texts, although it is seriously ambivalent within Nepali society. Shirokogoroff himself, however, meant by this only "social recognition—a group which distinguishes one of its members by bestowing on him their confidence," something that the numerous clients of a jhāṅgarī frequently do. Finally, as was demonstrated in the last chapter, they articulate, within their texts, a "general theory of spirits, their particular characteristics, and the practical possibilities of dealing with spirits."

All of these characteristics, along with technical details of their practices, clearly distinguish jhāṅgarīs from dhāmīs. What I advocate, then, is to use in its original form the definition of "shaman" provided by Shirokogoroff's description of Tungus, not the revisions attempted by either Eliade or Reinhard. Consequently, throughout this work, I use "jhāṅgarī" and "shaman" as synonyms. Dhāmīs I will refer to as "mediums," or I will leave the term untranslated. Using a word borrowed from Tungus does not, I hope, diminish the linguistic integrity of my study. That Tungus use a word of possibly Sanskritic origin to name their shamans should, after all, caution us if we speculate about historic origin or the direction in which influences flowed. When John T. Hitchcock first uncovered the distinct complex of jhāṅgarīs in Dhorpatan and the Bhujī

Illustration 3.2. Anarup Rokāya, Maṣṭā Dhāmī

Valley in 1961, he accurately labeled them shamans and called attention to some of their systemic resemblances with those of Central Asia (Hitchcock 1967), a point reiterated by David Watters (1975) and Reinhold Greve (1989). There are intriguing similarities, but however labeled, jhāṅgarīs cannot be seen as a simple derivative or historic vestige of the fictitious construct known as "classical Asiatic shamanism," whose disparate elements probably owe much to southern neighbors. Jhāṅgarīs exist, not just as another example of "shamanism," but as a set of unique persons with unique resources, with their own contexts and their own configurations in time and space.

4
Staging Interventions

There are three obvious components of every shaman's performance to which any observer has access. First, the shaman uses words. He sings, chants, prays, whispers, talks, mumbles, shouts. Second, he moves. He dances, trembles, squats, leaps, rolls on the ground. Third, he uses things. He drums, throws seeds, ties knots, pounds pegs, waves yak tails, smashes gourds. Here I take up the connections between these sets of activities, between what is said and what is done. Specifically, I now examine the reflexive character of shamanic speech and shamanic action, again using what is said to understand what is done. I am interested in the connections between what can be heard during a performance and what can be witnessed and reported both by outsiders (whether anthropologist or local audience) and by participants (shaman or patient). Sorting out the ontological problems involved among these three sets of accounts, I make use of ethnomethodology's realization that social situations are not necessarily ready-made or unproblematically available to their participants, but actively constituted by the continuing interaction of the participants, who work to arrive at a sensible construction of the situation. I support the methodological argument that the use of tapes, repeatable and public, offers the best approach from which the situational reflexivity of shamanic activity can be tackled. Most important, I show that most of the work that goes into making a performance performable as well as observable and reportable is contained within the texts themselves.

Shaman texts not only contain the rationale for the action performed in their ceremonies, describing the causal agents of the afflictions for which the patient is being treated, as Chapter 2 demonstrated. They also detail the ideal performance that the shaman strives to recreate. The texts are filled with precise "stage directions," straightforward accounts of what should be done as the ceremony unfolds. These directions do not necessarily occur as the actions they direct take place—text and performance follow intertwined but sometimes divergent courses. Like a musical score, texts do not explicitly supply every detail of a ritual; continuo must be supplied extratextually by the shaman or, in some cases, by assistants. These additions, as we will see below, tend to be points that shamans themselves insist are trivial. A shaman in performance is neither composer nor improviser, but a virtuoso soloist who reads vibrant life into a literal and fixed score. To the score, shamans must add the dramaturgic interpretations that transform words into gestures, episodes into performative sequences, and texts into lifesaving rituals. Performance is an important measure of a successful shaman. Who can recreate the cosmos who can't captivate the attention of a few dozen villagers? A good singing voice, powerful drumming, rigorous dancing, and effective dramatic technique were often cited by both shamans and their clients as characteristics that distinguished a better shaman. My analysis, however, concentrates on their "scores." Instead of commenting on a set of individual performances, posed as fragile, momentary point events, I concentrate on the notes. Therefore, even in this chapter, focused on a particular performance, I anchor my discussion with the texts. Setting words free from the accidents of individual performances, it may appear that I sometimes approximate a theological or idealist treatment of shamans, treating their texts as eternal and transcendental. I endeavor not to cross into such a theology, but am trying to demonstrate conclusively that shaman texts have been carefully crafted to appear exactly a theology, pure, perfect, sacred, and unchangeable.

Like any event, a shamanic session is neither uniform in its drama nor consistent in its intensity. Some parts are extremely captivating, others entirely boring. Alternations between these extremes do not necessarily occur randomly, however, but follow certain predictable patterns, patterns that are deliberately manipulated by the shamans themselves. When we compare all the ceremonies, each time there are key moments consistently more intense and more dramatic than the rest. In this chapter I first examine the three most important, most consistently spectacular, of such moments, and reflect on their contributions to the ceremonies as a whole. Second, to illustrate the directions found in texts, I concentrate on a detailed description of an actually performed event. Each performance is a unique, unreproducible event, but each such event contributes to a fuller understanding of the entire corpus of shamanic meanings, even as those meanings support each event.

In every ceremony, the first excitement comes, predictably enough, at the beginning, when the shaman shifts into the public side of a performance, having concluded the material preparation for the event and his whispering of mantars. He strikes his drum with single loud beats and begins the recital appropriate to the occasion. This requires some dramatic intensity, since at the very beginning the attention of the audience (and of the patient, if present and conscious) can be relatively easily obtained and, for a few moments at least, held by the shaman. The second such moments are the arrival(s) of the spirit(s), events that can recapture the audience's attention. Onlookers tend to be momentarily awed and respectful at the presence of something extraordinary and otherworldly, although mundane concerns—gossip, a chance to share a smoke, flirtations—soon intrude, as the performance settles back into predictable routine. This inevitable loss of attention helps account for relatively spectacular endings, the third set of moments I examine, when the shaman tries to recapture and focus the audience's (and patient's) attention, fixing in place the order that the ceremony has reconstructed.

How these three consistently most intense moments of every ceremony are structured and how they are fitted into the overall ceremony provide clues to their overall purpose. I suggest that the shaman's cure is a remedy for entropy, an attempt to force the world back into its original satisfactory arrangement by recalling that original orderliness and compelling its reemergence. Shamans manipulate the physical world of bodies and things by manipulating the linguistic world of words and spirits. These observations on language and purpose are further supported by an analysis in the next chapter of the mantars that initiate, conclude, and are inserted at crucial intervals into every ceremony. First, though, we look at those parts of a ceremony available to any observer.

How is the opening of the public part of the ceremony marked? Consider four examples, each from a different shaman, each the beginning of the Recital of the Nine Little Sisters, in order of declining complexity. The first is the opening that Karṇa Vīr most frequently used:

The eldest god is Skyfallen Mahādev,
the eldest age the Golden Age,
the eldest valley is the valley of Nepal,
the eldest level of the world is Tilīkarmā,
the eldest direction East,
the eldest month Cait,
the eldest weekday Sunday,
the eldest planetary conjunction Tuesday's conjunction,
the eldest lunar day the eleventh,
the eldest shaman Jumrātam.

(4.1)

The second example is one Gumāne used for major texts only:

Where did my Mahādeu originate, at Indra's house.
Where did my Sitāyā originate, at Nārāyaṇ's house.
Where was my Mahādeu's head, to the east.
Where were his feet, to the west.
His right hand to the north, his left hand to the south,
Mahādeu came into being.

(4.2)

The third example was used by Man Dev for all texts:

When Earth was mother, when Heaven was father,
as the Age of Truth passed, the true level of the world,
as the Third Age passed, the third level of the world,
on that day, at noon.

(4.3)

Fourth is the opening that Deo Rām Kāmī always used:

Yes, in the Age of Truth, on that very day, hai!

(4.4)

Every shaman uses a similar opening to shift the ceremony at its very beginning from the mundane present to a precise point in mythical time. That temporal point may be expressed vaguely, as "that very day," more precisely, as "the time of Mahādev's origin," or with the acute precision of an exact moment of astronomical time, as "the eleventh day of the waxing moon falling on a Sunday in the month of Cait in conjunction with Tuesday (Mars with the sun ascendant)." That such a shift into the Golden Age, the Age of Truth, is really intended is underscored by a set formula, variations of which Man Dev, and others, commonly used to interrupt a recital so that informal consultations with clients *(baknu)* can take place:

> In this finished time, when the strong shove,
> in this time of murder, what shall I say? Hai!
> In the king's house, in the God's house,
> there are disturbances. Hai!
> There are sins and greediness. Hai!
>
> (4.5)

The present age, for shamans as for everyone else, is the Kali Yuga, the Age of Destruction, a time when one hardly expects intercessions with gods to be successful, whether conducted by shamans or by anyone else. If someone is going to be cured, it is only because of a continuity that roots the present age in the Golden Age. This parallels exactly the continuity of modern shamans with the intercessors of that former age, when the world, freshly created, was still responsive to intercession. That world is explicitly described as "soft and fluid, unstable and muddy," and "just a few hours old," resting on a metal base but not yet hardened and impenetrable, oceans and land still confused into a marshy bog (a level of creation called *"jaltal"*). One version of creation begins:

> The eldest god, Self-created Mahādev
> designed the solid and liquid world.
> On the eldest metals,
> iron metal, zinc metal, the world rested.
> The world was just a disorderly place.
> "Be," he said, there were no men.
> "Speak," he said, there were no men.
> "How will time pass, how will there be a world?"
>
> (4.6)

Miraculous events occur in miraculous times. By shifting the banality of the everyday world back into the Golden Age, shamans establish a fresh sense of responsiveness to ordinariness. The most ideal age, the best day, the perfect moment—these are all conditions for a genuinely successful ceremony (compare Overing 1990 and Levy 1987). If they aren't here, they must be recreated and superimposed upon less favorable conditions. Shamans said, for example, that Tuesdays and Saturdays were the best days for ceremonies and that one must sit facing eastward. They would go ahead and perform on any day and face in any direction. The recital would then explicitly redefine the day as Tuesday, the direction faced as east. The words uttered take precedence over the accident of mundane details. By invoking the Golden Age, the ceremony is situated there, just as invoking familiar spirits compels their presence. Words shape and give substance to the accidents of the external world. The right words create the world anew, curing the victims of a stale, deteriorated world.

Another necessary condition for a genuine cure is to incorporate the best jhāṅgarī, a requirement met by the recurring invocation of the original shaman throughout the recitals and the detailed information on how he performed his rituals. Contemporary shamans may be able to cure, but only because their knowledge replicates the knowledge of the first shaman. Even the first shaman was affected by the world's decline, however. To explain the limits of shamanic knowledge, Karṇa Vīr told a story (in prose) of how that eldest shaman's knowledge was divinely curtailed. At first, Jumrātam knew everything, having received the gift of sight *(dṛṣṭī)*. From sunrise to sunset he knew everything that was going on. One day a client wanted to find Mahādev, who had retired to the Himalayas to make love in private with Pārvatā. No one knew where they had gone. Jumrātam told the inquirer exactly where to find the divine pair, hidden in which *kharsu* tree on Mount Kailās, and the searcher surprised them in an intimate condition. "Damn," exclaimed Mahādev, "this is our own fault. We've given seers [*herne mānche*] too much ability to see. Let them know some things, let them not know others" (4.7). And ever since, concluded Karṇa Vīr, they have known some things but have been unable to know everything.

Another straightforward explanation for shamanic failures, offered by Man Siṅgh Kāmī of Rāṛī, was that in this Kali Yuga even the gods have become corrupt and lie. They trick and deceive us. We can no longer trust their declarations and promises of assistance. Both this and the previous explanation suggest that one must somehow reestablish the Satya Yuga, must return to the time before the gods were offended or language corrupted, in order to produce a truly effective cure.

Not only do the Golden Age and the first shaman figure prominently in the beginnings of recitals; they incorporate the eldest (hence the most respected, the best) of many categories, as the first opening passage cited above illustrates. That example included ten categories. Such lists can be twice as long, expanding to include the eldest stones, metals, rivers, fishes, animals, birds, trees, grasses, grains, planets, diverse alternate intercessors (besides the first shaman), the eldest obstructions, even the eldest disease:

> the eldest disease *vāi jāgmī* [the vāi of injury],
> the eldest king, Sijāpati,
> the eldest grains, blacksoil black beans, *mimi* lentils,
> the eldest birds, the black crow, the slippery beak king crow,
> the eldest trees, black oilwood, bar pipal,
> the eldest rivers, Bhāgīrathī, Setīvatī,
> the eldest fish, *māgaluryā*,
> the eldest race, rich in thought,
> the eldest form, form of wisdom.
>
> (4.8)

When the eldest blacksmith, Tikhu Kāmī, forges the first agricultural implements, we even learn that the eldest temper is tempering to the color of mouse blood.

To introduce the eldest ritual specialists, Karṇa Vīr would continue the Nine Little Sisters after the opening cited above with another block of text that would also appear, slightly modified, in some of his other recitals:

> Where did Jumrātam Jhāṅgarī originate, he originated at Tārātālī.
> The eldest sage, Sāto Gyānī, originated at Chārkābhoṭ.
> The eldest paṇḍit, Bharṣā Paṇḍit, originated at Chārkābhoṭ.
> Where did Prajā Prakil originate, he originated at Chārkābhoṭ.
> Where did Ratan Pārkī originate, he originated at Tāgāserā.
> The eldest astrologer, Kālu Jaiśī, originated at Bāchigāũ.
> The eldest oracle, Maitī Dhāmī, originated at Tārābhoṭ.
> The eldest rammā, Jumrātam originated at Tārātālī.
> The nine great witch sisters, where did they originate?
> They originated in the east, at Hā̃gābāṅg, Pāṭan Melā.
>
> (4.9)

Perhaps Tārātālī is a corruption of Tarakoṭ or Tānātālī in southern Ḍolpā, influenced by the Sanskrit name of a particular hell, *talātala,* but Karṇa

Vīr claimed that it was in another world. Each other place mentioned is geographically real, located in either Ḍolpā or the Magar area of eastern Rukum. Each is relatively inaccessible from Jājarkoṭ. The trails are arduous, frequently closed by landslides or snowfall, and the inhabitants, Tibetans and Magars, regarded as untrustworthy and dangerous. Besides connecting the recital to the surrounding world, this passage establishes continuities between the ceremony and the past. It connects the contemporary problem of witchcraft with its origins, which the recital goes on to recount. It implicates the rest of the ritual specialists, the herneharu, even though they do not figure prominently in this particular recital. It shows, too, that not only do cures date back to the original intercessors, but problems likewise can be traced back to the original agents of affliction.

As is true elsewhere in Nepal (Gaenszle 1991; Holmberg 1989; Sales 1991; Strickland 1982), most shaman recitals involve stories of origin. They maintain their concern for the beginning of things not only at their own beginnings, but throughout. To cure acts of witchcraft, you retell the origins of witches; to repair a star obstruction, you recount the origins of the heavenly bodies; to counter acts of shamanic sorcery, you relate the circumstances of the original curses. In each case, shamans try to influence the history of the cosmos, to reestablish a natural order that has been disrupted, to produce a present time more favorable for his clients. Each of these activities battles entropy to resist the inevitable, accelerating descent of the world into chaos.

Shamans who use a variety of optional opening passages appear more impressive to a recurring audience of familiar villagers than do less versatile performers. Of the fourteen shamans with whom I worked, Karṇa Vīr was the most adept at this. He used five different ways to begin. His choice was not random, but responded to circumstances and was shaped by his training. The list of the "eldests," he explained, always precedes recitals of the Nine Sisters, the casting off of star crises (gauḍā phālne), and the binding of a house. Appropriately, the eldest witches would be listed only when witchcraft or troublesome vāi were going to be treated, the eldest planet and star obstruction only when their story followed. Furthermore, when using the creation recitals to treat in the most elaborate possible way a serious case of gauḍā, he would precede the two passages already given with three others, which themselves also occur elsewhere:

To cast off the planets,
to cast off the star obstructions, listen!

When self-respect has collapsed, when the heart is troubled,
if contempt was shown, if jealousy was concealed,
if a foundation stone is overturned,
if a pentagram has been transferred,
listen! to this old recital!

The star obstruction of birth,
the star obstruction of death,
the star obstruction of children's crises,
the star obstruction of configuration,
the star obstruction of the inner heart,
the star obstruction of what is hidden,
Death at the head, Niu [its reason] at the feet,
the Time of Death, the Messenger of Death,
Rāhu, Ketu, Śaniścar, Maṅgal,
Bṛhaspati, Ulkā, Saṁkaṭa,
to this ancient recital, listen!

(4.10)

All five opening passages also precede the beginning of the Recital to Juma Kāl and Juma Dūt, performed at the funeral of a shaman, and the *toyo khāne melā,* used at initiations (Chapter 6), the two most important events in any shaman's career. Thus, the degree of formality at the opening to a session indicates, at least for some shamans, the degree of importance with which they regard the session that follows. Multiple openings are not a feature of every shaman's repertoire, however. Man Dev and Deo Rām of the Bhujī Valley apparently always used the same opening lines (4.3 and 4.4) on every occasion and for every text.

The imperatives "Listen!" that mark each of the three sections of text last cited are common at the beginning of various recitals. They are directed both to the shaman's human audience (which is sometimes admonished to be quiet) and to the spirits or forces evoked, the listing of which fits together with each "Listen!" Shamans consider the cooperation of supernatural forces rather than help from the human audiences essential to improve whatever situation they are trying to improve, while a detached observer might reflect that the "moral support" of an engaged audience is equally important. While serious negotiations with the supernatural are carried out in the privacy of whispered mantars, not in public recitals, the drama framing those negotiations takes spectacular performative characteristics with enhanced audience appeal, ensuring that human audiences are never neglected.

A few standard lines of opening passages are used to connect one recital to another. For example, when the story of the Nine Little Witch Sisters followed one or more parts of the creation cycle, Karṇa Vīr would omit the formal opening (4.1), simply substitute the line "Arising in the Satya Yuga," and then begin the story. Another connecting line is "The truth of that day, the redemption of that day," while the shortest possible way to begin a new story is: "In the Satya Yuga." These phrases again demonstrate the importance of situating the recitals in mythical, ideal, time. They are also a minor way in which shamans do respond to circumstances and modify their meticulously memorized recitals when appropriate.

Besides establishing the performance in mythic time, it must be situated in mythic, consecrated, space. The second opening quoted above maps Mahādev's body as geographically vast, coextensive with the earth. The Recital of the Nine Planets tells us that the planets originated from a leprous skin which Mahādev cast off when he took a new avatar, establishing his vastness as cosmic (3.8). (For counterparts in the Hindu theory of *yantra,* see Padoux 1989 and Rosu 1986.) Some way of incorporating the cardinal directions, with a spirit assigned to each, figures in every ceremony, at the very least in the opening and closing mantars, if not always in the publicly recited texts. The permanent opening of the rāyā sarsu mantar, replacing the temporary passage first learned at the beginning of training (1.2) goes:

> Come from the Eastern Direction, Guru Gorakhnāth!
> Come from the Western Direction, Bhakti Mātā, Bhakti Pitā!
> Come from the Northern Direction, Ogari Gogari Gosāī!
> Come from the Southern Direction, Maicananāth!
> Come from Kāśī Kasmerā, Guru Gorakhnāth!
>
> (4.11)

Nāths are temples dedicated to Mahādev, closely associated with kānphaṭa yogins, and eponymous aspects of Mahādev himself. The texts frequently identify Mahādev with these wandering mendicants, "Ogari Gogari" (restless, unsettled) Gosāīs, as in the story of the witches' origin (3.3), or in the following opening to several different mantars:

> Awake! Awake!
> In the east, Candannāth, awake!
> In the north, Bhairabnāth, awake!
> In the south, Gorakhnāth, awake!
> In the west; Ratannāth, awake!
> Of the four directions, of the four nāths,
> yogi who travels around, awake, go there!
>
> (4.12)

This second example shifts immediately from the nāths to the yogin who visits them, commanding him to act. This recalls the mother's curse on the wandering soul of her departing child (2.11), when each nāth is called upon by name to stop the soul and send it back. As in these cases, four or six directions are mentioned in practically every one of the public recitals, and occur in most of the longer mantars. The burial of lingams in the four directions is part of the world's creation (2.26); shamans spit kacur root (along with a mouthful of words) to the six directions in the ceremony to raise a masān (3.34). Every seduction of the Nine Little Sisters takes the witches on a tiring journey covering every direction; stakes of wild plum wood are pounded in the four corners of a property when binding a house. The emergent pattern is not just an ideal topography of sanctified earth, but an active incorporation of geographic elements into the cure as prototypic order. The original patterns of the earth have a sacred order, the same order that every shaman must recreate in a patient's life. Entropy, rather than evil, emerges as the true enemy of a shaman. He cures not by attempting to alleviate individual, superficial symptoms by which chaos disorders particular lives, but by returning the patients' current universe to its original well-ordered pattern.

After the opening passages, texts launch either into narratives, telling of such things as how witches came into the world or how the land was divided into wild and cultivated, or else into enumerations, such as lists of places or plants. The *jarman karman melā* names 130 different plants and trees, repeating throughout the refrain:

> you've gone to look for a place,
> you've gone to look for a space,

I've brought you back to your place,
I've brought you back to your space.

(4.13)

Audience attentiveness fades throughout these sections. For a long time I thought that most villagers did not even know what shaman stories were about, despite having heard them so often. Villagers themselves vigorously sustained this inaccurate conclusion. Whenever I tried to discuss the contents of recitals with them, they would insist that these were things which only shamans knew. In any case, they said, the language used was that of the spirits, so how could they know anything of it? One day, however, while I was working outside on a transcription, attracting a dozen onlookers, some younger villagers started to amuse themselves by guessing, with remarkable accuracy, what the next line would be. It turned out that they could not only parody the recitals but could reproduce them word for word. Even after I had found them out, they still would not discuss the texts, out of both respect for and fear of the supernatural powers involved, certainly not out of ignorance of them.

At least three factors underlie their reluctance. First, a common belief throughout Nepal, well documented anecdotally, holds that if you begin to learn any form of secret knowledge, whether that of shamans, or witches, or Tantric specialists, you must learn it in its entirety. Otherwise the partial knowledge will eventually drive you crazy. This belief contributed to my loss of several potential transcribers, who quickly discovered that they were too scared even to listen to my tapes of mantars. Others persisted until they started to dream every night of the taped material. When I gave a copy of my thesis to a friend, Yogīśwar Kārki, his relatives warned him not to keep such dangerous material as the recitals it contained in his house. Second; shamans, like witches, may take offense and seek revenge if your accounts of them are unflattering. They may possess the power to overhear what you say in private. The further from home people were, the more open they tended to be about these subjects. Some of the best stories of witchcraft and sorcery that I collected were told by Jājarkoṭ residents whom I visited in Nepalganj and Kathmandu. Third, admitting that you know a great deal about practices like manipulating spirits for personal power exposes you to suspicions that you perhaps do those things yourself. Not only shamans and witches, but otherwise ordinary people, may be accused of nursing a bīr (an enslavable demonic spirit), which in return for being regularly fed helps them and afflicts their enemies. It is better to claim that you know nothing at all than to admit you know too much.

Attentiveness seems low at shaman performances, I conclude, because of excessive familiarity, not from lack of interest. Sheer attendance remains high at these ceremonies, although nothing but the thrill of the spectacle compels uninvolved onlookers to assemble each time a shaman performs, which can be several evenings a week. Seances provide entertainment, whatever else they do, to communities for whom an early bedtime is the usual way to conclude the day. Once the villagers have assembled, though, protected by the shaman from night-roaming spirits that might otherwise trouble them, they take advantage of the occasion to visit with neighbors, gossip, and flirt, their attentions straying easily from the ceremony.

A good way to recapture an audience whose attention has been lost, whether spirit or human, is through spectacular possessions. After his preliminary preparation, a shaman calls one or more classes of spirits to begin a session. Every shaman normally uses at least two mantars for this. The first places specific, named protecting spirits at his head, feet, navel, left, right, front and back:

> Having effect in front, Fire Demon [*agni betāla*],
> having effect behind, Black Horse Hoofprints,
> having effect on the right, Narsiṅgh Bīr,
> having effect on the left, Hanumān Bīr,
> at the head, Head Gorakhnāth,
> at the sole, Kulmināth,
> at the navel, Navel Bhayar, Solitary Bhayar.
>
> (4.14)

The second is the "summoning the spirits" *(deutā bolāune)* mantar, a list that can include hundreds of spirits. Although every version affirms that the shaman controls the spirits, not vice versa, their arrival is always marked by a few moments of uncontrolled trembling. The shaman actively demonstrates his power over the spirits whenever they appear. He grimaces and shouts, then drums vigorously and dances back and forth in a frenzy, struggling to bring the spirits under control. While such a dramatic possession is an inevitable part of every session, it need not occur at the beginning, and, in many cases, is repeated several times throughout the ceremony. Moments of possession allow the shaman to establish some momentary physical power over the human audience. He scatters fire onto onlookers who have settled too near, sending them tumbling as he breaks out of the circle of onlookers to dance. He may even manage to kick those who have fallen asleep.

Besides specific mantars that summon various classes of spirits, some passages of the public recitals apparently must be accompanied by possession, as I found when taping these texts outside regular performances. Such a point regularly occurs in the middle of Tilīkarmā. Taking up the story where we left off in the preceding chapter, in all versions, Jumrātam descends to the underworld after cursing the king (or the prince, or the entire royal family). He leaves behind a tomb and monument (Chapter 6), tells his wife to display all the signs of mourning, and disguises himself as a copper worker or blacksmith. When messengers seek him, his wife eventually reveals his whereabouts by means of a riddle (6.5). When they find him, he strenuously denies being a shaman even though the messengers point out revealing signs, such as calluses left on his hands and knees by his drum and those on his head left by his leaves and feathers:

> "I am not the shaman of your world, attendants," he said.
> "But respectable copper worker,
> what are those calluses from on your head?
> They seem to be from the matted locks of hair,
> from the pheasant feathers, from the fragrant leaves."
> "No, attendants, an unhappy man's work,
> I carry charcoal, I carry ore,
> those calluses are from the headstrap," he said.
> "What are those calluses from on your hands?
> They seem to be from holding the complete drum."
> "No, attendants, an unhappy man's work,
> I carry charcoal, I carry ore,
> I pound metal, I sound metal,
> those calluses are from the hammer," he said.
> "What are those calluses from on your knees?
> They seem to be from the complete drum."
> "No, attendants, holding with my knees,
> I make plates, I make pots," he said.
>
> (4.15)

Finally, following the jhagrenī's instructions, one of the attendants throws a bunch of fragrant leaves *(surkā rejī)*, or in some versions, kacur root, into the smithy's fire. Its fumes force Jumrātam to become frantically possessed with dozens of his spirits (an unusual case of substance-induced possession):

> He began to tremble lightly,
> began to tremble more heavily,
> with twelve bīr, twenty-two māphī,
> twenty-two barāṅg,
> the fields shook, the forests shook,
> Rammā Jumrātam began to be possessed.
>
> (4.16)

I taped seven variations of this passage, and five times the shaman recording it began to tremble as he recited it. Only Gumāne Kāmī, the most sophisticated of the shamans, who practiced regularly in the district center and included various district officials among his clientele, and Sibe Damāi, who was no longer a practicing shaman since losing his equipment in a house fire fifteen years previously, were not susceptible to its force. Apparently, just mentioning the agents of possession in such a context as this where they are possessing the eldest shaman induces a state of possession as effectively as can any other technique. This method also works in mantars that summon bīr, māphī, and barāṅg. They demand that those spirits move, as in the following example:

> Hey, twelve māphī, move; twenty-two barāṅg, move.
> Atop my head, move; atop my shoulders, sit.
> Shaking the earth, move; shaking the world, move.
> Coming, shame the mouth; going, press upon the back . . .
> Make the truth known, mend any falsehoods.
>
> (4.17)

One explanation is that spirits come when they hear their names called. However, names are not just words, they are also things, and may be substituted for the objects they ostensibly represent. The evocation of a spirit does not just summon a force, it *is* that spirit. The spirits are present because their naming presents them. This is another reason why ordinary villagers are reluctant to discuss shaman texts. Such a discussion might result in the unwanted presence of spirits. Throughout South Asia, names are personal property. Their casual use is avoided, being disrespectful. Whenever possible, one uses a (real or fictive) kinship designation, a formal title, or a teknonym to address or to refer to someone. Even shamans prefer terms like "the twelve bīr" or "the twenty-two barāṅg" instead of individual names, such as Kālyā Bīr, Kaile Bīr, Dhaulyā Bīr, or Chaḍke Bīr, to name a few. In the Recital of the Nine Little Sisters, the moment when the shaman first addresses the witches by their names takes on special prominence. When their attack on him fails, he begins his triumphant seduction of them. "He did their names" *(nām garyā)*, the text explicitly puts it. Discussing how to summon Mahākālī and other goddesses, Śiva Bahādur even changed the verb in this phrase to a causative, *"nām garāunu pāryo,"* in the sense of "you must cause their names to be done."

In any particular ceremony, only a few spirits are declared present. Those spirits not summoned must have their locations fixed, to establish a further web of connections between the present situation, mundane geography, and the sensational, miraculous events associated with divinities. When Abi Lal named the 240 major spirits that he could call, he coupled each name with the site of its shrine. It began:

East, West, North, South.
Bāyu burmā called, come here!
From the southern quarter,
At Kālī Maṭh, Patthar Mālā, Lāṭu Mālā, Lāṭu Kāilī, Gaṅgā Mālā.
At Bāgār Jiuli, Lāṭu Mālā, Lāṭu Kāilī.
Above, at Kaingār, Gār Mālā, Satru Mālā.
At Khār Kholā, Gaṅgā Jaisī . . .

(4.18)

It continued in this way through the four cardinal directions. This was not simply a geographical enumeration, however, though we were just conversing and no ceremony was under way. Having invoked them, he needed to address them:

Come when I say come, go when I say go.
Give me honor, give me strength, give me a good name.
Put brightness in my patient's eyes,
put life force in my patient's body.
Return his spirit, return his soul.

(4.19)

This invocation resembles a prayer, except that every mood is imperative. It continues with a request to the spirits to return any lost wits and then to swoop back to their shrines, demonstrating that one does not casually name spirits without doing something with them, if only to send them away again. These spirits, the bāyu burmā (haunting vengeful spirits of polluted corpses and high-caste suicides), each have their own shrines where supplicants attempt to enlist their assistance to correct social wrongs. Many have their own dhāmīs attached to those shrines. They are rarely summoned collectively to possess the shaman. After all, each would demand a blood sacrifice, and no one could pay for hundreds of animals to be slaughtered.

Instead of immediately using major spirits, a shaman first calls only his familiar spirits and those of deceased shamans, agents who make smaller demands and can be collectively fed at the end of the ceremony, often with the blood of just a single chicken. Still, explicitly mentioning the ranks of divinities establishes an additional level of order in the world, one more orderly grid to superimpose on the disorderly present. As with time and space, a shaman utilizes the order of the spirit world, each divinity in its own shrine, to reproduce the balance they represent in his patient's currently unbalanced situation.

Besides passages within recitals that require an accompanying act of possession, some recitals require a fresh possession before they can end. The performance (though not always the telling) of Tilīkarmā ends with a possession for all shamans. It occurs when Jumrātam has returned to this world and lifts his curse from his brother-in-law, the king. The toyo khāne melā, used for initiations and the yearly village prophecy from atop a pole, is an even more vivid example. Shamans were regularly unable to reach the end of even a casual telling of this recital without becoming possessed. To avoid this, they just broke off midway: it just doesn't end otherwise. This was true even though it concludes differently in different versions. Some versions, for example, repeat the weaving of the pyre/net/fence done by the first shaman when finally curing his brother-in-law the king at the end of Tilīkarmā. This time, the numbers go higher and higher until the shaman begins to tremble. Other versions conclude with the negotiations with the sacrificial animal, but these, too, go on, including dialogues with more and more animals, until the trembling begins.

Endings that involve possession usually fit into the recital through the narrative device of summoning the first shaman, Jumrātam, to perform a particular ritual, which the contemporary shaman reenacts as he recounts it. The House-Binding Recital, for example, tells the story of a father and son who search for yogins who will take away their pollution. Nowhere until the very end of the recital is any mention made of shamans, until abruptly at the very end:

> They went to Tārātālī,
> brought back the great Rammā Jumrātam.
> He danced and drummed out to the crossroads,
> he danced and drummed back from the crossroads,
> began to bind the house.
>
> (4.20)

The contemporary shaman, at these lines, also dances and drums, while possessed, out to a crossroads near the house and returns to conclude binding the house, so that as Jumrātam completes his ritual, the contemporary ceremony likewise ends.

Transitions that suddenly involve the original shaman do not occur only at the end of recitals. They can be quite complex, involving stories within stories, quotes of other texts within a text. The Recital to Postpone the Star Obstructions recounts the creation of the original experts and their testing by the gods. When Jumrātam is summoned to Indra's heaven to cure the goddess who has felt the touch of death, he recites the Dowry Recital to cure her. He begins by naming the eldest of each category, using the first opening quoted above (4.1). Sometimes the entire recital may be embedded here, with the recursive result that Jumrātam tells his own story as part of the cure. Continuity between the activities of the first shaman and those of his modern descendants is thus reemphasized throughout the performance, not just noted in the openings and closings.

Many endings symmetrically parallel the time shift of the openings, returning from mythic time and space to the present here and now. More emphatically, they eliminate residual distinctions between the real and the ideal. Jumrātam's negotiations with the original witches merge with those between the contemporary shaman and the contemporary witches. Following the dance that creates the vāi (2.18), Jumrātam banishes the Nine Little Sisters, declaring: "I'll stomp you into the underworld." He does so to eight of them, but the youngest manages to negotiate:

"No, my elder brother, leave me breath and life,
you were born inside, I was born outside,
we've done so much together,
leave me breath, my brother,
leave me life, my brother," all of this was said.
"What you throw toward me,
I'll take with great respect,
what you give to me carefully,
I'll carry with me always,
I'll come as would a supplicant,
leave as for my parents' house,
set a time for me, that time I will observe,
set a promise for me, that promise I will keep,
I will do all this, my brother, leave me breath and life."
All of this was said, one level of oaths,
[through five levels of oaths]
All of this was set.

(4.21)

Suddenly, the tenses shift from past narrative into present imperative. No longer is the story of the original witch sisters being told, it is their present descendants who are being addressed:

You were bound by oaths and promises,
all of this was set.
Charms that are your fault, spells that are your fault,
ills that are your fault, deceits that are your fault,
set away all your curses, set away all your afflictions,
set away all your attacks, set away all your abuses,
heaven and the stars compel you,
from this crossroads here,
move to the far four corners!

(4.22)

A similarly sudden shift into the present occurs at the end of the Drongo Recital. The mother of the dead child has prophesied that it will find no place to stay, no matter what form of birth it takes. In each form, it suffers an untimely death (2.10).

He took a birth in a pigpen,
he was sacrificed to honor a jhāṅgarī,
he found no place to stay.

He took a birth in a chicken coop,
he was born as a good cock,
he died at the right time and at the wrong time
[that is, at his own appointed time and as a substitute for others],
he found no place to stay.
He wandered around,
he came to stay in his mother's lap,
he came to be born in his mother's lap.

[Then, with tense changes but without a break, the recital addresses the contemporary child.]

Don't let your heart wander, don't let your mind wander,
your mother's lap provides protection,
your father's lap provides protection,
your gold and silver provide protection,
your home and land provide protection,
so, make your place in your mother's lap.
Where would you go, son?

(4.23)

Having striven throughout his ceremony to achieve the complete superimposition of the mythic upon the present, the shaman has the final task of preserving the new reality that he has constructed. To this end, whether or not a concluding possession is needed to end a particular recital, the overall ceremony is finished with dramatic lists of witnesses, oaths, and bindings:

The edible offerings have been made,
my good knowledge has been displayed,
Bhūmī Basundharā a witness,
the bār pipal tree a witness,
Bhāgīrathī River a witness,
fresh leaves a witness,
Dhartī Mātā a witness,
Jwālā Devī a witness,
Sijāpati Rājā and Jumrātam Jhāṅgarī a witness,
my own lord Mahādev's oath.

(4.24)

At the end, the shaman again scatters grain in the six directions. He repeats the level of oaths in increasing numbers and the initial bindings, now trying to hold in place the newly achieved order. For a moment, the ongoing disintegration of the world is halted, even reversed. No shaman, though, is powerful enough to compel it to resist entropy for very long, and cosmic disintegration, with its performative equivalent of audience disinterest, inevitably returns.

Now, having outlined the key structural features found in every ceremony, I want to examine how they work within one particular, actually performed ceremony. Jhāṅgarī Man Dev Kumaĩ performed the specific event that I examine on October 5, 1967, in the Bhujī Valley. It was recorded by John Hitchcock, who also taped the recital without an accompanying performance. For additional details of the ritual I rely on notes which Professor Hitchcock and his assistants made of the performance. I also draw on my own familiarity with nearly identical rituals in Jājarkoṭ and commentary that contemporary shamans I know provided. This is the best occasion to include an extended example from Hitchcock's material, for three reasons. First, there are technical considerations. He used two tape recorders, one inside and one outside the house, and had several assistants who could not only operate the machines, but were also trained to record their own observations, resources beyond my own limited ones. Second, using this recording opens up points that I want to make better than do any similar cases from my own fieldwork, for by examining a situation at which I was not personally present, involving a shaman now dead whom I never met, I demonstrate how applicable my preceding analysis is beyond the specific cases that generated it. Finally, it expands the diachronic depth of my study, illustrating the extreme similarity between events of a quarter century ago and those that continue to be enacted in the present day, a continuity demonstrating the conservative nature of both texts and practices.

The particular ceremony is one of "killing siyo" *(siyo mārne).* Its recital is very simple, telling no story whatsoever. By examining one extremely simple text in greater detail than I have any other text so far, I hope to give a more accurate impression of what a shaman's performance is really like, with its lapses into boredom as well as its dramatic intensity. I concentrate on the text in the chronological order of its performance, along with the shaman's asides to his assistants. When it offers some potential insight, I examine differences between the performed and the dictated versions, and offer some possible reasons for the discrepancies.

Shamans perform this ritual when an individual or family is persistently troubled by a siyo, whose malignant influences the shaman is expected to disperse. The general issue is a shattering of self-confidence, a loss of personal balance and integrity, and fragmentation of personal wholeness and well-being. In recent studies, Roberte Hamayon (1990), Anne de Sales (1991), and Robert Desjarlais (1992b) have suggested that this is the major activity of shamans among, respectively, Buriats, Kham Magars, and Yolmo Sherpa. While this is not true in Jājarkoṭ, where the treatment of witchcraft victims and sufferers of star obstructions dominate shaman activities, concentrating on it here may offer complementary insights into those three stimulating studies.

The text on which I concentrate did not begin the evening's events, so I will first outline the preliminaries. The first thing Man Dev did was to take a brass tray and put on it a measure of rice along with nine smooth round black stones. He lights a small lamp and places it on the tray, along with strips of red and white cloth. He then puts the tray at the base of the central house beam. At the back wall of the house, an assistant hangs a wooden jug filled with water, and puts the drumstick into it. Man Dev mixes kernels of corn, wheat, and rice in a drinking vessel, and says a mantar over them. He then throws grain in the six directions. Next he takes a little clarified butter and rice, rubs them between his hands as he blows on them another mantar, and throws them into the fire. A large leafy branch from a *kāthe kāulo* tree has been cut earlier and put in the room. Man Dev now picks it up and gives it to an assistant, who selects the best twigs from it and bunches them together.

Man Dev next applies his body-protecting *(aṅg bandhnu)* mantar, then another mantar to a twig that he singes over the fire and tucks into his turban. He follows this with mantars over ashes that he applies to his eyelids and streaks over his costume. He heats his drum over the fire, testing it with three loud twangs! He repeats the body-protecting mantar, telling his patient and the patient's family to shake their bodies (as if dusting off their backs) while he says it. He next recites his summoning the spirits (deutā bolāune) mantar. Most important of these spirits was a barāṅg named Laṭṭe Siddha, whom Man Dev called his shaking spirit *(kapāune deutā)*, and to whom he yearly sacrificed an uncastrated ram.

Next comes a predictive ceremony *(richaṅg phālne)*, throwing leaves and water out of a water pitcher to see if they land shiny or dull side up, another ritual that seems arbitrary, since the shaman simply keeps tossing until he gets a favorable throw. He then dons his costume, burns more leaves in the fire, and, as he begins to sing aloud a few lines of the deutā bolāune, becomes possessed. Man Dev often sang his deutā bolāune publicly while beating his drum, as though it were a recital. Sometimes he quietly hummed it, as he did at first, and will also do later in this performance. When discussing it, he called it either a mantar or a recital *(khetī)*, depending on the context. During these opening lines, it becomes clear that the shaman listens to his own recital. When he mentions extending protection over the bronze and copper utensils of the house, he abruptly stops and exclaims: "What! We've forgotten to put in Mahādeu!" *(khoi mahādeu rākne bhule cha)*. By this he means a copper coin placed on the tray with the rice, stones, and oil lamp to denote that god. He then waits until someone comes up with a Nepali ten paisā coin, which he puts in the plate. He then bites a small piece of kacur root and resumes singing where he paused.

He continues to sing until his body shakes with the spirits' arrival. He shouts "Yes!" *(ho!)*, quits singing, and offers some general consultations including some rather redundant remarks about the need to treat siyo, though it has been decided in advance that this will be done. The patient, the son of the shaman's younger brother, fell from a cliff while drunk. Although he physically recovered after a few weeks, he and his family remained disturbed by the incident and desired treatment.

When the consultations end, Man Dev performs a long version of the Ban Bhampā, the story of Gorāpā and Serāpā dividing the wild and the cultivated lands between their descendants. In this way, several hours elapse between the beginning of the ceremony and the preparations for siyo mārne. It is nearly midnight when the following events begin. Before Man Dev undertakes the final part of the ceremony, women of the family cook flatbreads fried in clarified butter (a special treat), ten to feed the assistants necessary to carry out the ceremony, and nine miniature ones (the size of small coins) put inside the gourd to entice the siyo to enter it.

While the breads are frying, Man Dev smokes, and directs his pupil and the family as they begin the final preparations. First they soften white clay in water and use a stick to paint a simple pattern on the drum (Fig. 4.1).

Next, they strip the bark off the freshly picked tree branch, cut it into three approximately equal lengths, and warm them in the fire. One becomes a handle inserted into the top of a bottle gourd *(chiṇḍo)*,

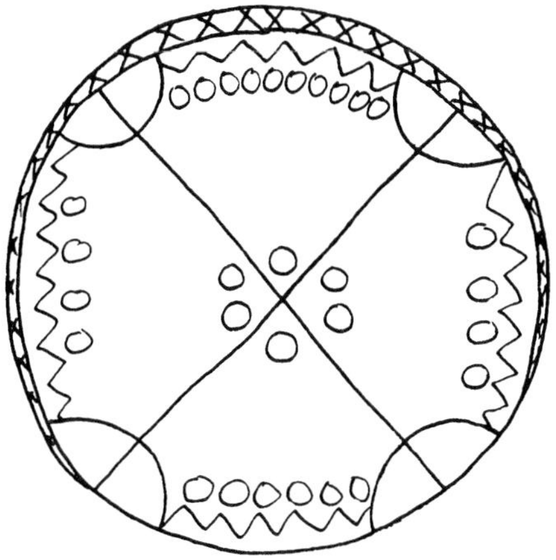

Figure 4.1. Decorations on Man Dev's drum

another is given to the shaman, the third becomes the "sword" later used to smash the gourd. Both the handle and the gourd are also painted with the white clay (in Fig. 4.2).

The pupil asks if he should use black ash as well as white clay, but

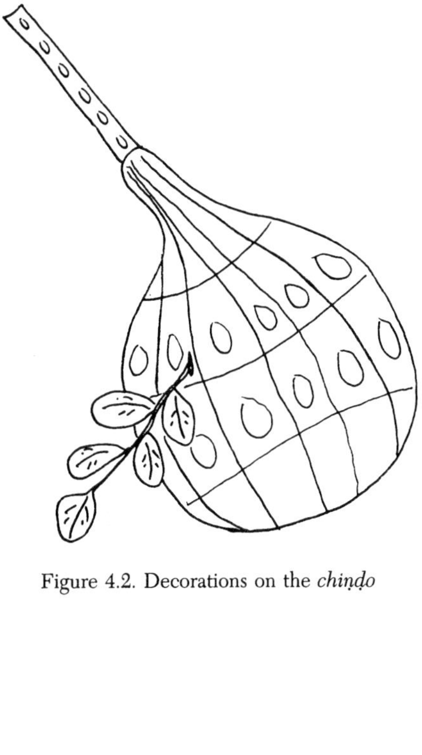

Figure 4.2. Decorations on the *chiṇḍo*

Man Dev says no, just clay. The pupil next cuts a small hole into the side of the gourd, and inserts a leafy twig.

Once Man Dev has dried and heated the sticks in the fire, he takes one, taps his drum rim with it, and inserts it into the rim. Having taken up his drum, he begins the recital as his pupil completes painting of the gourd. He has told the men to cut the chicken once he begins to sing. The text as performed begins with a general list of afflicting agents including siyo, though without giving it particular prominence. It affirms the shaman's ability to quell these forces with the help of tree branches. Because this text follows the Ban Bhampā, which opened with 4.3, it does not have a formal beginning of its own. Instead, it begins with an address to the branch just inserted into the gourd:

> O, branch of the kāṭhe kāulī tree [twice],
> approved by the spirits, approved by the powers,
> you who drive away witches, you who drive away bewitchers,
> you who drive away rāh, you who drive away siyo;
> branch of the kāṭhe kāulī tree [twice],
> approved by the spirits, approved by the powers,
> you who drive away asān, you who drive away masān,
> you who drive away *siure,* you who drive away *biure;*
> branch of the kāṭhe kāulī tree,
> you who drive away sirum, you who drive away bārum . . .
>
> (4.25)

Siure is the Kham equivalent of *siyo,* while sirum, bārum, lul, and lulapā (4.26) are all (general classes of) descendants of Serāpārun (2.16). The dictated version lists several additional forces: bāyu and batās, asān and masān, *jal* and *mul* (a set that associates mūl with its common meaning as a "water source" in addition to its astrological significance), ched and bhed (the tricks and deceits of witches), and moc.

After these few lines, the men, who are preparing to cut the chicken, call out and interrupt Man Dev. He quits singing to resolve their argument over how to put the blood in the gourd, telling them that it doesn't matter, either through the hole in the neck or the one cut in the side. He resumes where he left off:

> you drive away lul, you drive away lulapā,
> you drive away rāh, you drive away siyo.
>
> (4.26)

He stops again after a few lines to remind them not to forget to put in the little breads. He then starts over at the beginning, and pauses at the same point to ask if they've put the blood in yet or not. They haven't, and after a few more lines they interrupt again because they think that it does matter how the blood should be put in. Again he tells them it really doesn't matter. He himself stops after a few repeated lines, to test each of ten whistles freshly cut from bamboo. Man Dev clearly does not want to begin the next section of the recital until all the preparations are finished. He tells everyone several times to be quiet before he finally begins it. As opposed to just four times in his dictated version, he has addressed the kāṭhe kāulī branch sixteen times, giving it extreme prominence in the performance. He has also repeated the line "you drive away rāh, you drive away siyo" four times. This coupling of siyo with rāh is not arbitrary, for the ritual treatment of both is very similar. A rāh must also be lured into a gourd that will be shattered. Rāh, as noted in Chapter 2, are spirits of children who die at birth or at an early age, before the second teeth appear, and whose corpses are buried, not cremated, so that they may more easily find rebirth. But just what is a siyo? The next section of the text obliquely provides an answer, by listing many of the most prominent varieties of siyo, acting as a summons as well:

siyo of one who has fallen from a tree,
siyo of one who has fallen from a cliff,
siyo of one who has fallen from a bridge,
siyo of one who has fallen into a hole,
siyo of one who has been struck by a rock,
siyo of one who has been struck by a log,
siyo of one who has been eaten by a tiger,
siyo of one who has been eaten by a bear,
siyo of one who has been bitten by a serpent,
siyo of one who has been struck by a stone,
siyo of one who has been eaten by a serpent,
siyo of one who has been burned by a fire.

(4.27)

It is minimally clear that a siyo results from a misfortune, and would seem to be the result of an unnatural death. I first thought that a siyo must be the soul of someone who died in some such way, but both shamans and nonspecialists in Jājarkoṭ corrected this impression, explaining that such a spirit would be called a masān. If it troubled its former family, it would either have to be worshiped as a pitār (ancestral spirit) or treated as a bāyu (spirit of someone who died by accident or suicide, or whose corpse was polluted). A siyo, they insisted, is the result of someone's having narrowly escaped such a death. This ceremony is performed after a severe accident, when the person remains shaken up by the event, and when the family also remains upset. As a consequence of the close call of death, a nonphysical part of a person, the siyo, has become detached and wanders throughout the world, having obtained a malicious and threatening aspect that must be quieted. This interpretation, the most common in Jājarkoṭ, equates siyo with sāto, as in "sāto gāyo"—to lose one's wits. It would seem to fit the situation under discussion as well, since the individual who fell survived. Unfortunately, applying this solution is clouded by remarks that Man Dev made during the baknu, when he referred to a *siyo rāh* that resulted from being killed by a tiger. Also, at the end in the divination, he referred to siyo that remains from the time of the ancestors. Further, in his rāh killing recital, the child becomes a bird and lures his father high into a tree, from which the father falls and dies:

> Falling from the pipal tree, he dies right there.
> Oh, Father Nilawaṭā, went to become a siyo.
> His son also, oh, Kālu Bhaṇḍāre, oh, Kūrjā Bhaṇḍāre,
> became a rāh, a moc. Oh, Kūrjā Bhaṇḍāre [said],
> "You have become a siyo, I have become a rāh,"
> thus he said then.
>
> (4.28)

The issue has no clear, unambiguous solution, for the passage further equates rāh and moc, a casual conflation also found in the Jājarkoṭ area. "It's breath, it's life force, it's life breath," Karṇa Vīr tried to explain, and then told a story about *"hiyā"* that further complicates the issue (in Jājarkoṭ, as in Jumlā, *s* often becomes *h,* while *hiyā* is the plural of *hiyo*): "Satī Barbā and Luwā Naṅgrayā were two brothers. The king of Khātī climbed a *pharsā* tree [a type of fodder tree]. They shot a golden pellet from a pellet sling and it struck him in his heart. The *ḍāmnyā* disease rose in his heart and he died, he became Hiyā Rāj. When he takes a hiyo, we can awaken the victim. And when hiyā go to stay in the forest, we can retrieve it" (4.29). This implies that what is really important is to placate the king of hiyā (mentioned in 2.14) who has captured the one now in question, so that the place where the present hiyo (or siyo) happened to originate remains incidental. Hiyā Rāj also commands animals, whose hiyo can be summoned by a shaman and dispatched to plague enemies.

The variety of siyo particularly relevant on this occasion, of one who fell from a cliff, receives no special emphasis here—Man Dev does not alter the text to fit the circumstances, but recites it exactly the same as when he dictated it. Siyo, it seems, are more important as a collective force or as aspects of relational selves than as individual entities or fragments of an individuated self.

A definitive explanation does not emerge, and does not, I would suggest, exist. However, the crucial factors seem clear: some aspect of personhood has become detached, either from the patient or from close relatives of the patient, sometimes including those who have died. The result is troublesome, and the entire family must be involved to resolve the disturbance. Unlike sāto, which is eventually reunited with its source, siyo are driven off, "killed," as the title of the recital suggests. Even Man Dev's text (4.31) mentions a "golden sword, a silvery shield," used for bringing the siyo back, more appropriate as offerings to a king such as Hiyā Rāj than as lures for the wandering siyo.

The siyo is certainly something that wanders detached from its source. The next section of the text clarifies this. It enumerates a long list of places where the siyo might be resting, and searches through each of them. In each locale, the shaman offers the local minor spirits *(simī-bhūmī)* a share of the sacrifice in return for compelling the siyo to return. Simī-bhūmī are marginal divinities, usually named by their location alone; they occupy, explained Man Dev's pupil, a lowly place in the divine hierarchy comparable to Kāmīs in the human social order. Calling them, the shaman maps his "travels" in search of the siyo:

> Ai, O simī of Tamghās Garkhā Wetlands,
> O bhūmī of Tamghās Garkhā Drylands,
> your share is here, your portion is here,
> Simī Sa La La La La, Bhūmī Sa La La La.
>
> (4.30)

He subsequently mentions 164 more specific places, gradually approaching from afar the site of the ritual. As it sounds, the "Sa La La La La" refrain onomatopoetically imitates the bamboo whistles that call the siyo. The text addresses some important shamans of each quadrant. They, too, are told to force the siyo to leave there and return home. As places in the west are named, the spirits of two deceased but influential jhāṅgarīs, Kusan Rammā and Bethan Rammā, are told to block the path of the King of Death, Yama Rājā:

> Going to the Western House, Kusan Rammā, going,
> Bethan Rammā, going, to Yama Rājā,
> you don't give a path, you don't give a way.
> In the doorway, the door, into the bottle gourd, going,
> the white clay, going, with that began to write,
> with a branch of the paṭkā tree, going,
> made a golden sword, made a silvery shield.
> The white clay, going, with that began to write.
> O branch of the kāṭhe kāulī,
> approved by the spirits, approved by the powers,
> you bring the siyo, you drive the siyo,
> into the bottle gourd, going.
>
> (4.31)

There are more spirits mentioned in the dictated version, adding the shaman's personal twelve barāṅg and nine dhuwā, whom he failed to include, or whose assistance he didn't need, in the performance. After mentioning a few distant places to the south, west, and north, Man Dev pauses and tells the family where to sit, then begins to round up his ten helpers. Some have fallen asleep, others have wandered off, but eventually he finds nine of them. Man Dev says, "Nine are enough, give each one a bread." As each receives a bread from the patient's family, the shaman gives them a ṭikā (forehead dot) of ashes, for protection. He then gives them directions. Two should take bowls of sand and water to throw at the family, two more take nettle fronds with which to beat the patient, the rest are to position themselves outside with whistles, as the text directs (below). Finally everyone is in place, and the shaman resumes his litany of place names. He breaks off after naming a few more and tells the young men that they should be outside and ready. They argue about who should take the third stick and have the responsibility for breaking the gourd, a task finally assigned to the shaman's pupil.

Along with the gourd, a small model of a plowshare, a long needle that will be driven into it, and a stake of wild plum wood *(pā̃iyũ)* will be taken to the crossroads, to bind the siyo there. The text directs what materials to use when making the plow and spike. These are carefully followed. Like the net (below), the plow attains mythic proportions by associations with the first blacksmith:

> Of the kharsu branch, going, making a great plow,
> of a paiyā branch, going, making a great spike,
> atop the three-pronged one [the plow],
> chips were cut out. O Tikhu Kāmī, Elder Brother,
> you hammered the great plow,
> you forged the great plow.
>
> (4.32)

However, unlike the description of the net, included at the end of this performance, this passage about the plow and spikes appears only in a much longer coda in the dictated version, all of which Man Dev omitted that night. The directions are in the text and were closely followed, but they were not recited on this occasion. This is reasonable, for clearly you can't wait for a passage about sacrificing a black goat, for example, and only then start looking for an appropriate one, for this could easily result in a delay of days. Even a simple ceremony like this one requires a goat, a chicken, a bottle gourd, fresh leafy branches, white clay, a model of a plow, an iron needle, and a fishing net. However, it is obvious that other people, not just the shaman, know what is needed and what should be done, even to the extent of challenging the shaman's own version of the instructions, as in the dispute over how to fill the gourd with chicken blood. By repeatedly attending the same ceremonies, at least sometimes observing and listening, members of the general population acquire specialist knowledge. The shaman needs only to remind clients what to do. He does not have to give meticulously detailed instructions to the participants for them to enact the ritual exactly as the text says it should be enacted.

As Man Dev sings the long list of place names, two men inside the house break a long iron needle into three pieces, and pound each piece into the model of the plow. The common word for "needle" in Nepali is *siyo,* which probably contributes by catachresis to its appearance in this ceremony. Yet another common homonym means "border." This meaning prominently occurs throughout the Ban Bhampā, recited earlier in the evening, helping connect that text to the siyo mārne. The siyo (the fragment of soul) has crossed the boundary (siyo) to join the forces of the wilds, now falling under the jurisdiction of Serāpārun's descendants, who are regulated by that recital.

Once the pieces of needle have been driven into the plow, the men carry it outside. Man Dev now stops singing the recital and instead quietly hums his deutā bolāune text. Suddenly, he shakes hard, demonstrating the spirits' powerfully disruptive presence. Man Dev's pupil blackens the faces of the patient and his immediate family (five people in all) with soot. He wraps them together in the fishing net, and suspends the net from the main house beam. One assistant throws sand at those in the net, another sprinkles them with water, and then both beat them with nettle fronds, discouraging the siyo from joining them. Man Dev, still trembling, moves outside and squats next to the gourd. He resumes singing the list of place names, until at last he locates the siyo at a place called Kāule Garkhā. This is not, as one might expect, the spot where the original fall from a cliff took place, but a place where kāule trees grow. (I would have liked to know what other significance the place might have, but this question wasn't raised at the time.)

When the shaman locates the siyo, he makes this known by calling it by the apparently meaningless name "Garan Kāle Garan." Meaningless, that is, to the shaman and his audience. Man Dev suggested it might be borrowed from Kham, but Kham speakers were also unable to explain it. Perhaps it is an example of what Malinowski (1965) called "the coefficient of weirdness." Anticipating the arguments of Wittgenstein's *Philosophical Investigations,* Malinowski observed: "A word is used when it can produce an action and not describe one, still less to translate thoughts. The word therefore has a power of its own, it is a handle to acts and objects and not a definition of them" (1923:322). An exemplary ethnologist, Malinowski never allowed his theory to constrain too rigidly his data, so that his best work dilutes these theoretical extremes. Although his conclusion that all meaning is completely indexical suggests that oral texts become meaningless removed from their contexts, he nevertheless produced clearly understandable, word-for-word translations of Trobriand texts. Tambiah (1985:31) suggests that this apparent contradiction was the result of Malinowski's "histrionic talent." Malinowski concedes that untranslatable words were untranslatable only because he failed to get the services of a "competent commentator." That, too, is all I will concede with phrases like "Garan Kāle Garan," and the similar phrase, "Garan Sele Garan," used to address rāh in the parallel ceremony of rāh mārne.

The siyo is invited to its meal:

O Garan Kāle Garan,
in the doorway, the door, in the golden door frame,
in the silvery door, O Garan Kāle Garan,
going into the bottle gourd, going into the white clay,
feast on this blood, feast on this flesh,
eating the bābān bread, eating the yogi bread,
O Garan Kāle Garan.

(4.33)

The "golden door frame" and "silvery door" refer to the decorated gourd into which the siyo is lured. As the siyo is being trapped in the gourd outside, inside the house the family of the patient remains bound inside the fishing net, also trapped. The net not only puts them physically in the shaman's protection and demonstrates that the family is a unit but also affirms their ties to the greater society around them, by detailing the net's mythic construction. This again invokes the original blacksmith, Tikhu Kāmī, who forges its iron sinkers, and the first potter, who weaves the net itself. The net brings the family actively into the ritual and weaves mythical characters into their presence. Mythic prototypes occur throughout the recitals, but here, where there is no story whatsoever, it requires considerable artifice to incorporate them. They appear only in a coda sung at the end of the ceremony, after the siyo has been trapped, the gourd shattered, and the pieces disposed of at a crossroads:

Tikhu Kāmī, Elder Brother,
from a black she-goat, stripping off the great skin,
made a bellows, was pumping it.
Tikhu Kāmī, Elder Brother, carries coal, charcoal,
having set up a forge, having set up a firepit,
the bellows from the black she-goat he pumped.
Dhurkoṭe iron, carrying that, he brought it.
On the True Forge, he begins to forge sinkers.

(4.34)

Tikhu Kāmī forges various types of sinkers—round sinkers, flat sinkers, and axe-blade-shaped sinkers. Here, they are not enumerated, but in the dictated version they are counted, slowly and clearly, to one hundred. The potter *(kumāle)* prepares the net:

Brother Kumāle,
of nettle fiber, of flax fiber,

with white clay, you begin to cook it.
From the nettle fiber, going, pulling out a great thread,
O Brother Kumāle, you begin to weave a net.
He put in the first line of the warp,
shifted the first line of the woof, wove the first woof.
He put in the second line of the warp,
shifted the second line of the woof,
wove the second woof.

(4.35)

The weaving continues, fading off into rapid mumbling, up to at least twenty strands. In the dictated version, the weaving of one hundred strands is counted one by one. Perhaps, being able to count to one hundred is a notable achievement in a nonliterate society. It is also a device to lengthen the ceremony, so that preparations can be completed while the recital continues. This time, everything is ready, so Man Dev doesn't need the extra time. When necessary, the recital can further expand by attaching each of the hundred weights that complete the net. Such repetitive passages are common throughout the shaman recitals. Their effect is more profound than simply killing time. So many repetitions and enumerations in the texts help induce and maintain trance states, despite their dulling effect upon inattentive audiences. Even that dulling effect may have a purpose within the overall manipulations that must be achieved if a patient is to be cured, by increasing susceptibility to the moments of active intervention. Discussing the border between the normal and the abnormal, the sane and the insane, a theme running throughout *The Book of Laughter and Forgetting*, Milan Kundera notes, "the border is not a product of repetition. Repetition is only a means of making the border visible. The line of the border is covered with dust, and repetition is like the whisk of a hand removing the dust." Uncovering this border, which also separates the natural and the supernatural, the real and the ideal, is imperative for a shaman to affect the world.

Tied to the main house beam, close to the hearth, the fishing net connects the patient and his family to the cosmos:

Its top was in heaven,
its roots were in hell.

(4.36)

The dictated version of the recital provides directions as to who should be put in the net, and by whom:

O my patient, going, and the householder,
and the whole family, and the children, going,
and all the male and female servants,
tie [the net] to the main beam, then cover them.

(4.37)

With the family inside the net, the text invokes the major protecting spirits of the six directions and of the house, trapping the siyo. The shaman has already protected everyone else present, by scattering mustard seeds over them at the beginning of the ceremony. The one exception is the goat. Since it will be sacrificed at the end of the events, the shaman does not extend his protection to it. It was tethered in the doorway covered by a blanket specifically to exclude it, a point also covered by the text:

Atop the four-footed one [the goat],
in the door, the door frame, covered this there.

(4.38)

This, Man Dev explained afterward, is because otherwise the siyo now present might trouble him. To ensure that the siyo enters the gourd and not some other receptacle, the family covers all other containers in the house, such as water jugs and cooking pots. The (dictated) text finally gets around to the chicken, which has already been cut:

Of the cock [Kham: *pui bājā*],
of the hen [Kham: *tirī bājā*],
the cock, going, then cutting this,
in the bottle gourd, going, having put this there,
put in Bāban bread, put in Jogi bread.

(4.39)

Once the shaman locates the siyo and addresses it, the ten villagers, who have been assembled to assist the shaman (and by doing so, express their solidarity with the afflicted family), carefully follow through their directions. These again occur only in the dictated version and not in the evening's recital:

> Some of the men, going, then with sand,
> then begin to scatter it.
> Some of the men, going, holding nettles, strike.
> Some of the men, going, with pure water, going,
> then begin to scatter it.
> Of Deva Niṅgālī bamboo, going, making great whistles,
> two men above, going to the Eastern Direction,
> going to the great conjunction [gauḍā],
> one turning to this side, one turning to that side,
> having joined their buttocks, then begin to blow.
>
> (4.40)

Two men go to the west and blow their whistles there. The spot where the pairs of whistlers bump together and whistle is a gauḍā. Here, rather than being a "star obstruction" or a "crisis," gauḍā simply means "meeting place," establishing a concrete overtone for this otherwise esoteric astrological term. The directions continue:

> Two of the men, going,
> climbing atop the great roof beam,
> having joined their buttocks,
> then begin to blow.
>
> (4.41)

Two men do this, and as all six blow their whistles, Man Dev drums fiercely and dances through the courtyard. Every few minutes, he sings a few lines citing places closer and closer, calling on their local spirits for help, but mostly he drums and dances as the whistles resound. The commotion intensifies as he announces that the siyo is in the courtyard, hovering around the gourd. The spirits, he shouts, give it no other path. One of the two men with sticks unplugs the gourd and holds it in his left hand. The shaman squats next to him. Here the only major variation between the way the ceremony is performed in the Bhujī Valley and in Jājarkoṭ occurs. In Jājarkoṭ, instead of being cut at the beginning, the living chicken is hung head downward over the gourd. When it suddenly flutters and trembles, it proves that the siyo has entered the gourd, which is then stoppered. The chicken is cut only later at the crossroads, and a goat is not required. In Bhujī, the shaman himself trembles when the siyo arrives. He shouts Hoi! and points to the gourd. As the audience joins in with shouts and whistles, the men shatter it.

O Garan Kāle Garan, in the door, the door frame,
in the bottle gourd, going,
striking the bottle gourd, shattering the bottle gourd,
while going "hā hā," while going "ho ho."

(4.42)

They carry the broken gourd along with the plowshare to the crossroads. The sticks they used to shatter the gourd are stuck into the plow, to act as handles, and the plow is used to dig a shallow hole. The assistants toss the pieces of gourd into the hole, and ram the plow into the ground next to the hole. The whistlers bite through their bamboo whistles and throw them in, too. The shaman's assistant slits the goat's neck so that its blood drains onto the plow and into the hole.

At Sātai [True] Crossroads, doing this there,
of the kharsu branch, going, the great plow, going,
turning its face toward the forest, burying that there;
of the paiyā branch, going, burying the great spike;
of the deva niṅgālī, going, shattering the great whistles;
the great goat, going, at Sātai Crossroads,
going to the great obstruction, going to the great plow,
then cutting this there; *ārulā, bārulā* [meaning unknown].
The paiyā spike, the iron spanner,
I'll strike it, I'll bury it!

(4.43)

Man Dev dances and drums, then returns to the house, where he hums the deutā bolāune mantar again. The patient and his family are released from the net as the shaman concludes the performance, reciting the fragment of text about the construction of the net. At this point, he should have knotted a string around the wrist of each member of the patient's family, and slit upward through the knot with a large knife *(khukuri)*, but he forgot this and had to do it the next morning instead.

The assistant extracts the goat's spleen and hands it to the shaman, who carefully examines it. Everyone crowds around to get a look. Man Dev concludes that the siyo has survived the ritual and may still trouble the village, if not the family. Perhaps, he predicts, it will bother the daughter-in-law's house, or the houses of daughters who have married away. As evidence, he points to a dark red spot at the upper edge of the spleen and a white vein running vertically across it. This shows that the siyo still lives among the *bhāi-bandu* (the extended family). He concludes, though, that perhaps this is a siyo surviving from the time of forefathers, not the one from the most recent cliff fall. With these remarks, the ceremony is over.

Various aspects of this text illustrate flexibility toward the performance and its appropriate materials. In the dictated version, three other trees, *paṭkā, khaniyā,* and *tusāro,* as well as the kāṭhe kāulī, are named, with sticks and leaves from all four designated acceptable to the spirits. If a branch from one is unavailable, another could be substituted. The dictated version includes a passage about inserting a dry, leafy branch into the side of the gourd (Fig. 4.2). During the early preparations, the shaman's assistant silently did this without Man Dev's comment. This branch rustles when the siyo enters, announcing its arrival, a detail overlooked on this occasion.

What have I shown by this detailed account of one ceremony, besides giving some sense of its complexity and developing a cautionary warning against seeking meaning exclusively in performance? First, a performed text can diverge from the text as memorized by the shaman, not just in trivial ways. Here, the most detailed passages of the text were not included in that night's performance. Second, the directions for performing a ceremony that a text contains can be closely followed even when they are omitted from a particular ceremony. The reflexive relation established between text and performance can be summarized with Garfinkel's concept of the "documentary method of interpretation." At one level, the ritual can be read as the "document of" the text, while the text is the underlying pattern that gives sense to the ritual. The next level reverses these roles, with the text as document, the ritual as pattern (Garfinkel 1967:78). Each performance makes sense out of, and puts sense into, the text, just as each recital does the same for each ceremony. This is not surprising. One point that Garfinkel was trying to make, and to make problematic, was that ethnomethodology is what we always do but fail to recognize, so this reflexivity is necessarily as much a feature of shamanic activity as it is of any other activity. The difference, if there is one, is that process is less transparently taken for granted by shamans. Shamans not only battle witches and malign spirits, they also struggle against the inevitable indexicality and reflexivity of languages. Shamans endeavor to follow exactly a set of directions for creating order, even as they create the conditions for changing it.

5
The Sound of Things

While systematic inquiry into the properties of language flavors the Western philosophic tradition as far back as Parmenides, only in this century has such inquiry intensified, reaching a point where the philosophy of language seems to have become coextensive with at least metaphysics, and perhaps with all of philosophy. Minimally, the study of thought and of ideas has become the study of them through the intermediary of language. The social sciences are not exempt from these developments, despite lagging a few steps behind each shift in philosophical emphasis. Since I endeavor to clarify and bring to life a traditional anthropological abstraction, "shamans," using this modern emphasis on the mediating role of language, and since, at the end of this chapter, I sketch a shamanic theory of language, I will begin by outlining some of the various steps that have led to philosophy's own reorientation. While these twists and turns of theory mediate my entire study, they have remained for the most part unemphasized background until now, allowing my exploration of the specifically shamanic worldview, and especially the worldview that emerges from shaman oral texts, to be more emphatically accentuated. These notes "signpost" the way that I have conceived my study and may provide a mirror reflecting distinctive features of specifically shamanic discourse.

Much of the most recent redirection of philosophy results from the logical positivists, who sought to delineate "the form of any possible language." Logical positivism wished to construct a logically perfect language of well-formed propositions about the world, propositions that could be completely analyzed, bounded between tautologies and contradictions. Each such proposition would be defined by an ostensible reference to the objective world, and each proposition would be self-sufficient ("atomic"). All nonreducible, synthetic propositions could then be dismissed as nonsensical. Wittgenstein sums up this approach as: "To give the essence of propositions means to give the essence of all descriptions, therefore the essence of the world" (1963:95; 5.4711).

However, in trying to construct such a language, an irremediable need for untestable sets of "protocol" statements emerged, elusive limits apparently never part of the system whose boundaries they form. So too, did an awareness that so-called "elementary" propositions required such properties as number or color that express only different degrees of the same quality. Consequently, these propositions form open-ended systems of affiliated propositions, related, as Wittgenstein put it, as are the marks on a ruler. If elementary propositions can contain numbers, they can exclude one another. Therefore, such propositions are not logically independent. Developing an argument against his earlier efforts, Wittgenstein observed: "It isn't a proposition that I put against reality as a yardstick, it's a *system* of propositions" (1975:110). This increasing awareness of unclosable gaps between logical grammars and formal theories of language on the one hand and the events of naturally occurring speech on the other led to new analytic approaches to discourse. An investigation into ordinary language began to replace the reductive analysis of sentences. J. L. Austin characterized ordinary language philosophy as the examination of "what we say when." While warning of the traps that words set for us, of their inadequacies and arbitrariness, and showing little concern for the dilemmas possibly raised by linguistic relativism, Austin was nevertheless confident that "our common stock of words embodies all the distinctions men have found worth drawing, and the connexions they have found worth making, in the lifetimes of many generations" (1979:182).

Much of the way in which an investigation into ordinary language proceeds relies on "Wittgensteinian semantics," characterized by his famous suggestion that often, to discover the meaning of an expression, we need to look to its use (1953:43). Instead of seeing language as a set of pictures, Wittgenstein suggests that we look at it as a set of tools, each appropriate to certain purposes. This view dispels the idea that there is one necessary form of language, one necessary source of meaning. Wittgenstein introduces the notion of "language-game" to suggest that meaning results not from logical properties intrinsic to language, or to the mind, or to the world, but from custom and training. Language games are rule-following social constructions, so knowledge, along with properties such as objectivity and rationality, grows out of social uses. David Pears summarizes as "extreme anthropocentrism" Wittgenstein's insistence that only linguistic processes preserve meanings. Language games gain a certain stability from the rules, "but even the rules do not provide a fixed point of reference, because they always allow divergent interpretations. What really gives the practices their stability is that we agree in our interpretations of the rules" (Pears 1970:179).

Social scientists are increasingly receptive to Wittgenstein's therapeutic reflections on language as games, and on language games as forms of life. However, his own work was more edifying than constructive. Wittgenstein helped others break free from outworn conventions and unprofitable lines of inquiry without systematically providing new conventions. Attempts to formulate a philosophic system out of his varied remarks are self-contradictory. Instead, I read the *Philosophical Investigations* as the most sustained set of sarcasms ever recorded. Wittgenstein himself compares it (another sarcasm?) in its preface to an album of sketches made on a journey. Consequently, it is not always obvious, to say the least, how these meditative reflections might assist a task like ethnological research, though a number of authors have tried to demonstrate their relevance. Peter Winch (1958, 1970), for example, has outlined some ways that these ideas minimally challenge conventional social science and provide new directions for inquiry. Winch's basic argument is that "the central problem of sociology, that of giving an account of the nature of social phenomena in general, itself belongs to philosophy . . . this part of sociology is really misbegotten epistemology" (1958:43). Arguing that human action rests on the views that actors themselves hold on what is the case concerning the world around them, Winch claims that "social relations are expressions of ideas about reality" (1958:23). By discussing language, we discuss what counts as belonging to the world, and what doesn't. Stability depends on following rules, but even more crucially, on agreeing how the rules should be interpreted. While Winch concludes that to study social behavior is to elucidate the rules which people follow in their behavior, he recognizes, as did the ethnosemanticists, the importance of procedures that identify when things are the "same" and when they are "different." That is, the most important rules are those for establishing equivalency, and for determining the correct use of expressions. These rules exist within the playing of some particular language game, not in some atemporal eternity, since languages are products of particular, historical, contexts. Accepting Wittgenstein's metaphor of languages as games, Winch insists that rules necessarily rest on a social context of common activity. This orientation connects his perspective with that of Alfred Schutz, who undertook to anchor Max Weber's social theory within Husserl's phenomenology. In his Fifth Cartesian Meditation, Husserl recognized that the phenomenological perspective applied to different levels, one of which is the social world. There, one deals with the constitution of social acts and their surrounding world of culture, and with the "genuine, though restricted, kind of objectivity belonging to such a world" (Husserl 1960:131–32). Schutz concentrated on this plane of Husserl's phenomenological method. It closely resembles the locus of Wittgenstein's reflections. Within it, rules are one, very important, aspect of the "stock of knowledge at hand," out of which participants in a social order construct their explanations of that order. While Winch's interests remain those of a philosopher, not of someone investigating particular social events, Schutz addresses actual social phenomena, yet their orientations are similar, as when Schutz observes that "the answer to the question 'What does this social world mean for me the observer?' requires as a prerequisite the answering of the quite different questions 'What does the social world mean for the observed actor within this world and what did he mean by his acting within it?'" (1964:7). Schutz insisted that we must not accept the social world as "ready-made," but must pay close attention to how actors in the social world understand one another and themselves. In a radical way, ethnomethodologists follow exactly this recommendation. Ethnomethodology studies "commonsense" knowledge: phenomena used to construct the social world and its factual properties—the processes of sense making. Its purpose is not to show that anyone's naive, common, taken-for-granted sense of norms, values, intentions, or whatever, is false, but how participants create and sustain their intentional lifeworld as objectively real. Ethnomethodologists do not attempt to establish "causes" for what people do, but ask how it is that people come to accept that their behavior does have causes. As Schutz directed, it identifies the natural attitude of everyday life, the practices of commonsense reasoning, the stock of knowledge at hand (recipes, rules of thumb, social types, maxims, definitions . . .), and particularly relevant to this study, the way in which all of this stock depends upon and is expressed in everyday language, especially in its vocabulary and syntax. Commonsense knowledge is not simply a static body of such ready-made features, however, for each feature has what Schutz called an "open horizon of meaning" (1962:14). That is, each element is plurivocal. Each acquires particular meanings in particular contexts.

The whole idea is to try to get some general sense of how things hang together, of meanings locally created and maintained, without forcing those meanings to correspond within a system judged by either empirical or transcendental standards of what is "true." The history of language use is the history of metaphor. We cannot view behavior as meaningful because it somehow corresponds with the world, for a pragmatic perspective drops the concept of necessary correspondence, such as of thoughts to things or of words to thoughts. These issues of theory become acute when it comes to the study of shaman texts. My discussion emerges from my descriptions, even as those descriptions are themselves founded within a "discursive space" created by shaman texts themselves. Nor is it simply descriptions that emerge from within the investigation; the very framework of that investigation evolves as my inquiry proceeds. Pragmatically, there is not, and cannot be, some fixed, eternal theory that can be first isolated and then systematically applied to some other equally well determined body of knowledge ("data"). The framework of any investigation must change as the investigation continues. A pragmatist refrains from comparing descriptions of the world in terms of how adequately those descriptions represent the world. Narrative must take precedence over theory, telling us to listen well before beginning to interpret. A corollary is listening to the debates of theory as those unfolding in another literary genre, often influential but not intrinsically privileged. I accept the attitude that meaning exists strictly within discourse, rather than in a relation between language and things outside it. Things do exist outside texts, but none of them, whether of soul, mind, or matter, has an intrinsic nature that strives to find expression in words. The world, as Richard Rorty insists, "cannot propose a language for us to speak" (1989:6).

The contrary, I argue, is true. For all of us, languages speak a world. Language speaks our being in that world, as we, as mediating agents, do propose a language to speak about the world. Shamans effectively demonstrate this perspective with their texts. This is most clearly heard in their private, secret, whispered tools of direct intervention, their mantars. In the remainder of this chapter, I examine the ways that shaman mantars speak a particular world.

Every shaman has an extensive collection of secret formulas, which they call either mantars or *japs*. They draw no distinction between these two terms, though jap is more commonly used as a verb. In most cases, these terms appear completely interchangeable—to jap means to repeat over and over, but a mantar gains effectiveness with repetition, and a text titled a jap may conclude with the line "Blow, mantar!" The lexical meaning of jap, "muttered repetition esp. of a god's name or a religious formula" (Turner 1980:208), is quite appropriate. The multitude of "ordinary" meanings for "mantra" fit these texts less well, not only because there is no single accepted definition. The simplest way of defining a mantra, as an "instrument of thought," is, I will show, quite inappropriate to the ways that shamans use them. Hence, I have preferred to retain the less familiar Nepali "mantar" when discussing texts that the shamans so named, trying to avoid semantic controversies that are peripheral to my study. As a rule, I use "jap" when the shaman who supplied the text called it a jap, and likewise "mantar" when that was how they labeled it.

However designated, these texts form an extensive subset of any shaman's repertoire of oral texts. Alternatively, they also constitute an extensive subset of the oral material known to everyone in Nepal, for it is no exaggeration to say that all adult villagers, both men and women, know and use at least a few mantars. Some individuals may claim, at least when they are themselves free of severe problems, that jhāṅgarīs and dhāmīs are just frauds, fakes, but I never heard anyone deny the potential efficacy of a properly recited mantar. Mantars, after all, figure prominently in all life cycle activities among anyone in Nepal who claims to be either Hindu or Buddhist, so only the most severe apostates would theoretically deny them entirely, a rejection I could never provoke even among my most radical friends.

The pervasive role of "mantras" in South Asian religious life goes back at least to the Vedic period, linking Vedic, Hindu, and Tantric (whether Indian or Tibetan) practices, all of which share the conviction that the world can be transformed by a correctly uttered formula. Providing a common theme in those traditions, the practice of mantras has received surprisingly little attention by researchers. A review of critical efforts can be traced through the excellent annotated bibliography that concludes Alper (1989), supplemented with references found in Padoux (1989, 1992). However, I mention this possible secondary orientation in passing, for I am interested less in situating shaman mantars in the labyrinth of South Asian religious life than in examining their specific contribution to defining shamanic practices and shamanic identity. To this end, I have chosen to analyze a few dozen exemplary texts. As will be seen, these texts are clearly not derivative repetitions of Vedic passages, nor have they much in common with the sophisticated metonyms of the *mahāvākyas,* such as the famous *"tat tvam asi"* or *"oṁ maṇi padme hūṁ,"* beginning as it does with the ideographically unique phoneme ॐ whose sound is the entire cosmos. It is equally true that the subtle discussions of sonic mysticism found in Indian linguistics and philosophy would seem more foreign to the practical orientation of the shamans themselves than do remarks made by Western ontological hermeneuticists such as Gadamer (1965), whose epigrammatic "sense in which language speaks us" earned a nod of the head from Karṇa Vīr when I attempted to explain it, using Vedic hymns to Vāc as examples. While my own discussion is partly informed by the intersections and divergences of Vedic and Western traditions, both remain for the most part as background. It seems appropriate, though, to recall one of the premises against which the goddess cautioned Parmenides in his vision: "That which can be spoken and thought needs must be; for it is possible for it, but not for nothing to be; that is what I bid thee ponder" (Kirk and Raven 1963:270, no. 345). This fragment shows how this divergence between Eastern and Western traditions can be documented as far back as the pre-Socratics. Every shamanic ceremony is an attempt to prove wrong the advice that the goddess gave to Parmenides, directly asserting the premise that she criticizes—what can be spoken must be. Logically, shamanic formulas take the unproblematic form, *p,* and, if *p* then not not-*p,* but where *p* stands not for a proposition or assertion, but for an imperative. A paradigmatic example might be: live! and by living, don't die!

To put these assertions in context, I concentrate on showing, first, that shamanic mantars are remarkably intelligible and sense-filled. True, they do make use of a few nonsensical, "abracadabra"-type phrases, which give them a more exotic flavor than that of the public texts. Such phrases are, however, never more than a line or two in any given mantar. Second, I argue that mantars set out to achieve the same ends as do the public texts, the reconstruction of order in the present world. Finally, I suggest that they do this by forcing the everyday world to conform to the world as expressed in language. I demonstrate that the private texts are not in any essential way, whether in design, purpose, or comprehensibility, different from the publicly recited texts, just more laconic, less in need of material representation, and, of course, private.

This last key characteristic, that mantars are always secret, makes appropriate here a few remarks about the ways in which I acquired my own, now very extensive, collection of them. I remain surprised, when I listen to my tapes, at how willingly shamans taught me their mantars. They volunteered them in long sets in response to a single question that I would ask. For example, I would request a mantar to use against witches, and they would recite without pause five or six japs for that purpose, when I would have expected, and been satisfied with, one or two. This is less surprising when it is realized that this is how they originally learned them, and that I had been working with them for four or five years by that time, but it still shows their willingness to teach me whatever they were taught. At least three factors were involved. First, as I noted already, there is the causal association between partially acquired secret knowledge and madness. Gore Sārkī explicitly cited this as the reason he felt compelled to teach me all the mantars that he knew, and it probably influenced others as well. Once I could recite the public texts, shamans had a moral responsibility to teach me their private ones. Otherwise, their karma would be burdened by having contributed to my insanity. The second decisive factor was that I gathered information from a relatively large number of different shamans, each of whom had a professional interest in my acknowledgment that he possessed significant knowledge. Knowing that I was cross-checking, it is unlikely that they would deliberately falsify material, though concealings through omissions, accidental or deliberate, remain possible. The third reason they taught me so much is simply that this is how shamans do things. Many years after I began working with Karṇa Vīr, he told me a story about his father, Lāṭo Jhāṅgarī, who remains one of the two most famous shamans to have practiced in Jājarkoṭ. (The other was Gore Sārkī's father, "Kālā Jhāṅgarī.") Nearly thirty years ago, in Vikram Saṁvat 2023, a cloth merchant, Karṇa Bahādur Rāul, passed through Churī Village. He met Lāṭo Jhāṅgarī on the trail and asked to hear his recitals. Lāṭo Jhāṅgarī asked the merchant to light a stick of incense, sat down in front of him and began to recite. He became furiously possessed, and continued for hours. The merchant became distraught, fearful of the wraiths responding to so many recitals, and begged him to quiet the spirits. Lāṭo Jhāṅgarī went on and on, until finally Rāul presented him with a new turban cloth, three hands of the best *markin* (commercial quality) cloth, at which the spirits finally became peaceful.

This parallels the way that I first began to collect Karṇa Vīr's recitals outside their performances. Having initially collected texts from Gumāne, the first time that I interviewed Karṇa Vīr, I challenged him to prove that he knew more than did any other shaman in Jājarkoṭ. He complied by taping texts for the rest of the night and through the next morning. Perhaps he was disappointed that I only gave him cigarettes and a bottle of locally distilled alcohol, no turban, but he waited nearly ten years before telling me this story.

No shaman wants to admit that another knows texts for some purpose that he doesn't, for that would be a confession of lesser powers, but the only conclusive confirmation of the extent of anyone's knowledge was to recite the texts. Once I knew, for example, that *putlā tānne* (removing the substances that a witch has put into a victim) is always accompanied by a mantar, I could expect to learn it from each shaman. My own experience confirms Evans-Pritchard's remark that "in the long run . . . an ethnographer is bound to triumph. Armed with preliminary knowledge nothing can prevent him from driving deeper and deeper the wedge if he is interested and persistent" (1937:152). Once I learned my first mantar, it was only a matter of time (admittedly, it's involved fifteen years now) before I learned many.

Until my return trips in 1989 and 1992, I could never reward my informants financially. The Mahendra Scholarship provided me with 500 rupees a month, about U.S. $30 at the time, even less than the Peace Corps subsistence allowance that supported me for three of the previous four years. (During the other year, I emulated a yogin, living on "nothing.") As a result, I could not purchase the cooperation of informants, nor that of transcribers or field assistants. Those burdens fell on my friends. Only when I recently revisited them did I reward shamans and assistants for their help, but still only with small gifts. Shamans seemed, however, to benefit directly from the prestige attached to my inquiries, resulting in increased numbers of clients. This was, I think, another reason they were so cooperative. They eventually recognized my persistent interest in them as a useful advertisement of their abilities, with their enthusiasm for this project increasing enormously. Prestige was involved in another way when I began my research, in the form of the keen support that I consistently received from a local historian, Yogīśwar Kārki, who as former district chairman of the "Back to the Village" campaign and chairman of the District Education Committee had considerable authority. When I first met Karṇa Vīr, he was an assistant village leader trying to build an elementary school in his village. When Yogīśwar told him to cooperate with my investigations, Karṇa Vīr cooperated, setting a decisive precedent for other shamans of the district.

Mantars are muttered in undertones, not recalled in complete silence. Clients and human audiences know when one is being applied, everyone recognizing them as the most important moments of any ceremony. The shaman shows signs of intense concentration. He pauses in his drumming and dancing, if they had already started. The muttering sounds rather impressive, with a lot of breathy snorts and puffs, possibly opening the way to an entire semiotics of mumbling. Often, they end with a spectacular possession. The distorted syllables of the words disintegrate, phonemes stretched to their breaking points, nearly achieving a climax where their soundings might overtake their meanings. Yet enough meaning must be preserved to demonstrate to the audience that the shaman remains in control, that he hasn't succumbed to the disorder that constantly threatens the world. As Marina Roseman notes of Temiar shaman songs: "The transformations wrought upon speech disguise and augment, yet never obliterate it . . ." (1991:148). Just as the possession by spirits is rapidly brought under control, so too is the delivery of a jap. I am convinced that onlookers commonly overhear much of their content, though no one was willing to confirm this directly. Again, there were occasions that contradicted villagers' claims of ignorance. For example, as I traveled throughout Rukum in 1992, I halted one afternoon in a high pasture where shepherds were camped. As he cooked our rice, my friend Citra Prasād Śarmā played part of a tape that he was transcribing. Even though I recorded it from a Kāmī in Jājarkoṭ, one of the Magar shepherds immediately recognized it as a "bīr calāune" mantar (below), supposedly one of the most secret shaman texts. He even observed, correctly, that it was incomplete. Perhaps this was exceptional, or perhaps its simple structure made it transparently obvious. As the following examples show, however, if the words are occasionally uttered loud enough to be heard, and they are, then they can also be understood, for their content is not exceptionally obscure or esoteric.

To begin with what is probably the simplest form that any mantar can take, consider one to calm the planets, Nar Siṅgh Kāmī's "*graha santa garne.*" This is a formula borrowed from Brāhmans. Karṇa Vīr used it only to parody priests, and by extension, any shaman who himself used it, such as Nar Siṅgh (who had once treated Karṇa Vīr's nephew more successfully than had Karṇa Vīr). It is, nevertheless, illustrative of a key feature of mantars. They undertake to compel, to restrain, and to change. This text consists entirely of a list of rather general terms, each coupled with the repeated imperative. Nar Siṅgh identified Ulkā as a planet (and Bilkā its rhyme), though the term more often means any natural phenomenon, a meaning that also fits here:

> Obstructions, be peaceful! Earth, be peaceful!
> Planets, be peaceful! Nine Planets, be peaceful!
> Ulkā, be peaceful! Bilkā, be peaceful!
> Land, be peaceful! Ground, be peaceful!
> House, be peaceful! Home, be peaceful!
>
> (5.1)

This illustrates perfectly what Roman Jakobson called the magic, incantatory function of converting an inanimate "third person" into an addressee of a conative message (1981:24). Even in content this mantar resembles Jakobson's example from Joshua 10.12: "Sun, stand thou still upon Gibeon; and thou, Moon, in the valley of Ajalon." This same conative structure, addressee plus imperative, can be seen in many shaman mantars, such as Abi Lal's Jap to Cause the Bīr to Move (bīr calāunu jap):

> Kālyā Bīr, move [*cal*]! Dhālyā Bīr, move!
> Kaile Bīr, move! Chaḍke Bīr, move!
> Arjun Vāṇ, move! Laṁkā Vāṇ, move!
> Ubā Bīr, move! Ghunimaṭyā Bīr, move!
> [more names follow].
>
> (5.2)

I expressed surprise that this was enough to summon one's familiar spirits, but Abi Lal succinctly commented, "You say 'Move, barāṅg!' They move. Having said, 'Come here!' they must move on your body."

When I remained unsatisfied, he supplied a more elaborate text, which has a formal beginning, a formal end, and incorporates flattery and bribes. When each bīr is named, it is promised "there will be a sacrifice for you," and they are called "beloved of the sun and moon." The longer version still preserves the dominant structure of the above passage, featuring most prominently the imperative "move!"

> Seven pines, nine doors, creaking open.
> For Chanimunṭyā Bīr, there will be a sacrifice.
> For Kālyā Bīr, there will be a sacrifice.
> For Kailyā Bīr, there will be a sacrifice.
> Move! Narsiṅgh Bīr. Move! Narsiṅgh Bīr
> [each Bīr is named, with a promise and command].
> Beloved of the Sun and Moon,
> darling of the Twelve Bīr.
> Chanimunṭyā Bīr will play on my body,
> will play on my headdress,
> will bring soul, wits, into my belly.
>
> (5.3)

A third version is even more elaborate, connecting each bīr with its place of origin and elaborating the bribes:

> Where did Hanumān Bīr originate,
> he originated in Ladudha city.
> The crop-producing lands are yours,
> the fruit-producing lands are yours.
> Act at my head, act at my shoulders!
> [more bīrs are named].
> Hanumān Bīr, Laṁka Bīr, you, come here!
> Act at my head, act at my shoulders!
> (So saying, you summon all of them.)
>
> (5.4)

The bīr may also be unresponsive, requiring the mantar to expand to include taunts and threats:

> You may be hiding after climbing into trees,
> you may be asleep in the water or springs,
> you may be asleep on the cliffs or rockslides,
> I'll grab you by the nose!
> I'll tug you by the ear!

I'll pull you by the wrist!
Move! Twelve Bīr!

(5.5)

These threats may even escalate into threatening to break the bīr's arms.

Having at least two forms, one simpler, one more elaborate, turns out to be a common feature of many mantars. Rather than being completely fixed and unchanging, they too, like public texts, expand and contract. If you begin to shake after naming a single bīr, or by appealing collectively to the "Twelve Bīr" (or the "Eighteen Māphī," or the "Twenty-Two Dhuwā"), it is superfluous as well as impertinent to call upon each of them by name. As Roseman discovered of Temiar healing arts, "To sing the true name of an entity in ceremonial performance animates the presence of that identity" (1988:814). While lists of potentially active agents may be deliberately curtailed, lists of the world's features to be quelled or protected are thoroughly elaborated. Such lists feature prominently in mantars, just as they do in the recitals. They become exhaustively comprehensive. They name each of the obstructions and each of the planets, each part of the body, each part of a house and all the objects in it. More than just a simple acknowledgment in passing is going on here. Naming is an assertion of authority. To know the correct name of something is the first step toward controlling it. The second step is to utter the name, transforming air into breath, breath into sound, sound into meaning. To speak is to apply one's knowledge. Naming assigns the word, and by extension its referent, a specific place in the order that is being constructed. Adding a command, such as "Be bound!" fixes it to an assigned place, fixes it to an assigned role.

A line that I quoted earlier (3.29), "Come when I say come, go when I say go!" is, I suggest, the paradigmatic form of mantric utterance. It delineates the relations between the shaman and his spirits, clearly telling them that they are subservient agents expected to serve his purposes, that he, not they, controls the ceremony. The spirits that possess the shaman are expected to follow his orders. The shaman takes complete responsibility for the consequences of the ceremony. He does not share that responsibility with the spirits, but tells them what is expected of them.

Other summonses are more delicate:

Hey, twelve māphī, move!
Twenty-two barāṅg, move!

Atop my head, move!
Atop my shoulders, sit!
Shaking the earth, move!
Shaking the world, move!
Coming, shame the mouth!
Going, slap the back!
Make the truth known, mend any falsehoods!

(5.6)

This passage elegantly expresses both the powers that auxiliary spirits possess and their intimacy with the shaman who calls upon them. The text clarifies what the initial expectations of them are. Spirits contribute to, indeed are typically seen as constitutive of, the shaman's power, but it is a power that the shaman focuses, administers, and manipulates, not an overpowering force to which he passively submits. Imperatives are the standard mood of shamanic mantars and japs. Supernatural assistance is not requested or pleaded for, it is demanded.

Commands are not restricted to spirits, however. Shamans direct them toward diverse entities, including physical pains. A perfect example of this is a mantar that Gumāne used at the culmination of ceremonies to relieve victims of witchcraft. It transfers away from the patient's body pains that witches have induced in their heads:

[That] consuming the head, I take out to the throat.
Consuming the throat, I take out to the heart.
Consuming the heart, I take out to the lungs.
Consuming the lungs, I take out to the liver.
Consuming the liver, I take out to the lap.
Consuming the lap, I transfer to the hips.
Consuming the hips, I transfer to the calves.
Consuming the calves, I transfer to the thighs.
Consuming the thighs, I transfer to the nails.
Consuming the nails, I transfer there!
I send across the four rivers, I reduce to ash!

(5.7)

This mantar shifts the throbbing pain of a headache away from the head, through vital organs of the body, collecting on the way other pains that may have accumulated elsewhere, down to the toenails and out of the body. Pain is ordered out with a forceful gesture to accompany the deictic adverb "there!" *(ṭhā)* of the penultimate line. "Crossing four rivers" *(cau gaṅgā tāru)* is a conventional way to express great distance, but "I reduce to ash!" *(bhasam pāru)* is unquestionably and uncompromisingly emphatic.

To transfer through stages is a standard technique of many different performances, found in public recitals just as in mantars. The public text to treat star obstructions moves them away in the following fashion (see also 6.33):

> The deadly star obstruction of the house pinnacle,
> was transferred to its foot.
> The deadly star obstruction at the foot,
> was transferred to the doorstep.
> The deadly star obstruction of the doorstep,
> was transferred to the edge of the porch.
> The deadly star obstruction of the edge of the porch,
> the Time of Death, the Messenger of Death,
> was transferred to the Ocean of Tears,
> to the Cremation Ground of the Dead,
> to Riverside Graveyard, to Barmā Crossroads.
>
> (5.8)

Much more than an inventory of anatomy or of architecture unfolds in these passages. Shamans create the world in which they act through the speech that they use, detail by detail. In the classic Western sense of language as a system of denotative signs that convey meaning through representation, shamanic speech, a constitutive exercise of power, of healing, and, sometimes, of terror, is not language. When all tropes are literal, metaphor evaporates. Figures of speech become the blueprints and maps of a transformative reality, resembling what Ruth Murray Underhill noted for Papagos: "The describing of a desired event in the magic of beautiful speech was to them the means by which to make that event take place" (1938:6). Gary Witherspoon noted the same for Navajo theories of language. "The symbol was not created as a means of representing reality; on the contrary, reality was created or transformed as a manifestation of symbolic form. In the Navajo view of the world, language is not a mirror of reality; reality is a mirror of language" (1977:34). A shaman's language does not attempt to describe how things are. It determines how the world will be.

The lengthiest part of the rāyā sarsu jap consists of another constitutive inventory. (For a somewhat similar but very short version, see Gaborieau's introduction to Oakley and Gairola [1977:27].) After the formal opening (4.11) and the story of the seed's origin (1.3), the seeds bind an extensive list of suspect forces:

> With this rāyā sarsu, bind the four directions.
> Bind the river spirits, bind the human ghosts.
> Bind the giant ghosts, bind the other ghosts.
> Bind the masān of timely deaths,
> bind the masān of untimely deaths.
> Bind the masān of those swept away in rivers,
> bind the masān of those who fell from cliffs.
> Bind major witches, bind minor witches,
> bind spells, bind charms,
> bind the threats from waters, from springs.
>
> (5.9)

The listing continues with both new entries and extensive repetitions (1.6). More than fifty different objects and forces must be bound. Most of these are predictable, following closely the lines suggested in Chapter 2, but a few inclusions are particularly interesting. Perhaps the most remarkable, which would fit well in Borges' delightful antitaxonomy of *Other Inquisitions* (1964:103), is "species that shake," foremost of which are listed, not shamans, but cows. Anyone who has observed a cow has perhaps noticed that it often trembles, its sides rippling with involuntary shudders, but here we find an explicit connection between this shaking and its sacredness. The category includes pipal trees, also revered, which shake without a perceptible breeze. This could offer a starting point for a "superstructural" revision of materialist theories of why cows and certain trees are sacred, since jhāṅgarīs sometimes call themselves *viprālī*, using a diminutive of the Vedic term *vipra* (one who trembles, a particular kind of priest). This term shows up in some mantars, such as at the conclusion of Nar Siṅgh's jap to awaken masān:

> Come, Brother Kaṁsa,
> accompany this viprālī!
>
> (5.10)

Hindu influences in these two lines are reinforced by identifying as an important masān the demonic maternal uncle of Kṛṣṇa, Kaṁsa, who ordered the slaying of his sister's children.

The rāyā sarsu text continues, binding threats from the assembled audience, a passage that can be transformed into a curse (5.33), and reappears in the ashes mantar (6.1):

> Bind the hand that strikes,
> bind the tongue that speaks,
> bind the eyes that see,
> bind the soles that stomp.
>
> (5.11)

The mantar binds ghosts who stay in waterfalls, masān who stay at cremation grounds, their cousins the *syāuryā* who hover at graveyards, barmās who stay in shrines, and various spirits who stay in springs, cliffs, and forests. The "seven doors" (the entrances to the head) are bound, the patient is bound head to foot, and the jap concludes with violent threats, including ones against dhāmīs and their assistants. In the middle of this sequence we find "jhāṅgarīs who stay in gels" (shamans who stay in trees planted over a shaman's tomb), explicitly associating dead shamans with other generally malevolent forces.

> Bind solitary demons of ridges,
> bind shamans staying in shaman tombs,
> bind masān of crossroads,
> bind syāuryā of the floodplain graveyards,
> first bind this courtyard seat where it is pressed,
> bind the Ālaṅg seat, bind the Mālaṅg seat,
> bind seats where experienced hags [*klaṅkenī*] have pressed,
> bind villagers staying in the village,
> tricks, deceits, minor witches,
> major witches, striking, killing,
> pulling out eyes of the living, breaking arms,
> I drive into hell!
> Break open those staying at the crossroads with a plow tip!
> The important syāunyā staying in the floodplain graveyards,
> Rājā Masān, Karbir Masān, Bhiudal Masān, Gaṅgārām Masān,
> Marbir Masān, Little Brothers Uraṭhā Juraṭhā,
> asān streams, masān streams, Little Brother Bindu,
> died at the right time, died at the wrong time,
> impaled, netted, swept away in rivers, fallen from cliffs,
> honored and respected mediums [dhāmīs, *dhumārās*],

their assistants striking, killing,
I drive into hell, I kill with an iron staff!

(5.12)

Karṇa Vīr's version adds a distinctive passage after the call to awaken both the deities of the four nāths (shrines) and the wandering yogin. It fully describes that yogin, using the same description that appears in the Recital of the Nine Little Sisters, where it is the disguise that Mahādev takes to play a trick on men and create the first witches (3.8). This is one of several cases where a passage of a jap is the same as a passage of a recital. Other shamans, including Abi Lal, Nar Siṅgh, and Kamāro Kāmī, all used this description within both their japs and their recitals:

You, yogi, have come!
Where can you be sated, where can you be stuffed?
Worn on the head, a tiger's skin,
worn on the forehead, sandalwood ashes,
worn on the ear, a large pendant,
worn around the neck, a rudrākṣa necklace,
slung over the shoulder, a pair of begging bowls,
held in the hand, a thunderbolt staff,
slung in the waist, a double-edged knife,
put on his ankles heavy anklets,
dressed in frayed saffron cloth,
began to do knowledge, began to do meditation,
began to exclaim in disgust,
began to exclaim in contempt.
Barren cows, lame cows, the cow of wishes,
from the burned dried cowdung, ashes . . .
he began to put a jap on the ashes.
Indra, God of Heaven, Vāsu, God of Hell,
Kālu Jaiśī, Maitu Dhāmī, Satava Gyānī, Bharṣā Paṇḍit,
Rammā Jumrātam began to put a jap on the seeds.

(5.13)

In these last lines, not only the yogin, but also major divinities and even other experts share the responsibility for applying the jap to the mustard seeds. Finally, the first shaman, Jumrātam, puts in an appearance, as he commonly does at the ends of public recitals.

A jap to suppress witches, used at the beginning of every ceremony to protect the shaman, again contains this description, but further elaborates the yogin's rudrākṣa necklace. The text strings onto the necklace twenty-two berries, one by one. Each has a different number of faces, and the text asks, then answers, what different divine force or astrological configuration wore that berry:

> Who wore the one-faced rudrākṣa berry,
> who wore the two-faced rudrākṣa berry,
> who wore the three-faced rudrākṣa berry
> [through twenty-two].
> The twenty-two-faced rudrākṣa berry
>   was worn by Vāsu Deu,
> the twenty-one-faced rudrākṣa berry
>   was worn by the Twenty-One Lāmās,
> the twenty-faced rudrākṣa berry
>   was worn by Viṣṇu's Throne,
> the nineteen-faced rudrākṣa berry
>   was worn by the Eighty-One Lāmās,
> the eighteen-faced rudrākṣa berry
>   was worn by the Eighteen Goddesses,
> the seventeen-faced rudrākṣa berry
>   was worn by the Seven Ṛṣis,
> the sixteen-faced rudrākṣa berry
>   was worn by the Sixteen-Hundred Cowherdesses,
> the fifteen-faced rudrākṣa berry
>   was worn by the Five Bhuwānī,
> the fourteen-faced rudrākṣa berry
>   was worn by the Fourteen Goddesses,
> the thirteen-faced rudrākṣa berry
>   was worn by the Thirteen Three-worlds,
> the twelve-faced rudrākṣa berry
>   was worn by the Twelve Barmā,
> the eleven-faced rudrākṣa berry
>   was worn by the Eighty-One Lāmās,
> the ten-faced rudrākṣa berry
>   was worn by the King's Chariot,
> the nine-faced rudrākṣa berry
>   was worn by the Nine Hundred Thousand [stars],
> the eight-faced rudrākṣa berry
>   was worn by the Thirty-Three Rooms,

the seven-faced rudrākṣa berry
  was worn by the Eighty-Eight Goddesses,
the six-faced rudrākṣa berry
  was worn by the Fifty-Six rooms,
the five-faced rudrākṣa
  was worn by the Five Bhuwānī,
the four-faced rudrākṣa
  was worn by the Fourteen Goddesses,
the three-faced rudrākṣa
  was worn by the Three Three-worlds,
the two-faced rudrākṣa
  was worn by the Goddess Durgā,
the one-faced rudrākṣa
  was worn by our guru, was worn by us.
On the head, a tigerskin . . .

(5.14)

The yogin description repeats another time. This text, uniquely, ignores local divinities and shamanic spirits in favor of Hindu astrological references, each one wearing a berry. The rudrākṣa *(Elaeocarpus)* berry necklace is one of the most important accessories designating wandering mendicants. Briggs (1989:15) discusses the symbolic importance of berries having from one to twenty-one faces for kānphaṭas, though none of the designations overlap with those in this mantar. Important dhāmīs wear such a necklace, but it is not part of the standard shaman costume. Although every shaman that I asked knew a version of this mantar, including Magars as far east as Tākā, whose versions were in the Kham language, none wore such a *mālā*. It is present only in the words of this mantar. Other preliminary mantars are directed to equipment that the shaman has, such as his wooden seat, his drum, or drumstick. Only this one is worn in words alone. The next section of the text resolves this apparent puzzle. It describes again the wandering yogin, who wears this necklace, telling him that he has arrived. Invoking the yogin makes him present at the ceremony, exactly as does the naming of any spirit. Signifying so precisely this transcendental mālā leaves no room for terrestrial imitations. Objects stand in subsidiary, indexical relations to words, to entire classes of concepts. Sometimes, in public situations, as when Man Dev could not proceed without the copper coin that is Mahādev (Chapter 4), visible denotation takes precedence, but here, as part of a private text, the referents are too important to be apprehended in the syntax of concrete objects. Mustard seeds may denote life and growth, feathers the sky and flight, and kacur root the underworld and its hells, but the cosmic order *(ṛtā)* that binds even the greatest gods is too grand for any physical symbol to represent it.

The two overlapping sections of the rāyā sarsu jap and this rudrākṣa jap, the call to awake and the description of the necklace and the yogin, have obvious similarities to opening passages of public recitals. They immediately introduce the points of the compass, each associated with a particular spirit, and the introduction is followed each time with a casting of various experts. Not only in structure but in content as well, these preliminary japs parallel the public texts. Though most mantars lack narrative, they make sense, so clearly that it might be described as hypersense, language in its purest expression, so lucid and elementary that animals, spirits, and even the dead understand it. As Laderman notes for Malay spirits (1991:65), the nonhuman and no longer human audiences of a shaman's sacrifice often seem like ignorant children, and are often addressed as though they were rather stupid.

Like mustard seeds in this example, japs are often applied to some common physical substance, such as rice, water, a mixture of various grains, or iron shavings, and then that substance is physically distributed to convey the words' power more widely. "Wherever you go, there you protect!" An onomatopoetic *"Phū"* or *"Phūk!"* (Blow!) conveys the application:

May you who cause trouble be turned to ash!
Phū mantar!
Śrī Mahādev's oath!

(5.15)

These lines conclude many japs, particularly those blown onto something. At times, a substance that has been japped, usually water, but sometimes milk, yogurt, or herbal leaves, is fed to the patient, extending its force internally as well as externally. This is especially true in the treatment of pregnant or childless women, cases where the treatment of the disorder most often locates it inside the body rather than in an external source. Sometimes, small children are fed these things, though this is less common. Children's problems are usually entwined with those of their mothers (Chapter 2). The jap that concludes the Drongo Recital to treat stillbirths, miscarriages, and other obstetric problems explicitly transfers the child's heart back into the mother, replacing the poison of a pregnancy gone wrong:

> Aum! The fire's plan,
> in the woman's stomach a dead child's span,
> amid the guru's comings and goings,
> I pull out this poison, I kill that poison!
> Rām Candra's deep supplication,
> sharply affected, sharply corrected.
> You, child's heart, I transfer into the mother!
> Blow, mantar! Śrī Mahādev's oath!
>
> (5.16)

Villagers may put seeds treated with a mantar in the bedding of someone troubled by unsettling dreams, or they may throw treated sesame and barley into a fire to dispel the lingering fear of a particularly troublesome dream, such as one of farming fields of cotton, a premonition of leprosy. They scatter potentiated grains on their property and cattle to protect them, and sometimes sew them into pouches to be worn around the neck.

As each ceremony begins, the shaman scatters mustard seeds to protect himself. Before he summons selected spirits, themselves potentially threatening, he binds the surroundings to limit the variety of threats and problems that confront him, allowing him to deal with a single aspect of the whole deteriorating world. This self-protection continues with the japs that he next applies to the fire in front of him, to the ashes that he streaks on his forehead, to his body, his drumstick, drum, guava or cinnamon leaves that go under his seat and onto his head, his costume, and, for certain ceremonies, the piece of kacur root that he keeps under his tongue. All of these japs are similar, with many lines overlapping, often identical to passages of the rāyā sarsu text. That to bind the body begins:

> Bind my side, bind my hide,
> bind my vitals, Head Rāhu, Head Yāhu,
> Deep Pond Sarasvati,
> bind my nine pulses, my twelve organs,
> bind my complete hand, bind the dirt under my nails,
> bind Agni in front, Prajā Jyānī in back,

Wood-splitting Bīr,
Asān Body, Masān Body,
Blood Ghost, Minor Witches, Major Witches,
assembling all composed,
they are disposed!

(5.17)

The most distinctive section of the mantar mumbled as a shaman picks up his drumstick connects it to his wooden seat *(pirā)*, where it drives a wedge beneath potential enemies, including representatives of secular authority and any in the audience who might strike him, slander him, or get up with ill feeling and leave before the ceremony ends. Through a quick series of synecdochical expansions, the mantar succinctly connects the drumstick to the sound coming from the drum, to that sound's effects on the senses, to the ways these sensory impressions rattle the teeth during the recitation of a mantar, finally changing the heart of him who recites the formula:

Under the crowd summoned by the king,
under the couch of the queen,
under the striker's blow,
under the speaker's tongue,
under the riser's sole,
under others, under druthers,
under the drumstick, under the drum beat,
under the five [senses], under the teeth,
swaying the mantrist's heart . . .

(5.18)

The short mantar for the wooden seat itself primarily protects against witch attack. It threatens witches of the sky and the underworld as well as their human counterparts, and concludes:

Awakened dead witches [*uṭhe ḍaṁkīnī*] of the four directions,
Nine Little Sisters Gunāmenī of the Eastern Direction,
killing your eyes, I drive you through seven hells!

(5.19)

The jap for picking up the drum identifies it as the owner of the planets, naming four of them and the two nodal points of the moon. Most drums are made of sadān wood (which bleeds a thick blood of coagulating red sap when cut), and covered with a wild goat's skin, but the text contradicts this:

> *gobri* wood, yak's hide,
> come, little brother, to the shaman's side!
> My drum's Ulkā, Saṁkaṭā, Rāhu, Ketu, Śaniścar, Maṅgal,
> distance all of these, destroy my enemies!
> Ghosts, specters, witches big and small,
> haunting suicides male and female,
> protect me from them all!
> Blow, mantar! Śrī Mahādev's oath!
>
> (5.20)

Every shaman wears a piece of kacur root around his neck. The leading shaman of Tākā, Bal Bahādur Buddha, was horrified to hear me recite a mantar without first biting on a piece. I wanted to know if he knew the rudrākṣa mālā jap, so I quoted part of it to him, but he insisted that I take a piece of his kacur before continuing. In Jājarkoṭ, however, this protection is considered essential only when summoning masān, suppressing vāi, supplicating goddesses, and sucking out poisons, though the jap offers wider protection:

> Forest kacur, skinny kacur, fat fist kacur,
> dedicate my mouth!
> You, kacur, big witches smaller witches,
> spells tricks, māī masān,
> little witches bigger witches, ghosts wraiths,
> female haunting suicides male haunting suicides,
> forest shaman field shaman, all be effaced!
>
> (5.21)

For the ashes mantar, see 6.1.

In each case, the protection holds potential threats in check while assembling other powers. Supernatural forces must be enlisted, commented Karṇa Vīr, just like the troops of an army, a description also found in his texts. Like the interventionary mantars applied outward onto the world, these mantars that a shaman applies onto himself and his equipment compel orderliness. Like the recitals, they attempt to halt and reverse the world's progressive decline.

Mantars that conclude every session directly parallel the ordering function of the opening formulas. Now that the ceremony has repaired the world, it needs to be fixed in place once more. The new order must supplant the old disorder. Every conclusion incorporates lists, collecting as shaman's words all the disparate elements that his performance has affected. Each concluding jap enumerates the things, persons, spirits, natural forces, and supernatural concepts that are to remain secure and stay within the jhāṅgarī's protection. Mantars that open and close any ceremony protect by systematic prescription, ordering chaos into an inevitable, comprehensively inclusive taxonomy of all possibilities. At the beginning of a ceremony, the world receives shape and form, molded into an initial holding pattern of bound elements. The shaman's recitations and rituals improve selected elements in that pattern. Finally, the resulting system is fixed in place and held there with oaths, promises, and threats. "Seeds of truth" *(sat byū)*, a mixture of grains, are scattered over patients, their families, their homes, animals, and property, to sprout into a reinvigorated life of reinvented meaningfulness. The final gesture is known as *"chānamā."* Karṇa Vīr insisted that this word, repeated in every phrase of the concluding formula, means the "grain that is scattered." It is probably derived from *chānnu,*" to choose, select, sort out" (Turner 1980:195), so that "chosen," or perhaps even "that I've chosen," could replace "grains" throughout the following lines:

> Drum skin grains, tap water grains,
> well water grains, spring water grains,
> tree notch water grains, tap water grains,
> bent planets grains, bent star obstructions grains,
> Barmā afflictions grains, Barāh afflictions grains,
> Bajyū afflictions grains, Devī Deurālī and lāmā afflictions grains,
> water and spring grains, Maṣṭā and Mahākal grains,
> Bhayar and Pitār grains,
> body and diseases [*rog*] grains, body and afflictions [*dokh*] grains,
> drum skin grains, wealth and dirt grains . . .
>
> (5.22)

The list often seems to go on forever, before the spirits finally depart and the ceremony ends, always concluding with oaths in the name of the guru and of Lord Mahādev.

Within distinctive ceremonies, both the sense and the expression of mantars can differ widely. Constant beneath these fluctuations, all undertake to compel something. J. L. Austin's theory of speech acts (1965,

1979) offers an effective tool to discuss these differences. Austin conceived this theory as the study of specific meanings of utterances in use by actual speakers in concrete contexts. He convincingly showed that sentences have other purposes than just making assertions or "stating facts," a belief that he labeled the "descriptive fallacy." Austin demonstrated that sentences not only have constative functions but also have performative qualities: they are not just propositions, they are also actions. He distinguished three dimensions of the performative aspect of speech acts: "the locutionary act (and within it the phonetic, the phatic, and the rhetic acts) which has a *meaning;* the illocutionary act which has a certain *force* in saying something; the perlocutionary act which is the *achieving of* certain *effects* by saying something" (1965:121, italics in original). Performatives, observed Austin, are not simply true or false. He suggested that we instead measure them in terms of felicity and infelicity. A speech act properly done is felicitous.

In these terms, all mantars are speech acts in which the specific perlocutionary force differs, but in which the primary illocutionary force is compulsion. They compel spirits to be present. They compel things to stay in place, to be bound, to be distanced, delayed, destroyed. They compel dead spirits to stay dead, living villagers to stay alive. To accomplish these acts of compulsion, they incorporate perlocutionary aspects of any successful exorcism: they suppress and eliminate (Maskarinec 1993). First identifying the diverse unseen forces, they lure those forces into a vulnerable position, then demolish them. These characteristics can be seen in a pair of mantars for raising and then suppressing masān. First, to raise a masān:

> Guru Deu, Guru Maheś,
> I've brought sixteen cowries in my hand,
> I've given a sacrifice of blood,
> I'll give a flute to your right hand,
> I'll give a pipe to your left hand,
> your heart's cut, I'll give a chunk of meat,
> your skin's cut, I'll give a wrap,
> your head's cut, I'll give a pot,
> your hand's cut, I'll give a stirring stick,
> your intestines are cut, I'll give a string.
> Get up, get up!
> Mother Syāuryā, get up, Father Syāuryā, get up!

[masān who live in the sky rather than in the ground].
Chin culā, chin culā [said to be meaningless],
the force of the sky may knock you over,
split the earth, split it, masān, awake!
Awaking, awake!
If you don't awake,
be caught in the noose of birth!

(5.23)

The mantar concludes with names of nine different well-known masān (similar to 5.12) and a series of oaths. Shamans not only raise well-established masān but also undertake to capture new ones. Repeating conventional folklore of the week's most inauspicious days, Kamāro Kāmī explained: "If on a Tuesday or a Saturday, an important person of the village dies, then his pyre will produce soot. Take that soot and spread it on your body. Blow the mantar onto four grains of rice and strike with them." He recommended using white grains of rice to raise a masān, grains yellowed with turmeric to suppress one. He explained, too, that the most common reason to capture a masān is a desire for more power and control *(bal, kabjā)*. Everyone in Nepal seems to know popular horror stories of people enslaving a masān to plant their fields, move rocks, and plague enemies. Most tales end catastrophically when the masān becomes strong enough to subjugate and devour its owner. Shamans, too, tell such stories, obvious warnings that their powers are not to be casually applied by anyone.

Professionally, a shaman may want to discuss some issue with a masān. This is a major theme in the story of Payalpur. Since this is a recital used only in shaman initiations, it is not exactly a "private" or a "public" text," another convenient distinction that slowly dissolves as my analysis proceeds. Payalpur was the son of a very famous shaman, Syāulā Rammā. After his father's death, he began to experience fits of uncontrollable trembling:

The spirits wouldn't leave him in peace,
the powers wouldn't leave him in peace.
He shakes *dak dak* at night, he shakes *dak dak* at day.

(5.24)

He seeks his father's paraphernalia, but his stepmother hides it, hoping that her own son will eventually show signs of becoming her husband's successor. Payalpur seeks the advice of other shamans, but they fail to help him. Finally, he goes crazy:

> He really goes mad, he really goes crazy.
> Having been furiously [*ranga bhanga*] possessed,
> he descended to the sixth crossroads,
> descended to the Masān Ghāṭ.
> In the middle of the night, at the pitch dark time,
> masān began to lurk about.
> Going to the Masān Ghāṭ, Mājhā Payalpur [said],
> "I've had much pain, I've had much strain."
> Having then said this, oh, Syāulā Rammā, going,
> then waking, sat up.
> He met with Payalpur, his own son as well,
> they met at the ghāṭ.
> "You've had much pain, you've had much strain."
> To Mājhā Payalpur, shaking *kara kara, mara mara,*
> his own father as well, Syāulā Rammā, going,
> gave advice and ideas.
>
> (5.25)

This selection includes two untranslatable puns. The first is on *dukne-bhukne,* line 12, a common conjunction for "pain and problems." Substituting a retroflex aspirate *ḍh* for the dental unaspirated *d* changes the meaning "to creep and crawl, to lurk about," line 5. The second pun is on *bheṭ-ghāṭ,* line 11, a common phrase for meeting, but a *ghāṭ* is also a cremation ground, where this meeting is set. Shaking "kara kara, mara mara" likewise defies translation, along with the earlier "dak, dak." Both phrases use purely phonic tropes to designate uncontrollable possession, described as "going mad" *(aulāunda, baulāunda)* in the first line of the passage. Nepali has a rich vocabulary borrowed from Sanskrit to express subtle transcendental states, but shaman texts inevitably prefer more earthy representations such as these, delighting, too, in parallel constructions. Common also in spoken Nepali, these poetic parallelisms, using two words for a single idea whenever possible, feature in ritual language elsewhere in Nepal (Allen 1978; Höfer 1992; Sales 1991; Strickland 1987). This is as true of whispered mantars as of chanted recitals. Like enumeration, discussed in the previous chapter, this seems to be more than mnemonically useful. Rather, it demonstrates the primacy of language over a world in which the more names something has, the more fixed in place, the more real, the easier to order and manipulate it becomes.

The appearance of multiple puns in a "private" text perhaps helps to situate the shaman as a true mediating participant, not just a user of language, not just used by it, but genuinely in control. My attempts to explore this possibility never got very far, however. I would raise a pun I'd uncovered in a text and be met with grimacing disapproval of my apparent levity toward the sacred. I would attempt to explore a metaphor, a textual ambiguity, some striking evidence of polysemy or plurivocality. With stubborn logocentricism, the shamans would stick to a word-for-word rendition. Once I could repeat the words correctly, they were satisfied that I had at last "got" it. With mantars, there was no further to go than syntax.

Another reason shamans may raise a masān is to discuss whether it needs to be recognized as a pitār (ancestral spirit) and worshiped by surviving family members. In that case it would permanently reside in the family altar (ordinarily a triangular recess in the wall) and receive regular offerings. Alternately, it may only continue to covet some familiar household item, which needs to be identified and then delivered to the cremation ground, or some outstanding debt may need to be settled. Finally, a masān may be sent as a curse (1.5, 2.2). For whatever reasons a masān is raised, the promises made to it are strictly empty words. None of the items mentioned in the text are even assembled, let alone presented to the masān, not even as miniatures like the set of alternate bodies offered moc, the domestic utensils offered vāi (Chapter 2), or the dishes of unsavory food substitutes set out for witches (Chapter 3). Not even a noose is on hand to emphasize the concluding threat. Unlike the elaborate ritual accessories used to illustrate recitals for public audiences, mantars are rarely accompanied by visual devices, except for the grain or water that the shaman scatters (striking those physically present as well as those present in name alone). Material illustrations are a feature only of the public side of ceremonies, done for the benefit of visible clients. This seems to be true, too, of "mental" visualizations that might accompany mantars. Shamans were always puzzled when I tried to discuss "pictures," "images," or "diagrams" that they thought about or meditated upon. Their only solution to these lines of inquiry was to provide jantars, such as the one in Figure 3.1, or Figure 5.1, to be worn by people who have gone crazy. The imaginings so prominent in Tibetan

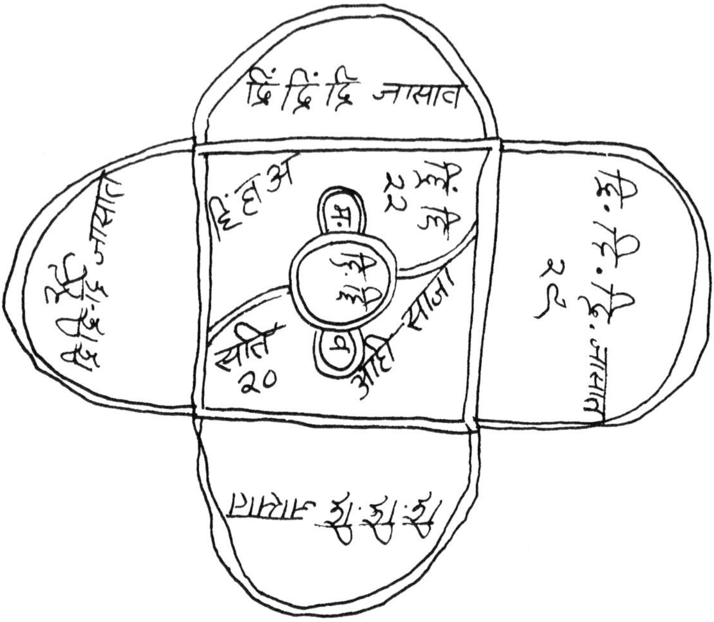

Figure 5.1. *Jantar* to treat madness

ritual (Beyer 1973) (or the spiritual exercises designed by Ignatius of Loyola) seem to have no role among Kāmī shamans.

Generally, words suffice for supernatural audiences, who only need to have things spelled out for them. There's a tempting hypothetical division here, placing speech and the supernatural on one side, action and the natural on the other. Attractive though this might be, it cannot, however, be advanced very far, since blood sacrifices clearly straddle it. The flesh and blood of sacrifice reunite the unseen with the seen. Even on this point mantars resemble recitals, reweaving a syntax of substance and sound, stitching them together with the power of grammar.

After a masān has been raised, and presumably, after it has performed whatever task the shaman assigned it or answered whatever questions he asked it, it is sent away by a related mantar. Honorifically addressing the masān as a guru and a god, this mantar tells the masān that now it has taken substitutes for its missing body parts, so it should be satisfied, and depart. Other than the flutes, which are not actually given either, the parts in this list with which it should be satisfied are not even those that were promised in the first mantar. Rather, they are what was left to the masān in the first place, such as a shoulder when it was promised arms, or a belly when it was promised a heart and intestines. Either masān must be dim-witted, that they would respond to these promises but then leave empty-handed (still armless would put it more accurately), or perhaps the compulsion of threats and oaths sufficiently overcomes the emptiness of the promises just as it overcomes the emptiness of the masān:

> Guru Deu, Guru Maheś,
> your intestines are cut, you've taken a belly.
> your hand's cut, you've taken a shoulder,
> your head's cut, you've taken a noose,
> your heart's cut, you've taken a belly.
> You've taken a flute in your right hand,
> you've taken a pipe in your left hand,
> you may have gotten up, you may have gotten up,
> you may be frightened, you may go back!
>
> (5.26)

Oaths in the names of specific gods and goddesses follow. This second jap enumerates body parts in the reverse order of the original one, so that the suppression is at least a partial inversion of the summons. At the end, the masān is bombarded with oaths, the same ones that conclude a public performance. These presumably scare it back to the cremation ground or crossroads. Like witch evil limited but not abolished, or crises postponed but not eliminated, masān are usually suppressed but not destroyed, their potential usefulness preserved.

Some japs do, however, use far more threatening language to suppress or eliminate something completely. This is best seen in the formulas used against witches and malignant ghosts. Troublesome masān that one has not oneself awakened may also have to be quelled, with japs that use more forceful language. A good example is the Narsiṅgh jap, which also allows for some bragging about one's guru:

> Om, honor, long life to Narsiṅgh Powerful Bīr.
> From resting in idleness, put on a necklace of banyan berries,
> bubbling ear, fluttering nose, flame twinkling,
> wherever has your ghost gone to be?
> With glimmering lamp, see my show [*dekhi merī tamasā*],
> the oath of Guru Lāmā.

Eight sarsu seeds, twelve rāyo seeds,
flint of nine ridges, may I be able to jap this!
You, ghost, be destroyed!
Other gurus play, our guru moves!
[*aru guru kheldā, hāmrā guru caldā*].
Other gurus' staffs are of cane, our guru's staff is of iron,
diamond-eared iron rod, striking, killing,
ghosts, masān turning to ash!

(5.27)

The text includes another pun, since *bar barkhanī,* line 2, means "goat droppings" as well as "banyan berries." Each resembles the other, of course, and the resulting ambiguity is unresolvable, paralleling the ambiguity between a "good" masān and a "bad" one. Although details of prosody fall outside this analysis, the monosyllabic puffs opening line 3 are sonically noteworthy. The line goes: *khaṭ khaṭ kān, phaṭ phaṭ nāk, jwālā jhili mili,* speeding up as the line advances. Karṇa Vīr once delivered the 187 words of this mantar in 45 seconds. On several occasions, he declared that it was one of his two most important mantars. Notably, this mantar recognizes the possibility of shaman impostors, those who inauthentically playact *(khel),* in opposition to genuinely moving (*cal,* command formed from *calāunu*). The nominative *cāl,* "movement, custom, behavior," sometimes puns on *chāl,* "trick," as when Mahādev plays a trick on mankind. "Play," especially as a transitive, "cause to play" *(khelāunu),* plays an important role in the vocabulary that describes relations between spirits and humans, as when Gumāne would declare: "I cause my māphī to play." Here, however, the text emphasizes the shaman's complete control over supernatural forces, including other shamans. The lines also recognize different qualities of equipment, but their real force comes in the language of striking, killing, causing to turn to ash.

Although the first shaman showed in the Nine Sisters recital a selfish interest in letting the youngest witch survive (1.4), japs used at the end of a ritual against witches show a much less flexible attitude. This initially hints that there may be an opposition of useful witches and useless ones, just as useful masān are placated while useless ones are turned to ash. The japs, however, use a language of uncompromising antagonism:

Wherever there are witches,
the tricks of you witches I attack!
Killing you witches,

transferring the spells of you witches into a hole,
stomping you witches beneath my sole,
you witches I kill!
Blow, mantar! Śrī Mahādev's oath!

(5.28)

Another version, specifically to treat small children upon whom a witch has gazed enviously, threatens to poke out the witch's eyes:

Your spells, be reduced to ash!
My spells, gain ascendancy!
Sundering the witches' eyes,
killing you witches, be reduced to nothing!
Blow, mantar! Śrī Mahādev's oath!

(5.29)

This suggests that the public recital lures witches near with seductive flattery (3.5). Once their defenses are lowered, the japs to destroy them are recited, reducing the witches to nothing.

The jap concluding the ceremony to bind a house contains a very forceful suppression. It even "kills" the King and Queen of Death, going on to kill all those who died in inauspicious situations. It shows how a jap to conclude a ceremony ends as well:

Killing Jama Rāj, killing Jama Rānī,
killing those who died at the right time,
killing those who died at the wrong time,
killing those hung on a pole,
killing those hung in a noose,
killing those swept off in streams,
killing those fallen from cliffs,
striking the eastern direction,
killing Bhasam Ghost of the Eighty maund iron rod,
striking the southern direction,
killing Kaṁsa Sur [name of a particular demon],
striking the western direction,
killing Maiyā Sur Demon [*dānvā*],
striking the northern direction,
killing Long-Ear Demon [*lāmkānyā dānvā*],
take away, driving east, driving east,
take away, driving south, driving south,
take away, driving west, driving west.

[then references to the kānphaṭa yogin and to seven, named, Bhairam].
May there be no tricks, may there be no deceits,
may there be no minor witches,
may there be no major witches,
the main oaths of the Nine Nāths, the Twelve Bhairam,
will strike the treachery of ghosts, ghouls,
will kill them, thrust them into hell,
will bind this house!

(5.30)

The harshness of these threats recalls a final subject, without which any discussion of mantars remains incomplete—those that administer a curse. Coming only at the end of training, these were, naturally, some of the mantars that shamans were generally most reluctant to divulge, even to admit knowing. They also hesitated to divulge those that consistently provide income independent of a specifically shamanic ritual, which other villagers could apply without needing a shaman. Leading this second category were those to heal snakebite, versions of which were known to many villagers. Abi Lal's wife rushed over and vocally objected to his taping his version. He ignored her, but whispered nearly inaudibly into my tape recorder, unlike his usually clear delivery. Whispering and mumbling were the only techniques to ensure inscrutability that I encountered, unlike the elaborate obfuscation that Taylor (1988) reports for Tobelo *mantaráa.* I obtained only four versions of the snakebite mantar from shamans (2.1 is one example), and one from a dhāmī's assistant. Each addresses the snake directly with lines such as "your poison is killed, my poison makes stiff," and each conforms structurally to the other mantars that I discuss in this chapter. Nar Siṅgh's version concludes:

Your poison I move,
My poison I prove!
Your two teeth lose,
my thirty-two teeth win!

(5.31)

Other texts that are not exclusively shamanic include mantars that blacksmiths use while performing their craft, japs used as charms for success in love or hunting, and a much wider "medical" set known to many, including those to treat hernia, colic, toothache, to remove dirt in the eyes, to stop a wound from bleeding, to assist digestion (especially in babies), to treat impotence, to dissolve knots in a nursing mother's breast, to reduce the pain of bee, wasp, and scorpion stings, or to treat cattle suffering from various ailments. Some of these include practical recipes, like the only unique line to treat scorpion sting, against which ashes are a reasonable treatment:

> Orpion scorpion, your poison, soaked up by ash!
>
> (5.32)

Another pharmaceutical recipe found in a mantar recommends treating bleeding by binding it with "white dog" vines. As far as my collection of strictly shaman mantars goes, however, these advice-giving phrases are rare. Some shamans have considerable ethnopharmacological knowledge. They collect many medicinal plants, especially from high-altitude meadows, and can prepare very elaborate concoctions. Again, however, this knowledge cannot be considered specifically "shamanic," for it overlaps with what is known by other local experts who are not shamans. In the shamanic world, words transform substance. Any medicinal properties of raw substance are trivial compared with the power of speech.

To curse, several jhāṅgarīs said that you summon your familiar spirits (the bīr and barāṅg) and direct them at someone. Others recommended the "Cutting of the Circle" ritual (Chapter 2). Both approaches are commonly attributed to witches. Gore Sārkī claimed that his own father, long deceased, who remains a famous jhāṅgarī around Jājarkoṭ, never taught him his curse to sicken enemies. Eventually I believed him, for he appeared genuinely troubled by this gap in his own training, and even proposed to come with me to Tākāserā to interview jhāṅgarīs there, where we could together complete this aspect of our training. Magars are popularly said to know the best curses, able to dry the throats of rival jhāṅgarīs. When discussing variations in drum rhythms and singing styles, Karṇa Vīr chose to parody the way Magar jhāṅgarīs sing with exactly this line: "Hai! Your father, guru jhāṅgarī's throat has gone dry, Hai!" He then chortled with laughter, for, like most other Kāmī shamans, he did not think much of the powers attributed to Magars, who, he insisted, simply sing louder and act more aggressive to conceal their lack of knowledge. Like every shaman, though, Karṇa Vīr took seriously the issue of drying up throats, having had it done to him twice during his career, once by a powerful witch and once by a mysterious traveler. He compared the helplessness of being speechless to being reduced to a congenital cretin *(lāṭo),* a complete loss of all power.

I have already quoted the key lines of two curses (1.5 and 2.2). Abi Lal supplied another typical example, and his brother Karṇa Vīr provided its reversal:

> All around the seven seas, shrines of the gods,
> you gods are the Lord God's agents [Īśvara's Vāṇ].
> You gods, do a possession! Do a concealed attack,
> Rājā Īśvara's Vāṇ!
>
> (5.33)

Clearly, curses do not significantly differ in structure or content from other mantars. They, too, list and compel agents. Instead of demanding those forces retreat or abate, they compel them to attack. The curse is lifted in a structurally symmetrical formula:

> All around the seven seas, shrines of the gods,
> you gods are the Lord God's agents.
> Wherever you are enshrined, to there be assigned!
> Wherever you go, go there!
>
> (5.34)

Another curse, known, I think, to every shaman, is directed toward malicious members of an audience. A shaman mutters it at any time during a ceremony when he senses that someone present bears ill will toward him. It intensifies a few lines of the rāyā sarsu mantar by replacing the commands to bind with more aggressive verbs:

> Pierce the eyes that look,
> cut the tongue that speaks,
> break the arm that bumps,
> cut the foot that moves,
> break the hand that touches!
> Go! Dry out their voices!
>
> (5.35)

Sometimes, the last line is further sharpened to "cut the tongue tip of the thinker, dry it in the sun!" as in 6.1. This is the worst possible threat, since a dry throat may be healed, but no shaman reports restoring a severed tongue, so the threat implies permanent loss of eloquence and power.

The illustrations that I have provided in this chapter seem sufficient to support two conclusions. First, the texts that shamans call mantars and japs are remarkably similar to their lengthier public recitals, which they designate melā, *okhā, dhūr,* or khetī. Exactly like recitals, mantars used at the beginning of a ceremony have formal introductions into ideal space and time. They draw explicit continuities with that time through artful devices such as introducing the eldest experts or an archetypal yogin. This opening is followed with either a brief narrative story of origin, or an enumeration of forces and objects. They conclude with oaths, just as the recitals do. Like the recitals, mantars address tensions between order and disorder in the world. Their common goal is to reestablish some balance in the world, to impose the shaman's sense of how things should be, or rather, the texts' sense of how things should be. Both public recitals and private mantars isolate the most problematic areas of the world's chaos and refashion general disorder into more hospitable patterns.

Second, mantars and japs are intelligible. They require no special insight or training to understand them. They may be spiced with a few "mumbo-jumbo" lines (like chin culā in 5.23, or ārulā bārulā in 4.43), though even these might be penetrated by a more acute philological analysis than I, the shamans themselves, or my Nepali friends have been capable of performing. Mantars use the same vocabulary and syntax, and have the same semantic purposes as do other shamanic texts. They retain considerable meaning even when divorced from context, allowing much of their character to be conveyed in translation. Most words of secret texts are clear and straightforward, just as a jap directed to witches describes them:

> Your spells are reversed, my spells are straight,
> Blow, mantar! Śrī Mahādev's oath!
>
> (5.36)

Like the recitals, mantars portray a world to which shamans expect our world to conform. They order the universe into a pattern that permits shamanic interventions to succeed, suppressing malign threats and encouraging benevolent powers, though never in an absolute sense. Sometimes, threats are made and "benevolent" powers dismissed, for shamans recognize the changing equations of power both in this world and between different worlds. Shaman texts seek not static equilibrium, but harmonic counterpoints of balance.

These points temporarily fixed in harmonic relation to one another, poised on a staff of the shaman's own creation, might be heard as a many-voiced fugue, where the theme itself is, of course, an aesthetic composition, not a representation fixedly anchored to some underlying "natural" universe. This image of healing as an aesthetic endeavor points to some fundamental divergences between mantars and our traditional views of language. Earlier in this chapter, I suggested that shamans are highly logocentric. This designation is misleading, resulting from my Western substitution of linguistics for metaphysics. For shamans, a text is in itself a thing, a highly circumscribed form of language, insofar as any language must be referential, predicatory, and reidentificational. As Favret-Saada observes in her analysis of witchcraft in the Bocage, "these spoken words are power, and not knowledge or information . . . For a single word (and only a word) can tie or untie a fate, and whoever puts himself in a position to utter it is formidable" (1980:9–10). Mantars are structured presentations of life, not references to it, their recitations becoming ideal dramas behind the accidents of casual performance that create shaman and patients as organized actors. "A drama is not only the *mimesis* of an action, the enactment of a story that represents actions by actions and in actions: at its best, it also brings us to an understanding of the shape *(eidos)* and boundary *(horos)* of human action" (A. Rorty 1992:4). Concentrated at the shape-giving boundaries of action, mantars resist attempts to separate signifier from signified. Their words fuse, refusing to separate, sense, reference, and meaning. Preferring syntax to semantics, they weave a metaphysics of what is really "real." Again like musical notes, their words cannot mean anything else, for nothing can improve on the power of the words themselves. Like a poem or musical composition, mantars express something only by certain words in certain positions, whose relations must be preserved if their viability is to remain intact. Heteroglossia is an affliction against which shamans battle, armed with semantic fusion, a formal A = A of word and world aligned in perfect, one-to-one isomorphism. The words are things themselves, their sound the real substance of the world. "Sound releases the Ideal from its entanglement in matter" (Hegel 1975:88).

Having until now kept my discussion at a generally linguistic level, I want to conclude by suggesting some metaphysical differences between this shamanic universe and a Western one. To do so, I find it useful to begin by briefly reviewing Plato's attack on poetry.

In the *Republic* and later in the *Laws,* Plato attacked poetry on four grounds:

1. poets compose under divine inspiration, not by using reason;
2. poetry teaches us the wrong moral values;
3. poetry encourages the emotions of those who perform or listen to it;
4. poetry is a representation *(mimēsis)* at least two removes from "true" reality.

Motivating this attack is not just moralistic righteousness, but Plato's theory of forms. Plato argued, of course, that the reality that we perceive is not true reality, for its particulars derive, through mimēsis, from transcendental Forms, which we cannot apprehend with our senses, but only with our intellects. As our experiential world of appearances relates to the true world of Forms, art further fictionalizes the world of appearances. Art, imitations of imitations, misleads us to mistake its products for reality, the world of "make believe" against which Parmenides cautioned.

In his *Poetics,* Aristotle responded to the first three of Plato's criticisms, arguing that

1. poetry is a skill or art *(techne)* which can be learned, with rules comprehensible by reason;
2. poetry does work by arousing the emotions of the audience, but this can be beneficial (the concept of catharsis);
3. poetry is a useful copy of reality, from which we can learn.

As the third point shows, Aristotle let stand unquestioned Plato's insistence that the world itself is primary, that language represents things in that world, and that tropes—a further remove from reality—are no more than representations of language. They are, literally, just "figures of speech." That is, both Plato and Aristotle, and most Western linguistic theory until Wittgenstein, accept a doubly denotative theory of language, one that puts things at the center, words at the periphery, and metaphors in subsidiary epicycles, so preserving the transcendental signified beneath our *Lebenswelt* (the world of daily life). With such a metaphysical premise, shamanic curing is an irrelevancy.

I suggest that shamans deny this fundamental principle of Western metaphysics. Shamans use language to constitute reality, not to denote or to imitate it. Shamanic language is not a mirror of the world but a set of technical devices to give form to a new world, an experiential lifeworld in which the words of a correctly recited formula will alleviate corporal suffering, because they give form to pain, to the sufferer, its cause, to the entire world in which the sufferer experiences pain.

Instead of a denotative theory of language in which words signify the world, shamanic speech presupposes a generative theory of words creating the world. Things in that world stand in indexical relation to sounds. We hear the result not of a signifying theory of language, but of an aural one, in which "true" reality mirrors language. Sound is what is real. To paraphrase Wittgenstein, the limits of what we can say are the limits of our world.

My final example is another treatment of headaches, one involving a *padu binī*. This is a legendarily beautiful woman who never leaves her quarters (perhaps a corruption or a pun on the Sanskrit word *padminī*, first of four erotic classifications of women, though shamans thought this far-fetched). She is said never to use her feet, and so is "footless," or more figuratively, a "secluded one."

From the eastern direction
the "secluded one" comes and stays,
on a Jew's harp she plays and plays.
The sound of the harp causes headaches sharp,
it causes restless heat, causes loss of sleep,
causes burning fevers deep.
Banish the burning pains!
Banish the restless heat!
Banish the loss of sleep!
Brushing with a straight broom,
brushing with a reversed broom,
transferring these pains atop cow dung,
destroying these afflictions,
may they be sent across the four rivers!

(5.37)

To resort to an oxymoron, this is a completely literal metaphor. A beautiful, secluded woman, out of sight, plays relentlessly on a Jew's harp. The harp's persistent twang becomes the pain throbbing in the head. It doesn't just replicate the original pain that the patient is suffering, it replaces that trivial, illusionary, material pain with extraordinary, ideal, shamanic pain. As the harp, sounding in the mantar, causes profound, true pain, so do the words of this mantar banish that pain, transforming it through the toccatas of the banishings into the moderate tonalities and softer rhythms of the brushing. We hear the literalness of metaphors at work. They do more than establish grammaticality for a condition. They create the conditions in which they intervene. In this mantar, the Jew's harp is to be heard not metaphorically, but aurally, playing the sounds of throbbing pain.

Reading the *Golden Bough,* Wittgenstein noted, "In magical healing one *indicates* to an illness that it should leave the patient" (1979:6e, italics in original). A shaman does more. With his words, which are his power and his tools, he creates the illness, creates the body of the patient, and creates the world in which his patient experiences relief. As did Prājapati (ṚgVeda X.130), a shaman speaks us into being, insisting that "that which can be spoken needs must be," and we who are spoken, become as we hear.

6
Shaman Voices, Shaman Texts

Becoming a shaman transforms an individual's identity, his public and private selves. It changes his perceptions and formulations of the political and social relations that constrain the possibilities of his person, in so forceful a way that those relations are themselves creatively restructured. Simultaneously, shamanic training recasts an individual's private experiences to conform to ideal experiences preserved in oral texts. The texts shamans learn to obtain professional competence are not simply templates for the correct performance of rituals, nor just devices for communicating to others particular models of reality; they produce, clarify, expound, and maintain that reality for the shamans themselves. They go beyond establishing "a causal precedent for the current state of affairs" (Hutchins 1987:288) to produce a precise, unique, and explicit way of unifying self-knowledge and personal experience. That is, they produce a unique self, as in Rom Harré's definition of a "self," not a certain kind of being, but a certain kind of theory, a way of organizing "one's knowledge and experience of one's own states," just as we use physical theories to organize knowledge and experience in the physical world (1985:262).

Shaman texts are much more than sets of technical maps or fixed cosmologies. They are genuinely a language creating and maintaining sense and identity. Lévi-Strauss once commented (in a narrower context than mine), "the native who becomes a shaman after a spiritual crisis conceives of his state grammatically" (1963a:179). Though qualifying his sense of what a "spiritual crisis" might be, I accept his remark literally and explore the consequences of being conceived grammatically. As shamans learn and use their texts, they establish new relational possibilities in society, and acquire new identities, new "selves," to optimize those possibilities. The process parallels the way they add new "spirits" to their collections of possessing agents. They accomplish both activities at the same time as they apply, demonstrate, and participate in precisely those activities, simultaneously convincing patients and audiences of their validity.

In the past chapters, I have examined in increasingly detailed ways what Nepali shamans repeatedly do throughout their careers. This chapter puts those details in both a socially wider and a personally more narrow context. Here, I examine how a shaman enters and leaves his profession, the events of shaman initiation and shaman death. These ceremonies not only define the parameters of a shaman's career but firmly anchor him in wider sets of kinship responsibilities and new village relations. Further, these events are, I will show, paradigmatic of every other ceremony that a shaman performs.

Although I just called death ceremonies a parameter of a shaman's career, this is not an opinion that shamans share. From their own point of view, the career of a successful shaman, once begun, never ends, least of all with death. Death instead provides the outstanding opportunity to prove one's success, to reveal that one really controls spirits, especially one's own. Events following death allow a conclusive demonstration of one's ability to postpone crises, to deflect the ongoing deterioration of this world, and to manipulate forces in other, nonmaterial, worlds.

Shamans perform death ceremonies only for other shamans. They do not participate professionally in other funerals, nor do they guide souls to the underworld. As I noted in Chapter 3, this conforms to Shirokogoroff's observations about Tungus shamans, for he observed that journeys to the underworld were infrequently taken and relatively unimportant (1935:310). I therefore question how definitively "shamanic" Eliade's emphasis that every true shaman must be a "psycho-pomp" (a guide of the soul) really is. While jhāṅgarīs guide lost souls back to their owners, summon and dispatch souls of the dead, lead away malevolent spirits, and "cheer up" *(yalsī ṭipne)* bereaved family members, I have found no evidence, either in texts or in discussions with contemporary shamans, that jhāṅgarīs ever played a role in funerals of ordinary individuals. Perhaps more than for Tungus, "soul-journeys" do play important roles

Illustration 6.1. Drum feeding ceremony

in jhāṅgarī ceremonies, featured in nearly every ceremony and referred to in many texts. One path traveled by jhāṅgarīs (2.20) is the same that dead souls take, crossing Chirenāth, Ciplai Gaurī, Cāyāneṭī (Eye of the Needle, Slippery Slope, Shadow Pass), but shamans do not lead souls there.

Death ceremonies for a shaman have two parts. The first half of the ceremony is the "making a shaman disappear" (jhāṅgarī walpāune), while the second half is the "raising of the shaman" (jhāṅgarī ukāsne). The first begins as biological signs of life fail. A shaman should predict the moment of his own death, so that it can take place at his home, with his pupils in attendance.

Should a shaman die elsewhere, he may become a *ban jhāṅgarī*, a haunting "forest shaman," though these do not have the prominence in Jājarkoṭ that they do in eastern Nepal, where stories circulate of how they abduct and train new pupils. In Jājarkoṭ the only similar stories always involve a *siddha* (forest-dwelling Hindu ascetic), not a ban jhāṅgarī, hinting again at connections between jhāṅgarīs and yogins. Shamans that I asked found stories about ban jhāṅgarīs as kidnappers preposterous. There are only ten or twelve ban jhāṅgarīs in Jājarkoṭ. All are treated as descendants of Gorāpā (2.16), who would no more kidnap someone than would a wasp or a bear.

Dressed in his costume, a shaman dies sitting up, cross-legged. At death, relatives place a silver coin in his mouth, as is done for ordinary persons. If not spat out, it indicates that the dying person accepts the arrival of death. A final drop of *sun-pānī* (water purified by having had gold immersed in it) is poured through his lips. Relatives dig a shallow round grave not far from the shaman's home, at a spot chosen by him in advance. Pupils tie the corpse to a plow beam to support it, and carry it outside in this posture, upright. It is disposed of, explained Karṇa Vīr, "exactly like a yogi." By this he meant a kānphaṭa follower of Gorakhnāth, for the funeral corresponds closely to that described by George W. Briggs (1989:39–43). They place the corpse, in full costume, in the courtyard of his own home. They put a piece of kacur root under his tongue, a staff in his left hand, a drumstick in the right. They apply ashes treated with a mantar across his eyes, to protect him during his descent into the underworlds. The text can expand to include most of the bindings of the rāyā sarsu jap:

> Pinnacle power,
> seeing near, seeing far,
> lighting the night as the sun and moon,
> bind the reader's voice,
> bind the walker's foot, bind the striking hand,
> bind the speaker's tongue, bind the seer's eye,
> bind the tricks of village witches,
> bind [their] tricks [chedī],
> bind [their] deceits [bhedī],
> bind eyes in the four directions,
> cut the tongue tip of the thinker, dry it in the sun!
> Bind the Barmās of shrines,
> bind the ancestral spirits in nooks,
> bind the shamans of shaman tombs,
> bind the spirits of the dead of crossroads . . .
>
> (6.1)

They close his eyes and blindfold them. The pupils put cinnamon and guava leaves behind the dead shaman's ears and wrap his head in a new white turban. The former pupils, in full costume, sit facing their guru and sing the first half of Tilīkarmā. This section first describes the marriage of the first shaman, Jumrātam, to the older daughter of Gorāpā. Gorāpā tricks his daughters into parricide, so that as he becomes the first human death, they find husbands. Jumrātam marries the eldest, the king of Sijākoṭ the youngest. (In other versions, other daughters of Gorāpā marry the first Brāhman, Hunyā Bāhun, and the first blacksmith, Tikhu Kāmī.) Jumrātam seduces his sister-in-law and must hide from the king's soldiers. As he departs for the underworld, the former pupils dance around the body, counterclockwise. They address the next section of the text, Jumrātam's instructions to his wife, to the widow of their deceased teacher:

> Examining, consulting,
> "Imagine, dream,
> how much have I brought you, dear jhagrenī,
> who will give you skirts, who will give you blouses? . . .
> Put a tomb for me in the valley,
> put a monument for me on the hill,
> cry a fountain of tears,
> wear your blouse inside out,
> wear your skirt inside out,
> I am going, to Tilīkarmā."
> Rammā Jumrātam set out forthright.
>
> (6.2)

The text instructs the widow to break her bangles, remove her necklaces, and wear her hair disheveled, as is expected of any Hindu widow.

> Jhumā Jhagrenī took off her gold earrings,
> took off her nose jewel, took off her finger rings,
> wore her blouse inside out, wore her skirt inside out,
> took off her finger rings, took off her pointed bracelet,
> took off her necklace, moved her hair bun forward,
> wore her hair bun backward.
> She was really colorless,
> she was really without color.
>
> (6.3)

Distraught, she asks where he will go, and Jumrātam replies:

I am going, to Tilīkarmā.
On the trail I take,
there may be marks of a walking stick,
may be a loosely spun thread,
may be a line of turmeric.
On a trail for witches,
there may be a spun thread of nettles,
may be a line of ashes.

(6.4)

This is a simple version of a recurring riddle, to be solved by anyone who might try to follow a dead shaman (Watters 1975). The puzzle involves the difficulty of distinguishing the path of a departed shaman from the routes that witches use. Often, the riddle includes the trails of cremation ground spirits (masān), lost souls (siyo), and forest spirits (banpā). In each case, the trails are marked by representative debris:

The path the masān walk,
[there] may be charcoal, ashes.
The path the *siwari* [type of witch] walk,
may be a row of lumps, rice mixed with blood.
The path the forest spirits walk,
may be fragments of gourd, streaked with white clay.
The path the shamans walk,
may be at the crossroads, rubbish, dried leaves.

(6.5)

A dead shaman resembles other malevolent forces. He travels in the same secret spaces as those who harm villagers. These travels are not, however, unique to death, but are repeated in every major shamanic sitting. They occur when treating star obstructions, countering witchcraft, binding houses, seeking lost souls, and during annual prophetic ceremonies. That the funeral resembles other rituals is emphasized by dressing the corpse as for a performance. By using the same texts at initiations and funerals, shamans vividly remind their audience that the potential malevolence of a shaman is always near at hand, retelling on each occasion the afflictions brought down on the royal family who failed to respect their shaman.

Once the recitation reaches the riddle, male relatives (sons, grandsons, brothers, and nephews) pick up the body, and the former pupils, dancing and drumming, lead the way to the grave. The pupils recite to the point when Jumrātam becomes a blacksmith (or copper worker) in the underworld. The relatives place the body waist deep in the hole, facing north. Most of the costume is removed, "returned to its owners," explains the text, explicitly naming each piece of equipment and its origin. It begins:

> Rammā Jumrātam went, returning his pledges.
> "Take back the pledge of matted locks of hair, to the syālī tree.
> Take back the pledge of pheasant feathers, to Chārkābhoṭ.
> Take back the pledge of fragrant leaves, to Kālā Pāṭan."
>
> (6.6)

The former pupils remove each item as the text mentions it. They leave at least one string of bells and a few feathers on the corpse, along with the blindfold and turban, but, as the first line instructs, they cut off his long topknot *(laṭṭā)*. (Should a shaman have the misfortune to die away from home, his topknot is returned to his family, and the entire ceremony is performed for it as a substitute for the corpse. This is the only hint of any "ritual dismemberment" of a shaman.) Relatives and villagers lay out a foundation for a conical shaped tomb (called a *raṅg, maṭṭī ghauḍā,* or *haṁsa maṭṭ)* around the body. In front of the corpse, the dead shaman's sons-in-law secure a pole identical to the one he climbed at his initiation (the suwā, now called a gel). Some shamans reported saving the top of the original suwā for this, but most were less meticulous. The pupils align it between the corpse's crossed legs. One of his hands is wound around the gel, a staff or drumstick gripped by the other. They build up the tomb as high as the shaman's head and pack it with clay, aligning a flat stone over his head. Centered on this stone is a bamboo basket, in the center of which is placed a wooden jug of home-distilled alcohol. Around the jug nine small flatbreads are arranged, with grains of sacred rice scattered over everything. Another flat stone is set on top of this ensemble, and the tomb is then built up into a roomlike cubicle, with a triangular window open to the north above the shaman's face. The deceased shaman's daughters and daughters-in-law smear the entire tomb top to bottom with a mixture of clay and cow dung. On the protruding pole are hung the deceased shaman's topknot, some of his feathers and bells, and his drum, which is first shattered. The pupils sacrifice a chicken, and then dance two or three times around the completed tomb, beating their drums. All the funeral goers return to the dead shaman's house, where they are fed.

Now, leaving the shaman in his temporary tomb, I want to examine events leading up to a shaman's initiation, showing how personal experiences are supplanted by impersonal text. My demonstration is intended as a caution against seeking meaning exclusively in "performance," or "use," of practicing too Wittgensteinian a semantics in our interpretations of others less postmodern than ourselves. Washed ourselves by dialogic waves of Rabelaisian proportions, we anticipate everyone trapped in labyrinths of nuance and contested meanings, wandering in wastelands of cloudy metaphors and opaque doubts. Should we, though, be dismayed to find that there are those who do not suffer the same crises in their ontologies that we do? In a traditional society such as Nepal, many meanings remain lexical and ostensible, accepted without participatory interpretation by those who conventionally learn and apply them. Such acceptance is especially pronounced in the orally maintained world of shamanic texts. Learned by rote repetition, with linguistic and ethnographic evidence suggesting little change over centuries, these texts nevertheless become the source of currently relevant quotations upon which shamans rely not only to explain what shamans know and what shamans do, but also who shamans are. Lila Abu-Lughod (1986, 1990) has shown us how memorized verses of traditional poetry may be used to express deeply felt "individual" sentiments. I wish to extend her insights to show not only how traditional oral texts provide crucial means of expressing the self, but how such texts may actively construct selfhood. Shaman texts not only give order to the confusions of patients suffering affliction but also create shaman "selves." Taking a clue from Lacan's (1968) provocative shifting of "self" to "subject," we may say that selfhood and signhood are inseparable, as Margaret Trawick suggests for another South Asian context (1990:266). Learning traditional texts, shamans do not just acquire cultural models, do not even just acquire a well-formed worldview with its articulated ethos. By learning them they transform themselves. They find themselves participants in new semiotic universes in which they discover, and are discovered by others to be, entirely different persons.

Individual experiences take on articulate meanings in what I will call "discursive space." This is neither some mundane phenomenological world nor sets of abstract symbolic structures. It involves neither matter nor mind, requires neither of our Western constructs of consciousness nor an unconscious, but is created by speech itself, speech spoken to oneself and to others, speech through which one is spoken, through which others are spoken. I accept as axiomatic the traditional South Asian description of person as composed of mind, body, and speech. "Mind" must not be confused with Cartesian mind, however, but conceived more as the organizing principles of otherwise arbitrary dispositions and of biological functions. It is, in other words, a more or less explicit theory of being-in-the-world, a theory of signs of the self, holding together such diverse phenomena as "Inspiration and expiration (respiration), blinking of the eyes (reflexes), biological functions, movements of the psyche, shifting attention from one sense organ to another, impulses, concentration, mentally visiting another place, sound sleep as if dead, . . . desire, aversion, happiness, misery, will, consciousness, control, knowledge, memory, and I-ness" (*Caraka Saṁhitā* 4.1.70–74).

Mind guides and organizes body. As Rick Shweder put it in his meditation on Obeyesekere's essay *Medusa's Hair*, "The body not only expresses a state of mind, the expression of which has public effects; the body doing the expressing is also experienced personally as a state of mind by the person whose body it is" (1991:340). (For a sensitive and insightful discussion of the importance of the body and its "presence" in Nepal, see Desjarlais 1992a, 1992b.) To achieve theoretical closure in this work, however, concurring with the authority of the Vedas and with popular Nepalese ethnophysiology, I accept that the privileged element of the triad, where constructions of the self and of culture primarily occur, is speech. Personal speech may be regarded, as Paul Friedrich noted, "as a means whereby the individual displays, and even defines, his personality vis-à-vis the group" (1979:403). By identifying the locus of personal speech as discursive space, ruled by Vāc (speech deified), I decenter, but, I hope, resuscitate the autonomy of individual agents, without getting caught in anachronistic nets of Cartesian dualities.

Discussing Lohorung Rai in eastern Nepal, Hardman concludes: "Individual characteristics and a tendency for egocentrism are thought of as being innate: sociability and the control of self have to be learned" (1981:179). As shamans become professionals, they reverse this socialization, for they learn to be egocentric while losing control of their earlier "self." With a slight shift of terminology, this is consonant with Obeyesekere's observation that "in many ecstatics the initial attack by punitive demons forces them to behave unconventionally and thereby helps them to overcome their inhibitions" (1981:162). Here, I am less concerned with personal inhibitions than with structural constraints, but the process is clearly similar. Utterly different from the disgracefully ineloquent mutterings of the first man, the recitals of Himalayan shamans are polished, well-constructed phrases, breathing life into novices who learn them, exactly as they treat clients. As Obeyesekere (1990:xix) persuasively argues, symbolic forms are created and recreated in the minds of real people. Their formations and transformations produce a "debate": the work of culture. Here, debates occur between personal experience and textual paradigms, between constraining social systems and individual aspirations. Nepalese shamans agree that anyone with adequate training can become a shaman, that no remarkable childhood experiences or visionary dreams were necessary to qualify a pupil. Yet they also uniformly report experiencing similar sets of disruptive, disorderly events that precede their careers. These experiences include unsolicited, involuntary possessions and spontaneous eruptions of deviant behavior usually characterized, by themselves and by others, as "madness." Early possession states and crazy actions form precedents for later specifically shamanic types of ritual action. The standard formative episodes sharply contrast with both the highly controlled, deliberately manipulated "possession" states and the theatrical, performatively bounded "deviant" behaviors that are definitive of shamanic practice. Uncontrolled possessions and unsanctioned behavior in others become recognized as symptoms of afflictions amenable to shamanic treatment. As potential shamans mature, they progressively control and manipulate symptoms they once uncontrollably experienced, or, what later amounts to the same thing, must eventually claim to have experienced. They convert those symptoms into diagnostic criteria applicable to disturbances in others.

Accounts of early experiences are highly stylized. Their conventionality suggests extensive reworkings of memory, or minimally, very selective reporting of events. These accounts are used to establish bodies of evidence more than to recount actual experiences. In casual accounts, agents of possession are vague, unnamed entities, loosely identified only as "spirits" (deutā), attacks from which many people who never become shamans suffer. These generic "spirits" gradually acquire specific identities from the material that shamans learn in their training. That is, this training transforms the spirits as much as it does the individuals whom those spirits possess. The early, ambiguous agents of possession take on both specific identities and specific roles. Training leads individual shamans to refine their accounts and reshape their reports to conform to shamanic ideals. They emphasize control over the agents of possession who once controlled them: "Calling, it comes, dismissing, it goes" (6.8, below).

Consider four representative accounts of how shamans discuss the events that led them to become shamans.

Karṇa Vīr

> Nine days after birth, on the "Nyāran" day, I shake. "What's with this baby, it will die. This way it will whither away." Then my father said, "It's nothing. The house god [*gharko deutā*] has seized him, that's why he's trembling on the ninth day. He'll be a jhāṅgarī." After that, fifteen years old, fourteen years old, I was senseless like him (refers to Gumāne's son, Śiva Bahādur, who was just beginning his career). I would climb onto the rooftop and shake, "What's he doing up there, this fool . . ." After that I reached fifteen, I became a jhāṅgarī. I put on a costume. At seventeen, I began to wander about. Now I am sixty-seven. Even now when friends and neighbors summon me, anywhere, I go. How did we become shamans in my family? I'll tell you (formal recital begins): A Bāhun of Kauśilā gotra, to the East, Seti Gār, Uttar Gāṅgā, Hāti Hole, Jangal Kholī, Nigāla Jhaprenī, Hiraneṭi, Bhāisi Kharka, we had an animal shed.
>
> (6.7)

The transition to memorized text in order to elaborate personal accounts is inevitable, here accomplished by raising a rhetorical question that no one had asked. That it always happens is crucial to my overall analysis, but first I want to consider the paradigmatic issues of shaking and its causes. In every shaman's informal account of his early experiences that I have solicited, occurrences of trembling are prominent, but unelaborated. In their stories, the agent(s) of possession are just "spirits" (deutā), or, at most, one with widespread local fame. Most often this will be the chief oracular spirit, Maṣṭā, who regularly appears in many dreams and possesses many individuals, not just those who become shamans or oracles. The subtleties of possession agents are left vague, as in the previous account and in the next.

Śiva Bahādur

On the twentieth of Maṅsir, my father was sick. On that night, at the time to sleep, on the twentieth of Maṅsir, a spirit possessed me *(malai deutā āyo)*. After the spirit came, I took hold of Maṣṭā's own pure possessions. After I took hold of them, everyone got up. Getting up, getting up, then the illness left my father, my father was better. Then my father said to me, or then my mother said to me, take a red strip of cloth, I'll put it on Maṣṭā deutā, or take some raw grains of rice, I'll feed them to you. (Interjection: "Was this while you were awake or did you see it in a dream?" Śiva Bahādur seemed stunned by this question. He fumbled for an answer, unable to summarize what was probably a hypnomantic state. Hesitantly, he declared, "In a dream . . .," trailing back into his recollections.) After japping me, they fed the grains to me, and the spirit left me. Then on the eighth of Puṣ, my father passed away. Then since my spirit (mero deutā) was happy, it came onto my body. Having come onto my body, my father was buried. Nine days later, the spirit calls me, moves me. Sends me here, sends me there. "I go up the hills, go down in the valleys, wander around the house, wander on the trails" (quote from a recital) finally, carrying a red cock, "On the full moon of Jeṭh, I'll worship you." I began to tremble with the spirit. After that the spirit was somewhat peaceful. Calling, it comes, dismissing, it goes (another quote). That's it. Since then, I've been okay, nothing bad has happened. But I have to worship that spirit.

(I try to identify that "spirit.") Q: Was that first spirit then Maṣṭā, or Barāh, or your father's māphī, or who?

A: To me, it was Maṣṭā. At first it was Maṣṭā. It was Barāh, it was this Hanumān Bīr, and my own lineage jhāṅgarī, my lineage jhāṅgarī, Hanumān, Hanumān Bīr, all the bīr.

Q: What about māphī, what about barāṅg?

A: My own māphī is the Chauasi Lāmā. The Chauasi Lāmā also rides my body. (His father had told me the same thing years before.)

Q: What about barāṅg?

A: What? Barāṅg? Twenty-two barāṅg, twenty-two māphī, twenty-two bīr, Dhaulai Bīr, Chadke Bīr, Naulo Bīr, Suro Bīr (continuing with twelve more names, quoting directly the text that summons them).

(6.8)

Prodded by my questions, he relies on memorized texts to elaborate his account of the spirits that possess him. He next elaborates on the line quoted above, "calling, it comes . . . ," by reciting the entire deutā bolāune (spirit-summoning) jap. This names every spirit that he summons, another instance of how the names of individual spirits must be connected to a particular use, not uttered gratuitously and meaninglessly. Vague talk of shaking provides a perfect way to avoid this issue in casual conversation, as in the next account, in which even the word *deutā* is absent until Gajā Vīr Kāmī reaches the point when he becomes an initiated shaman. Nar Siṅgh, whose account I do not include here, also described all of the events leading up to his becoming a shaman using only words for shaking and none for spirits.

Gajā Vīr

When I was twenty-one, my father died. After he died, I began to shake. After I began to shake, when my father died, then we did the rites for nine days, at the *maṁsa maṭṭ*. After that I became a shaman. After the god originated *(deutā upanna bhayo)*, two, four years later, I went and consumed the *jal toyo* (preliminary offerings). (Then, without my prodding, he recites the rāyā sarsu jap).

(6.9)

The shaman of the next selection differs from the preceding three in not being son or grandson of a shaman, though he could trace distant relationship to several. His account of being kissed by a monkeylike creature is very graphic, but again reverts to the ambiguous term "deutā" at the critical points:

Kamāro Kāmī

The spirit came to me *(malāi deutā āyo)* when I was fourteen (long pause).

Q: At that time, what happened?

A: At that time, what happened to me was, when I was fourteen, the time the spirit first came to me, at a plot of land up above, a place called Jārī that we have family rights to, we went to cut straw. When we went to cut straw, we were three brothers, my younger brother (and I), and one of the sons of my father's younger brother. And there

> was my older sister's husband. The four of us went. Going, at a stream we camped. My older brother and younger sister slept at one place, and a friend and I slept on the other side. The three of them were sleeping, had fallen asleep. I experienced *aiṭhān* (a terrifying sensation of someone sitting on your chest and sucking out your breath). It was just like a monkey. Something just like a monkey came and joined its mouth to mine. And at that time, the spirit came to me (malāi deutā āyo). I went crazy.
>
> (6.10)

Each of these accounts illustrates my point that there is no way to speak informally about particular spirits. Early in my research, I realized that villagers were always nervous whenever I wanted to explore the names and identities of spirits, as if just to mention a spirit was somehow to evoke its meddlesome power. Even shamans, despite their assertions of being in control, did not want to list spirits by name unless I had a chicken ready for them. Obtusely, I would argue that I just wanted a list of names, not a complete possession event. It took me years before I realized that they were, of course, right. To mention a spirit not only invokes it but gives it immediate presence, living reality. Spirits exist in and through discourse, as immediate agencies of that discourse. A spirit and its name are one and the same thing.

The "spirits" become precise elements of the shaman's self, simultaneously parts of his professional person and parts of the world he creatively manipulates, simultaneously psychological forces and social symbols (Ortner 1978:98). They become parts of the theory that organizes experience. Shamanic texts reshape and rearticulate life experiences by reshaping and transforming the "selves" of those who had those experiences. The texts' formalized accounts emphasize, and at the same time are examples of, abilities to intervene and refashion reality in constructive ways. This power is straightforwardly discursive. The recitals are both the means for and the proof of interventionary competence. The descriptions of shamanic practices found in oral texts become accurate reports of real lives. The texts supplant individual experiences to generate a professional identity, not as an unconscious archetype, nor as a set of symbolic forms, but as speech.

The same process applies to the most important item of any shaman's paraphernalia, his drum. Taking a hint from Janet Hoskins, who suggests that through the recitation of its personal history, "the drum acquires the power to heal and becomes a symbolic double of the patient" (1988:820), I suggest that the text that creates a drum illustrates how texts create shamans. This text's detailed instructions illustrate a seamless blend of practical and cosmological knowledge. The text names the best hardwoods for a hoop, the best bamboos for liners, the best skins for a cover, the best leathers for thongs, etc., connecting each piece of practical advice with a supernatural context. First, the text describes the felling of the tree that will supply the hoop. Assistants, referred to as "logs of wood" (a disparaging term for a corpse, here contrasting the "living" wood with the "dead" assistants), are sent to a tree chosen by the novice. Some shamans report seeing this tree in a dream, others use the suwā khetī (below) to identify it, but most just send assistants out to locate a suitable tree, one "acceptable to the spirits, acceptable to the powers."

> The two went, the "logs of wood."
> Looking at the base, there was a coiled cobra.
> Looking at the top, there were black hornets.
> "They don't let us cut, they don't let us."
>
> (6.11)

They return without it to the shaman, who instructs them to make obeisance to it. They tie strips of cloth onto it, throw four-colored grains of rice at it (white, black, yellow, and green), and sprinkle it, and the six directions, with alcohol. Sakrante and Deo Rām claimed that the tree should also shake before it is cut, as must a sacrificial animal, but when I reported this (separately) to Karṇa Vīr and Gumāne, both thought this was ridiculous, that I was being sarcastic to suggest it. They regarded the unprepared tree as another "log of wood." To be sure, the wood must be treated with respect, but no more than a corpse must be. Before its life becomes significant, it must be transformed into a drum. The tree is felled:

> "Go now, yes, go now, O 'logs of wood.'
> Tie a pair of cloth strips in the four directions."
> The vāi of the trunk's power [*muṭhi śakti vāi*],
> the coiled cobra at the trunk,
> the black hornets, all turned to ash.
> Vanishing, they ignored the injury, they ignored the theft.
> They struck the first injury, made a second blow,
> a first chip fell out, they gave it as a share to heaven.

They made a third blow, a second chip fell out,
was the share of hell. They struck a fourth blow,
a third chip fell out, was the share of local gods.
They struck a fifth blow, a fourth chip fell out,
was the share of witnesses. They struck a sixth blow,
a fifth chip fell out, was the share of leaders.
They struck a seventh blow, a sixth chip fell out,
was the share for Good Rammā's untimely death.
They struck an eighth blow,
a seventh chip fell out, was the share of the world.
They struck a ninth blow, an eighth chip fell out,
was the share of the holy man [siddha],
was the share of forest spirits [sirum].
They struck a tenth blow, a ninth chip fell out,
of the good drumwood, the share of the nine planets.
The drumwood was felled,
its head to the east, its base to the west.

(6.12)

The felling of the tree is a sacrifice. Devoting each chip to some power or threat in the universe connects the drum, a metonymic *axis mundi,* to everything that matters.

The text then tells us of the drum's powers to curse and to cure. When the first blacksmith, Tikhu Kāmī, pounds in the iron nails and rivets to shape the round hoop, the effects are devastating:

Pounding in one nail, Lamjā Tikhu Kāmī,
his topknot became bent.
"O Lamjā Tikhu Kāmī, honor to you, my Father's Father.
Oh, this drum of mine, appears to be a great pain.
O Elder Brother Tikhu Kāmī,
finish pounding in the nails, finish pounding in the spanners,
I'll fix things up, I'll make things better."
He pounded in the second nail, his ears became deaf.
He pounded in the third nail, his eyes became crossed.
He pounded in the fourth nail, his nose became crooked.
He pounded in the fifth nail, his mouth became crooked.
He pounded in the sixth nail, his neck became crooked.
He pounded in the seventh nail, his hands became crippled.
He pounded in the eighth nail, he became hunchbacked.
He pounded in the ninth nail, his feet became crippled.

(6.13)

The shaman's first thump straightens the blacksmith's topknot, his second blow returns his hearing. Each beat has effect, until Tikhu Kāmī is cured of the afflictions caused by pounding nails into the drum. The sound is the agent of the cure, just as the blows of the blacksmith's hammer caused the problems. From a musicological point of view, Rouget may be correct when he insists that "the shamanic drum—or any other instrument used in its place—essentially functions to support his singing, to provide the rhythm that is the primary support of his dancing, and to dramatize or punctuate the action" (1985:318). Shamans, however, insist that their drums are alive.

Rituals that feed the drum most clearly show this insistence. Shamans should feed their drums once a year, or at any time that the drum needs purifying, such as after being touched by a dog or a menstruating woman, or if it has been cursed by another shaman. The shaman tells the drum the story of its creation, reminding it of its important place in the universe. At the climax, a chicken is beheaded, and its blood emptied into the overturned drum, swirled around by the shaman. Then he places the drum in front of him, skin up atop the chicken's body. "Chang, chang, chang," the drum beats by itself, as the headless chicken, dead but flapping, causes it to sound, a dramatic reminder of the drum's pivotal position between life and death, a potent crossroads of the soul.

Once all the texts have been learned (twelve years was the standard answer whenever I asked how long this process took), an initiate can undertake his first pole climb. In discussing issues of competence and evaluation, every shaman emphasized mastering the corpus of texts. As my four examples show, none had much of interest to say about private experiences that he might have had before deciding to become a jhāṅgarī. Nearly all followed fathers or uncles into the profession. Kinship, not any extraordinary adventures or possession events, was most frequently a decisive factor. Although many of the most notable shamans instruct pupils with whom they are not related, few of these go on to be complete shamans. Most novices trembled with possessing spirits at an early age, but this is commonplace throughout the populace. When describing the death rites for his father, Gore Sārkī reported that every relative, male and female, child and adult, trembled on the ninth day after his death. In the story that Karṇa Vīr was so eager to tell of his ancestors (6.7), his forefather, in need of wood for tethering pegs, inadvertently cuts a shaman's gel:

Near the shed was a paĩyũ tree on the Paĩyũ jhãṅgarī's tomb.
He cut this for tethering pegs.
Pounding in a peg, the peg also trembled,
the man pounding in the peg also trembled,
the tethered buffalo also trembled,
the pounding mallet also trembled.

(6.14)

Trembling is a physical paradigm shared by the shaman, his drum, fermenting grain, and sacrificial animals, all of which participate in the rituals of initiation and death. Embodied, threatening violence but always brought under the shaman's control, each represents the interface between the shaman's life and the world around him, those lines most clearly drawn and most thoroughly broached by one more form of trembling, that of speaking.

Most shamans reported childhood dreams involving visitations of spirits, but this, too, is something that practically every villager reports. Whenever I tried to collect significant dreams from friends, students, or others, dreams involving deutā were usually their first examples. Nearly every person who ever helped me transcribe shaman tapes reported dreaming of spirits after listening to them, a reason several cited to excuse themselves from that task.

Neither experience—neither dreams nor preliminary possessions—was considered formative for shaman candidates. Neither were any anomalies of birth. Arriving in a caul is highly auspicious (compare Ginzburg 1985), but none of the shamans I knew were so born. After considerable search for some commonalities, I could find no particularly definitive events in the lives of all shamans. Man Siṅgh Kāmī of Rāḍī had even first been a dhāmī before deciding to become a jhãṅgarī, incorporating his dhāmic god into his collection of shamanic spirits.

In the Bhujī Valley as well, shamanic training and initiation were straightforward, though Deo Rām commented that a jhãṅgarī who never climbs a suwā will never be reborn, and will instead become a ban jhãṅgarī, who, he noted, resembles a demon (rākṣas or *piśāc*). "Climbing a suwā" is the ceremony of initiation and its periodic reenactment. It is also known as the toyo khāne (blood-consuming) ceremony, not only because of the large number and variety of sacrificial animals, but also because of the fresh blood that the shaman drinks. Performed as an initiation, the approval of the new shaman's career is publicly given by his guru. When performed annually, it is as a reenactment of initiation in which the shaman's personal spirits are fed by the community, and they respond with a few visionary pronouncements. Ideally, every shaman insisted, this ritual must be done annually. In fact, it has become rare. In the past ten or fifteen years, forestry officials have become quite important throughout Nepal. Before anyone dare fell a tree, the local official must be bribed (usually, with considerable irony, with meat and alcohol, just as one might offer to forest spirits). Other factors also interfere, such as a death in the shaman's family, or other sources of ritual pollution such as a wife's pregnancy or menstruation, or the unwillingness of villagers to foot the bill.

As the large number of sacrifices heralds the importance of this rite, another measure of its significance is the number of texts specific to it. Foremost is the Recital of the Origin of Alcohol (variously called *lāru*, *chā̃kī*, *paglā*, or *jāḍ*). Alcohol plays a role in the drum creation, too:

> At Cuwai Crossroads, the drum hoop was prostrated,
> the drum skin was fastened on, the liner was attached.
> Attaching the drum hoop liner,
> the liner didn't agree, the drum hoop liner didn't agree.
> "Strike it with hard alcohol, strike it with corn beer."
> The liner agreed, the drum hoop liner agreed.
>
> (6.15)

Like the biography of the drum, this mythical history of fermentation supplies another extended metaphor for a novice shaman. The eldest ordinary people, the "Bent Old Man" and "Bent Old Woman," discover barley seeds in the gullet of a dove. Dying, the dove recommends that they sow the seeds. The barley grows month by month, ripens, is harvested and stored. "In three days, it was fizzy-whizzy." It bubbles, it thunders. They ask: "What kind of grain is this?" They consult Rammā Jumrātam, who "goes to Indra's house," searches from the top of a ceremonial pole, dreams, and consults. He cautiously recommends performing a few experiments with it. They feed it to a worthless dog, who tracks the spoor of wild animals over ridge and valley. They feed it to an aged cock, who crows the dawn, crows the dusk. Still wary, they keep experimenting:

> "Let's feed it to the lāṭā [male congenital cretin],
> let's feed it to the lāṭī [female congenital cretin],
> If the lāṭā dies, he dies, if the lāṭī dies, she dies."

They fed it to the lāṭī, they fed it to the lāṭā.
The lāṭā didn't die, the lāṭī didn't die.
The lāṭā went "hāhā," the lāṭī went "hīhī."
"Ah, it's something that can be eaten,
ah, it's a fruit that can be eaten,
it's an immortal feast."

(6.16)

They next feed it to local officials, the *rikhe* and *mukhye,* and later to more important ones, the *mijār* and *kaṭuwāl.* No one misses the comic allusion to the propensity of government officials to demand a drink before they perform their duties. Once filled with alcohol,

The rikhe, the mukhye, going,
in the towns and cities, in the neighborhoods,
began to give judgments, began to make decisions.

(6.17)

Finally the original shaman concludes that it is safe to consume. It proves to facilitate his performance immeasurably, transforming him from a dead "log of wood" into an effective ritual specialist. With a typically abrupt transition into the present, the recital concludes with the shaman directly requesting a drink from the women of twelve different alcohol-consuming castes. This, too, is part of the toyo khāne ceremony, further implicating the entire community. In the morning before drinking blood, the shaman goes from house to house, receiving meat and alcohol, or money as a substitute, from each family, an event referred to as consuming jal toyo (water blood). Ideally, each household offers a chicken to the descendants of Gorāpā (the spirits of the wild who surround the village) and the seasonal threats associated with them. Earlier (2.16), I discussed what became of Gorāpā's sons. As part of that recital, the two brothers divide the earṭh, setting out boundary markers in the middle of the monsoon. Gorāpā chose markers of fixed rocks, fixed trees, fixed springs, while Serāpā chose straw and logs. Each month afterward, Serāpā urges a reexamination of their landmarks. Each month Gorāpā has a different objection. He points out that in Asoj of the scorpion (mid-September to mid-October, Nepalese months corresponding more closely to houses of the zodiac than to the Western calendar), the ancestors must be worshiped, that it is the month for worries, the months for cares, "even the ḍānphe (a type of pheasant) from the ridges descend to the lowlands this month." Kārtik of the bow is the month to sow black barley, to sow white barley, there is fever-causing dew in the forest. Maṅsir is the month the rice rolls over, the month the paddy falls down, rāh wander, and may capture souls. Puṣ "just comes and goes, the nights are long, the days are short." Māgh is the month to honor Brāhmans, the month to honor virgins, the month to honor yogins, there is snow. Cait is an empty month, "there are no leaves on the trees, there is no grass on the ground." Only in Baiśākh, after the annual forest fires, do they finally venture out, with the predictable results that Serāpā's boundaries are gone, Gorāpā's remain. Gorāpā claims the entire earth for his descendants. Following a complicated cycle of murder and retribution, the boundaries between cultivation and wild, culture and nature, are finally reestablished (2.27). The shaman upholds those boundaries through these ceremonies, which contribute a calendric awareness to the year's cycle while placing its agricultural rhythms under the shaman's protection.

The money collected from the households helps purchase a ram and a piglet, both sacrificed later in the ceremony. The shaman's own family must contribute a goat. Responsibility for sacrificial animals must be negotiated, this time more fundamentally than my previous examples (1.8 and 2.21). The toyo khāne melā, recited when it is time to climb the pole, teaches how to do this. The shaman must rebuild the animal, providing it with a new form, its original having been singed away by the heat of the Nine Suns and Nine Moons that formed Candravatī's dowry.

> The Water Animal was in the watery water.
> While in the water,
> "Go, it's time to do toyo khāne.
> We need the Water Animal, go, bring the Water Animal."
> Going to bring the Water Animal,
> "Where is the Water Animal?" they asked.
> Speaking from the water, the Water Animal said,
> "I'm in the water, empty.
> I have no ears, no eyes, no tail,
> I have no mouth, no feet."
>
> (6.18)

The assistants return empty-handed to Rammā Jumrātam. He japs black seeds, tells them to throw them in the direction of the voice, and they become the Water Animal's eyes. He japs leaves to be ears, datura to be a mouth, bamboo to be feet, thread to be a tail. When the animal has been reconstituted and is ready to be sacrificed, the shaman raises his spirits and powers, reciting the weaving passage of Tilīkarmā (2.25). He becomes possessed and ascends the pole. In preparation, assistants have tied a living piglet toward its top. Shamans said that if your personal familiar spirits are ritually pure (choko), if your only barāṅg were, say, Sati Barbā or Barāh, a young ram would be substituted, but every shaman that I know has both clean and unclean helping spirits, māphī as well as "pure" spirits, and so use a pig during the pole climb. Without māphī you cannot effectively counter witches, since they, too, use members of that class of spirits. At the climax of the pole climb, the shaman will drive his drumstick into the pig's neck and suck out its blood. Like Teiresias in Hades, after drinking blood, he then prophesies the future.

However, before this point is reached, and before he dances and drums from house to house eating and drinking in the morning, the shaman first recites through the night. He must complete the lāru melā, the ban bhampā (the story of Serāpārun and Gorāpārun), and Tilīkarmā. If there is time, he may do the creation recitals and the Nine Sisters, but these may be omitted. When he reaches the crossroads where the ceremony will take place, charcoal ash that has been vitalized by a mantar, the same used to prepare his corpse for death (6.1), is rubbed on his eyes, hands, feet, and tongue.

Next, he is blindfolded and recites the suwā melā. A suwā, the most prominent ritual accessory of this ceremony, is usually the trunk of a pine tree, erected at a prominent crossroads. The text helps identify a suitable tree. It lists many "not acceptable to the spirits, not acceptable to the powers." The shaman becomes possessed when he names the correct one. Conveniently, it is inevitably a pine *(sallī)*, which villagers have erected in advance. The text redefines it as precious white sandalwood:

> The dead assistant, the living assistant,
> bringing, giving oil, White Sandalwood,
> from the Eastern House, brought a pine trunk,
> brought it, dragging it along, brought it, knocking it down.
> it was acceptable to the spirits,
> it was acceptable to the powers.
>
> (6.19)

Villagers decorate the suwā with strips of red and white cloth *(dhājā)*, and hang long *toraṇs* (cords of woven grass with rhododendron or marigold flowers inserted) from the pole to neighboring houses, creating a festive space resembling a wedding. Villagers bring dishes of rice grains and jugs of home-distilled alcohol to place beneath the pole. Near the top, assistants bind the live piglet, and tie a ram to a stake at its base. The shaman binds the pole and the space surrounding it with mustard seeds. He honors his teachers:

> Jaya Guru, Jaya Guru.
> Skillful Guru, Clever Guru.
> Vision Guru, Dream Guru.
> Forward Guru, Backward Guru.
> Which guru taught me knowledge,
> which guru taught me understanding?
>
> (6.20)

He recites his spirit-summoning mantar. Immediately upon entering possession, he leaps onto the suwā, with drum and drumstick in one hand, gripping the suwā with the other. In an initiation, the guru assists the novice upward, pushing from below, singing:

> In the sky, the sun and moon are witnesses,
> in hell Vāsukī, King of Nāgs, is a witness.
>
> (6.21)

Perched in a crotch of the trunk, the shaman drums and sings to the spirits:

> The time for *toyan* [blood feeding] is here,
> it's come, your chance,
> True Gods, your festival, your fair,
> your chance for toyan.
>
> (6.22)

He continues with demands that truth be spoken, lies banished, evils identified. His auxiliary spirits, bīr, barāṅg, māphī, dhuwā, and sawā, begin to arrive, summoned by name. Meanwhile, relatives place two metal bowls, one holding water, the other alcohol, beneath the pole on opposite sides, covered with white cloths, along with a copper dish filled with coins contributed by the villagers. They drive four iron rods (or wooden sticks) into the corners of the crossroads. The shaman trembles vigorously with the collective force of his familiar spirits, assembling for the blood feast. He becomes frenzied. His speech disintegrates into snorts and gasps. With a sudden scream, he plunges his drumstick into the pig's neck, piercing the vein under its chin. Amid its gurgling squeals, he sucks out its blood, trembling frantically.

After the pig has been drained, the jhāṅgarī, still blindfolded and trembling, contemplates shadows in the two bowls at the base of the pole. He empties out the honor of the village in front of his familiar spirits. The list begun in 1.9 continues:

> the Magar's neighborhood, the Magar women's honor,
> the Kāmī's neighborhood, the Kāmī women's honor,
> the Sārkī's neighborhood, the Sārkī women's honor,
> the Dolī's neighborhood, the Dolī women's honor,
> the Gāin's neighborhood, the Gāin women's honor,
> the Bādī's neighborhood, the Bādī women's honor,
> the Hurkyā's neighborhood, the Hurkyā women's honor,
> the Phurkyā's neighborhood, the Phurkyā women's honor,
> the Porā's neighborhood, the Porā women's honor.
>
> (6.23)

Emphasis falls on the lowest castes, whose underprivileged members tend to be more devoted patrons of shamans. Listing Kāmī directly after Magar reminds us that most jhāṅgarīs are Kāmīs, seeking as high a status as is possible. Included twice in initiation ceremonies, this list reflects the shamans' insistence that they undertake toyo khāne on behalf of everyone. Therefore, they simultaneously neutralize the untamed threats that surround the village and pacify, in the personae of his familiar spirits, any malign aspects of the shaman himself.

The shaman's position as intermediary between worlds is physically dramatized as he hangs halfway between the earth and the sky, on the pole whose "roots are in hell, whose branches are in heaven." He drums the drum that was first buried and then resurrected from the underworld, and takes through his own mouth the blood drunk by the spirits who penetrate his body. The demands of those spirits have become his demands, their appeasement his appeasement.

In an initiation, the guru interviews the novice, seeking proof of his visionary powers. The dialogue unfolds in a highly stylized fashion, as in this example, recalled twenty years later by Deo Rām:

"Tell me what is at the foot of the pole."
"In four directions there are four pointed sticks."
"Besides this what more is there?"
"There is Mahādev's wealth [a copper dish]."
"Anything else?"
"I find *jas khaṇḍa* [water]."
"Anything else?"
"I find a clean white cloth covering the dish."
"All right, can you say, how long will your guru live?"
"The guru who helped this pupil climb this pole will live for
as many years as there are coins in the dish."
"I've helped my pupil to climb this pole. How long will he live?"
"After seven years, the pupil's father will die.
The pupil will live to be seventy-five years."
"How long will your mother live?"
"When the pupil has lived seventy-one years, his mother will die."
(6.24)

In the annual pole-climbing ceremony, conducted either on the full moon of Maṅsir (mid-November to mid-December, the onset of the cold season) or Jeṭh (mid-May to mid-June, just before the monsoon rains arrive), the prophecies are equally simple. Nar Siṅgh included an example as part of his instructions on how to conduct that ceremony:

Below, you must put a bowl of water.
You must put an offering of one rupee.
From above, you look into the liquid.
If it's time for rain, it will be cloudy above the water.
If it is not going to rain, the water will be clear.
Then you must say, "La, it's not going to rain."
If the water looks cloudy, you say,
"On such and such day, on such and such date,
the rain will come."
(6.25)

Besides the onset of the rains, the shaman sometimes predicts the number of deaths and births for the coming year, vaguely summarizing how many he sees in each direction. He frequently admonishes the village that it is not paying sufficient respect to the spirits. The relatively trivial and unemphasized nature of these prophecies underscores that this is more a ritual of comprehensive supplication than one of divination.

Representing the earth and the netherworld, the untamed descendants of Gorāpā and the seasonal afflictions associated with them are offered chicken blood. In the intermediary regions on the pole, between heaven and earth, the jhāṅgarī's own māphī, barāṅg, dhuwā, and bīr are placated. Finally, the established village spirits, representatives of a heavenly "higher" world, are offered a goat and a ram at the post in the courtyard.

Having reaffirmed his freedom from ordinary time by predicting the future, the shaman descends the pole. Family members move the bowls of liquid to one side. Sometimes, a guru plays lighthearted tricks on his pupil, perhaps putting his own snake-bone necklace at the bottom of the pole. "I can't come down, there's a nāg below," complains the initiate. The guru coaxes him down slowly, assuring him that it is safe in every direction:

> Make my pupil as bright as the sun,
> make my pupil as beautiful as the moon,
> then I will get my fame.
> To the east, I put Bet Barāṅg.
> To the north, I put Kaput Khamba.
> To the west, I put Burmā Deo.
> To the south, I put Devī Bhuwānī.
>
> (6.26)

As each direction is subdued, the pupil descends lower. When he reaches the ground, the shaman puts his drum at the foot of the pole and prostrates his head to it. In one variation (reported by Man Dev), the pupil lifts his teacher onto his shoulders and carries him around the pole. Next, still blindfolded, he seeks out the members of his own family and carries each of them, one by one, around the pole, allowing them to share in his ascent. They ride him just as spirits did before he learned to control them. When everyone is back on the ground, it is time to sacrifice the ram. It is turned upside down and tied by its front legs and horns to the suwā. The shaman reminds it of its debts:

> Your fate is to lose, my fate is to eat.
> Having pounded iron, that became your hoofs,
> that became your horns.
> Of balls of cotton, going, those became your wool.
> Putting in *tiṭhā* seeds, those became your eyes.
>
> (6.27)

The text completely reconstructs the ram, yet another example of how texts give intentional form to originally unmediated nature. An assistant sprinkles water on the ram, and it shakes to signal its acceptance of death. Holding the rear feet, the assistant slices open the chest and removes the heart. He tosses it to the shaman or, in an initiation, to the guru. The recipient catches it in his drum. He takes it in his teeth, slurps up some blood, dances around and tosses it back to the ram, aiming so that it lands near the chest. The ram is then untied and beheaded. The pupil catches the head in his drum, takes it in his teeth, dances, and tosses it, too, back to the ram. It should align with the neck. Both alignments, of the heart to the chest and of the head to the neck, are considered auspicious if they fall properly in place, inauspicious if they don't. Like other divinatory acts, should they fall inappropriately, the new shaman may repeat the tosses until the desired result appears. While there are no tales of a shaman's ever restoring life to the dead, the proper alignment of the severed organs with the corpse here produces an ordered semblance of restored life, an aesthetically balanced composition. Order, more than curing, prophecy, or subduing evil in the world, is the key feature of the performance.

Next, the guru and novice examine the ram's spleen, seeking clues to their fates and the future of the community. Afterward, the guru and his pupil relax and drink the offered alcohol. The ram's meat is cooked and eaten. At dusk, a final offering is made. Villagers set nine dishes of the ram's blood mixed with uncooked rice on top of an upside-down winnowing tray *(ulṭo nānglo).* An unmarried man, dressed in a woman's shawl, skirt, bracelets, and necklace, will carry the tray to a prominent crossroads, dancing a "backward" *(bippe)* dance step, followed by men carrying the suwā. They should carry it reversed and themselves leave the village backward. At the rear of the procession comes the shaman, carrying a jug of alcohol. The villagers deposit the suwā in an unpolluted spot, leaning it against a tree. The shaman dips his drumstick into the alcohol and scatters it to the six directions as a parting benediction. The dishes of rice mixed with blood are set around it, to satisfy any remaining hungry spirits and keep them away from the village. That there are nine dishes suggests an offering to witches, who otherwise do not feature in the initiation, but shamans that I asked insisted that the number was just conventional and that witches play no role in initiations.

Upon returning home, the shaman's family sacrifices a goat for their ancestral spirit. In most cases that I recorded, this is Sati Barbā (called by some Sati Garbā). The recital relates that he was the son of a human father and a divine mother. He describes his mission in the world as:

> I will protect the world, protect the days.
> I will kill Forest Rāh,
> will kill their spirits, kill their descendants.
> witches [ḍaṁkī], ghosts, prets,
> the descendants of Kaṁsa,
> The Black Brown Nāg, the Earth Nāg,
> Female Nāg, destroying them I go,
> to the forest I go.
>
> (6.28)

Jhāṅgarī Jumrātam repeats this when he appears at the end of the recital. Sati Barbā wanders about destroying all threats, spells, charms, nāgs, and forest spirits. He grinds cliffs into plains and reverses wrong-flowing rivers. An evil lāmā tries to subdue him, without success (3.20). Instead, Sati Barbā impregnates the lāmā's queen and his four daughters. The queen's son follows his father's example, but his four half brothers plot against them and must be defeated. They are, and then seek release from the weight of their sins through the intercession of wandering mendicants (not from their father the lāmā):

> Kāsī Kasmerā's Alabya Talabya Brāhman,
> the pierced ear Gosāī̃,
> carried away all the bad days,
> poured out good days.
>
> (6.29)

One might develop the contrast between lāmās who plot and yogins who redeem, but what counts for villagers is that Sati Barbā indiscriminately suppresses all agents of affliction, protecting anyone who might be threatened by them. He even offers enemies a chance to renounce the consequences of their evil actions, summarizing the benevolent aspects of this entire set of ceremonies.

Before sacrificing it, the shaman reminds the goat of its obligations:

> My share, your share,
> your sacrifice, your sin of killing,
> it's not on me, it's not on my patients,
> it is your birth that has made it so.
>
> (6.30)

Water is sprinkled on it, too, and once it trembles it is beheaded. In an initiation, the guru receives the head in his drum and picks it up in his teeth. Sipping the blood, he circles it around the pupil's head three times, then tosses it back to the goat. Again, the alignment indicates the success of the pupil's career. The goat's liver and spleen are examined, and a few of its hairs are burned in the fire, to satisfy any spirits attracted by the smell of blood. Finally, the pupil's family cooks the meat along with huge pots of rice, which are served to everyone who attended the ceremony, concluding the events.

There are obvious parallels and inversions between these events and those that accompany a shaman's death. The shaman, again blindfolded, is again on a pole between two worlds, now half in the underworld, half in the surface world. The alcohol, which will again contribute to forecasting the future, and the offerings, formerly beneath his feet, are now over his head. Seeking shadows in still liquids (or in dishes of finely ground flour) is a fairly common fortune-telling technique in Nepal, known as "looking into a mirror." In the recitals, the young Jumrātam recommends it to his mother when he sets out in search of his father, Purācan, who was eaten by the original witches. Since all shamans insisted that their ancestors, including the first shamans, were of high caste, milk and water, rather than alcohol, feature in this passage:

> Mother, put water in one bowl,
> put your milk in another bowl.
> If I die, then the milk will turn to blood,
> the water will dry up.
> If I live, then the milk will remain milk,
> the water will increase a little.
>
> (6.31)

Some of the possible symbolism of a container of liquid placed at the bottom of a pillar or inverted at its top has been explored by Gerritt Jan Held. Held suggests that the container at the base of the pillar represents "the underworld represented as a woman, in which Śiva's *liṅga* turns round as a churning-stick" (1935:209). The container above represents the celestial ocean. Together, the three elements, the pole and the two containers, provide "a perfect representation of cosmic motion." While appealing, such symbolism, since it presupposes a metaphysics of mimetic representation connecting natural and theological worlds, seems inappropriate for discussing shamans (or yogins, who also incorporate it in their tombs). Existing in a discursive world, shamans play with tropes without producing symbols.

For nine days, the shaman's family conducts a simple ritual at the tomb. They keep oil lamps and incense burning. On the ninth day, the former pupils of the shaman gather around the tomb. They sing the Recital of Offering to the Messenger of Death and the Time of Death. This recital begins with the part of creation when, denied a dowry of nine suns and nine moons, Candrā cremates herself, becoming the first higher being to die. Out hunting in the middle of the forest, Bhagavān and Nārāyaṇ see the pyre burning and wonder whose funeral it could be:

> "At our Ocean of Tears,
> whose corpse is that, whose funeral is that,
> the smoke begins to rise, the pyre begins to burn,
> is it Wonderful Daughter Candrā, or some son, or not?"
> "Is it, father?" they said.
> "That damned daughter may curse us
> as daughter murderers, as sister offenders,
> it may be Satya Nārāṇ's little sister,
> may be Father Bhagavān's descendant,
> let's smear out the fire, she'll live."
> Truthfully doing a truth act they went to smear out the fire.
> They reached Ocean of Tears,
> came to Cremation Ground of the Dead.
> They scattered the ashes, they blew through a tube,
> they found the ring toe.
> "That damned daughter has cursed us
> as daughter murderers, as sister offenders.
> Go, attendants, bring back a black yak tail,
> bring back a white yak tail."
> They brought back a black yak tail,
> brought back a white yak tail.
> They gave the body blood,
> the arms strength, the legs marrow,
> eyes light, put in life breath.
> They tested the side of the forehead,
> tested with a cane staff,
> brushed downward with a black yak tail,
> brushed upward with a white yak tail.
>
> (6.32)

That is, they repeat the gestures of creation, when Mahādev shaped and animated the first man. The ritual revives her, and she receives her desired dowry. Soon afterward, the entire race of man requires exactly the same procedure of reanimation, for it has dried up from the heat of the nine suns delivered by Candrā. The eldest items, those that survived the searing heat, are listed (4.8). Then, in a passage similar to 5.8, the star obstructions are postponed:

> The black star obstruction at the foot of the bed,
> was transferred to the door step.
> The black star obstruction of the door step,
> was transferred to the courtyard.
> The black star obstruction at the courtyard,
> was transferred to Hari Gauḍā, to Barmā Crossroads.
> "What shall we eat if we go, what shall we wear if we go?"
> said the black star obstructions.
>
> (6.33)

The shaman's negotiations with the different animals who might be sacrificed (1.8) conclude the recital. Though used only for a shaman's funeral, there is nothing at all unique in this text. Rather, the Recital of Offering to Juma Dūt and Juma Kāl is simply a rearrangement of passages particularly relevant to this occasion. As I hinted when discussing opening and concluding passages in Chapter 4, the recitals themselves turn out not to be rigidly fixed. They are composed of episodic blocks of text that can be juggled to suit particular occasions.

Finally, the former pupils sing the second half of Tilīkarmā, beginning with the king's messengers being sent to summon Jumrātam. They ask the shaman's widow where to find him, but she shows them the signs of mourning and the tomb. They return to the court with Ghobre Rammā, a pupil of Jumrātam's who seems to have learned little from his guru. He uses a drum hoop of *tusārī* wood (whose sap is milky rather than bloody), a drum skin from a domesticated goat rather than a wild one, and has a lizard for an assistant. Despite his comic regalia, he performs moderately well as a shaman and correctly diagnoses the problem:

> He danced and drummed out to the crossroads,
> he danced and drummed back from the crossroads,

was seated in the underworld,
rose from the underworld.
"Having been cut, O king, be cut.
Having been killed, O king, die.
I am not your jhāṅgarī.
Your jhāṅgarī is in Tilīkarmā."

(6.34)

For this information, the king rewards him with the lungs of a goat, and he returns home. However, the pupil's wife, incensed by her husband's eating pieces of lungs out of the broth when she steps out for firewood, drenches him with the hot broth. Writhing and squirming, in parody of one possessed, he flees. Besides providing a comic interlude, the episode instructs clients to patronize "their own" shaman, not others. The pupil does not even attempt to cure the king once he realizes that Jumrātam is still (more or less) alive. It warns pupils not to assist patients who aren't theirs, not to practice before their guru has authorized them to, and not to innovate, for his subsequent scalding suggests that disastrous consequences may result from ungrounded professional innovations.

A third time the king's messengers return to the shaman's widow (in some versions, the queen herself goes), but now they approach in humble supplication rather than in anger. They promise that the shaman will receive half the kingdom, and his "widow" finally instructs them of the path to Tilīkarmā. When the messengers identify Jumrātam and cause him to be possessed, the passage that so often induces possession in the shamans when they recite it (4.16), the gel shakes, the bells ring faintly. The spirit of the dead jhāṅgarī has returned from the underworld. He possesses his successors and chants with them the conclusion of the recital, covering the curing of the king and the receiving of rewards. The shaman's spirit, now genuinely a "tutelary" one from whom instructions may be received, joins the spirits whom his successors summon whenever they perform. Continuing his career as a shaman, he receives a share of any blood that is sacrificed, and his voice joins those of his pupils whenever they recite.

The pupils now open the top of the tomb and take out the container of alcohol. They dip their drumsticks into the alcohol and scatter drops on the tomb, saying:

Honor to you, guru father,
tell us where, tell us what's left.

(6.35)

Drinking the remainder, they become frantically possessed by their guru. He now tells them where to construct his permanent monument. They carry away the stone and the shaman's topknot of hair, to provide the foundation of his permanent monument (*bisāunā* or haṁsa maṭṭ, "soul" tomb as opposed to the earlier "flesh" tomb). Dancing and drumming, the pupils lead the way to where their guru wants his monument. They set down the flat stone, and relatives build up a four-walled solid box, about four or five feet high. At the top, a triangular window is recessed into each side. The daughters and sons-in-law of the departed shaman smear the monument with white clay. They smear each other's faces as well, and throw containers of water colored with clay over one another, rather like the celebration of the pan-Hindu festival of Holi Purṇimā. A few branches of a tree "approved by the spirits and powers," usually pine or juniper, are erected on top by a male relative, who ties strips of red and white cloth to the branches. Other relatives add more strips. The pupils dance around the monument. Finally, they sacrifice a goat or ram at the foot of the stones as a substitute for the dead shaman (1.7): "Sense measured out for sense, breath measured out for breath." Everyone returns to the shaman's home, where they are feasted on rice and meat.

The sacrifice at the haṁsa maṭṭ should be repeated annually, though eventually it lapses, as the memory and power of the departed shaman fade. Deo Rām's instructions recognized this, saying that a ram should be offered annually for nine, or at least three, years, while afterward a chicken is sufficient. In practice, this is often reduced to just strips of cloth, unless the dead jhāṅgarī manages to reassert himself by violently possessing his descendants to remind them of their obligations. Otherwise, he seems to sink into the anonymous māphī called the "Twelve Grandfathers," which includes the Dumb Grandfather and the One-Eyed Grandfather, names that reflect their unresponsiveness.

If the dead shaman had many pupils, the night before they open the tomb they first gather at their former guru's house and recite together, covering the stories of creation, the Nine Sisters, and especially the Ban Bhampā and the first half of Tilīkarmā. This set of texts emphasizes the kinship ties of the various characters, placing the shaman in both the world of men and the world of spirits. While the Ban Bhampā illustrates the negotiated relations between the world of men and the malevolent forces of the forest, the beginning of Tilīkarmā makes explicit the relation between Gorāpā, the shaman, and the different castes of Nepalese society.

Tilīkarmā begins with Gorāpā (sometimes called Khanuserā), a widower with unmarried daughters, reaching the time of his death. He has, in different versions, two, three, or four daughters. He sends them to fish, to gather fern shoots, and to hunt. Each time, he assumes a form that is half himself, half what he has sent them to fetch, for the division between the world of men and the world of nature has not yet rigidly solidified. Weary, he seeks to die by the hands of his own daughters:

> His eyes had gone blind, his ears had gone deaf.
> "Descendant Somatā, descendant Gomatā,
> your father has no sons,
> the home is saying 'go,' the forest is saying 'come,'
> so daughters, go and get some meat, go and get some fish,
> my daughters, you are sons to me, you are daughters to me,
> the home is saying 'go,' the forest is saying 'come.'"
>
> (6.36)

Since no man has yet died, Gorāpā has no other models for dying than those supplied by fishing, gathering, and hunting. Each time, his daughters recognize him as part of what they were sent for. Each time they return empty-handed. When he sends them to fetch meat, they

> beat along the rivers, hid in blinds on the ridges,
> hunted in the forests.
> Half the body father Khanuserā,
> half the body a living deer, came,
> the elder sister blocked a narrow part of the trail,
> the younger sister shot,
> the arrow entered the right side.
> He pulled the barb out, put on an herbal poultice,
> went off with blood streaming out.
>
> (6.37)

Unable to find his tracks, the sisters interview various plants and animals, awarding those who saw him with a blessing, cursing those who didn't.

Animals that may be sacrificed are reminded: "there is no sin in killing you, there is no merit in keeping you." These blessings and curses establish reciprocal relations between the inhabitants of the untamed spaces and the plants and animals that the shaman uses. Finally, the daughters seek the advice of men, adding humans to these equations. In versions with just two sisters, one goes to the king, the other to Jhāṅgarī Jumrātam. When a third sister is added, she consults Tikhu Kāmī, the first blacksmith, and when a fourth sister is added, she consults the first Brāhman, Hunyā Bāhun. In every case, advice is promised if the girl agrees to become the consultant's wife. Each does, establishing the first shaman as the brother-in-law of, minimally, the king, and in the more elaborate version, of the three most important caste strata in Nepali society. By marrying a descendant of Gorāpā, the shaman becomes a brother-in-law of the malevolent forces that surround the village (the sons of Gorāpā's brother, Serāpā). As Anne de Sales (1991) convincingly demonstrates, he becomes a matrilineal son-in-law of the higher deities, ties that each initiation recalls. Just as the initiation ceremony emphasizes connections between the shaman and the wider (visible and invisible) societies in which he participates, these passages insist that the shaman's roles continue despite his physical death.

With the help of their future husbands, the daughters find their father's corpse. They prepare for his funeral, the first to take place on earth. Cremating the body requires fire, and a grasshopper goes to heaven to obtain it. Burned when he tries to carry it in a sack, he finally returns with flint and steel, making a permanent contribution to the domestication of Gorāpā's descendants.

Tilīkarmā further asserts the shaman's superiority over the rest of society. After Gorāpā's daughters observe a year of mourning and pilgrimage, each marries. Twelve years pass, and they meet at a water tap. Here, too, versions differ. In one, the elder sister decides to visit her younger sister, who is now the queen, unannounced, although the jhāṅgarī warns her not to do so. The queen accuses her sister of coming to bewitch her and orders her removed:

> "My little sister will come here,
> I will meet her, I will wait here," said the jhagrenī,
> and she waited at the tap.
> With music, with drumming, came the chief queen,

she saw the jhagrenī there.
"Hey, what evil witch, what little witch are you,
why have you come to my gold tap, my silver tap . . .
you want to curse me, put a spell on me.
Go, attendants, remove her from here,"
said the chief queen.
Crying and weeping she left.

(6.38)

To punish the queen for these insults, the shaman "jhāṅgarīes" and strikes the king down with terrible afflictions (2.3).

In other versions, the sisters meet after twelve years to reflect on their fates, comparing the merits and defects of their husbands. The younger sister, having become the queen, refuses to bow her head to her older sister, and insists that she receive homage instead, to which the elder sister objects.

"O little sister, I am the elder sister,
bow your head to my feet."
The younger sister said,
"I am now the chief queen.
The country is mine, the fields are mine,
bow your head to my feet, elder sister." . . .
"No, little sister, have you come to crush my head?
I've eaten the elder share,
your king collects fees, collects fines,
collects tithes, collects taxes,
your king is like the day, my jhāṅgarī is like the night.
He consults in unhappy homes, consults in happy homes,
he consults when fed, consults when not fed,
my jhāṅgarī is big."
"Make it known, have it shown,
a jhāṅgarī's house has what norm, what form,
what do you wear, how do you fare,
I will go home with you, big sister," she said.
"No, little sister,
your king will be shamed, will be inflamed,
a jhāṅgarī means being a sorcerer, being an ensorcerer,
one does not go to a jhāṅgarī house," she said.

(6.39)

However, the queen comes anyway to visit her brother-in-law's house.

"Examining, consulting," the shaman anticipates this, and again asserts his control over the dangerous elements of the world by magically using poisonous snakes and stinging insects to construct a beautiful dwelling, a passage that closely parallels Mahādev's construction of the first plow (1.3). The queen is so dazzled she faints. She moves in with the shaman, where she is richly dressed, fed only fresh foods, and even eats the offerings (*arni,* Sharma 1971) made to a bride at a wedding.

> The food was dazzling, the clothing was dazzling.
> Six months, a full year, she stayed.
> The chief king became shamed, became inflamed.
> The Sijāpati King said, "Go, attendants,
> bring me that longhair's warm heart, I'll eat it,
> he has confused my queen, confounded my queen."
>
> (6.40)

This initiates the dispute between the king and the shaman, returning us to his departure for the underworld. Jumrātam uses a mantar to cough up a cursed heart, which the king eats with devastating effect (2.4). When the original shaman is finally identified and returns, the currently departed shaman also "returns." The king humbly addresses him as "older brother" (2.19), declaring: "the rulings of the day are mine, the rulings of the night are yours."

At the beginning of this chapter, I noted that these ceremonies establish prototypes for all other shaman performances. In other ceremonies, journeys to heaven and hell take place by superimposing textual descriptions of such travels upon his sitting and getting up to dance. Here, he physically travels, first from house to house throughout the village, next into the region between earth and heaven, where he finds all of his familiar spirits, and finally, between earth and hell, where he joins those spirits. These rituals unfold as communal and family events, every household contributing, with the largest contribution made by the shaman's own family. Rather than treating a single patient or a single household, the rituals preempt dangers to entire communities. With each pole climb, and with his final descent, the shaman accepts his role as protector of the village, mediating between it and the threatening worlds that surround it. His performances are for the common good, controlling both the spirits who possess him and those that threaten others.

Illustration 6.2. Shamans dancing

There is a careful, deliberately equivocal positioning of the shaman in both the initiation and death ceremonies. Spatially, he finds himself physically suspended between worlds, his head in heaven, his soles in hell. Socially, his position is equally ambiguous, inferior by caste, superior by the powers of his profession, an ambivalence that limits shamans from converting their supernatural interventionary power into political influence the way that local mediums have. Shamanic power is signed with transgression. A shaman is not only an intermediary between the world of men and the world of spirits; he remains a commited participant in both worlds of life and worlds of death. His kinship ties cut through and unite those worlds. He intervenes in both, with cures and with curses. The Tilīkarmā text replicates these ambiguities through riddles that each initiate must solve, poising the shaman, at death, for a triumphant return, a welcoming as the king's acknowledged older brother, a return to the world of men in which he will continue, by balancing good together with evil, to take part. With his body in the "flesh" tomb and his life breath in the "soul" tomb, that participation continues in and through the most human and most divine component of every person, speech.

Models articulated in their oral texts transform a shaman's experience, changing anomic, disruptive, confusing, and baffling events into assured and productive competence. Shamans find themselves in paradigms that are simultaneously ready-made and of their own remaking, made anew in every performance but preserved as atemporal, immutable document. The self-creating context of the texts extends to the shaman himself. By repeated application of these texts, a shaman's self becomes so reflexive that it loses its original references, and is transformed into a replica of the original shaman's persona. Every shaman's initiation and death rituals reenact this transformation, demonstrating that shamanic speech is, at the beginning and at the end, shamanic self.

7
Casting Indra's Net

You couldn't call it day,
you couldn't call it night.

(7.1)

During the first years that I lived in Jājarkoṭ, events around me seemed extraordinary and mysterious, and I saw them as puzzles that required explanation. At different times, I would achieve distinct kinds of provisional understanding. In one, prompted by interpretive ethnographies I had read, I would discern some underlying pattern, of religious symbols, say, or economic relations, or environmental constraints, that would provide a foundational account by which Nepalese society and actions taken within it fit coherently together. Major theoretical organizations, such as those of caste proposed by Dumont (1970) or Marriott and Inden (1977) proved misleading rather than helpful, failing to encompass the fluid group redefinitions possible in Nepal, an ill fit recently noted by, among others, Lecomte-Tilouine (1993), Levine (1987), McHugh (1989), and Parish (1991). Each provisional pattern eventually dissolved, as I uncovered new information that wouldn't fit. The better I got to know "marginal groups," members of low castes, women, mediums, and, most obviously, shamans, the more these grand theories seemed fleeting, deceptive, and specious. They existed only by mirroring hegemonic constructs of the dominant Hindu worldview—Nepal as the world's only Hindu kingdom—in which there is little room for marginal groups like blacksmiths, no room at all for "deviants" like shamans. Sometimes a new pattern dialectically emerged from the old, as I critiqued and attempted to repair the models. At other times I just discarded one set of theories and tried out another.

In an alternate way of understanding, Blakean epiphanies would at times momentarily connect events within an intuitively striking illumination. The words of a folk song, a parent's remark to a child, and the bells of a caravan passing before dawn, would spontaneously fit together as perfect, pure, and apparently eternal (because intuitive) sense. These flashes would rapidly fade, the patterns they suggested retaining only hints and shadows of meaning. Gradually the strategies by which I sought understanding changed as the urge to find theoretically grounded comprehensive explanations diminished, along with diminished expectations of durable insights. Once I saw that, as Shweder puts it, "the objective world is incapable of being represented completely from one point of view, and incapable of being represented intelligibly if represented from all points of view at once" (1991:66), I discovered, not as convincing theory but as lived experience, that there are multiple objective worlds, each containing multiple, contesting rationalities.

After living in a Nepalese village for three or four years, a thick aura of normalcy suffused most events, so that they no longer provoked efforts to make sense. The very normalcy of daily events thoroughly discouraged such inquisitive efforts. I no longer contended continually with disconcerting confusion or awkward misunderstandings. It took several toe-stubbing years, but I did become a "participant" as much as an "observer." There remained provocative reminders, however, that I had not achieved expressible understanding of events around me. Through those persisting provocations, I remained intrigued by various particular issues, but I no longer tried to tie them together into a seamless whole. I abandoned a quest for determinacy, but still hoped to limit the field of, as Quine calls it, the "objectively indeterminate" (1969:34). Ultimately, I concentrated on these smaller, semi-isolatable, intriguing, and relatively sensational phenomena, points that did not disappear as "just ordinary," even after most events had become transparently "normal."

Meanwhile, I continued to improve my understanding of local dialects. I visited more and more villages, mapping differences of vocabulary and grammar. I taped songs and stories, collected proverbs, riddles, and figures of speech. Friends transcribed for me recordings of natural conversations, disputes, oracular consultations, and shamanic sessions, initially as heuristic tools to understand the language better, but gradually as the best examples of precisely those smaller parts of events that continued to fascinate me. I came to realize that repeatedly listening to such recordings not only provided the best method for improving my Nepali, but also the best method by which to understand better those phenomena of which they formed parts, being precisely those aspects most accessible and most open to analysis. At the time, I had not read Garfinkel or the conversation analysts, but I slowly approximated key features of their approach, which made me later so receptive to it. Language, as Bourdieu observed, draws the tacit boundary of the thinkable and the unthinkable (1977:21). Grammar, I concretely discovered, does precede facts.

As I retell the story, it seems that these two tendencies, to focus on smaller, more precise topics, involving relatively conspicuous phenomena, and to know that I really knew something when it came to language, coalesced into and sustained this project. As I said at the beginning, a decisive factor for selecting shaman texts for playing this *Glasperlenspiel* was my discovery, after years of thinking otherwise, that these texts with unremitting, relentless thoroughness make sense. When I first listened to shamanic texts, all that I heard was sound, the "ha, ha, hu, hu" that drove Mahādev to curse his creation. Had those meaningless noises not been a part of my daily environment for so long, my discovery of their grammaticality would have seemed less momentous. As it happened, the incredible detail, the elegant constructions, and the relative profundity of these oral texts continue to amaze me each time I replay tapes that once spoke nothing to me, but that now shape a world in which I sometimes live.

To write this study, I have made some effort, as a methodological device, to see daily events of western Nepalese society as "anthropologically strange," to separate the everyday from the extraordinary in ways that reveal their contours as they might be seen by those outside local language games. At the same time, I cannot, nor would I wish to, entirely discard the approximation of quasi-native competence that six years of daily interaction necessarily confers, an ability to draw the boundaries between words and worlds in ways similar to how Nepalese themselves do. It is this competence that permits me to write with a certain authority, to translate texts and to connect them to wider issues with some assurance that I have got things right. This claim is not particularly remarkable. Every ethnologist makes, at least implicitly, a similar claim in every ethnography, writing from some perspective unattained by native members and encompassing theirs in scope. Ethnographies are written for audiences more diverse than just the people who have been studied, and may be judged by standards unavailable to those whose world has been rewritten. Parisians who happened to live through 8:00 P.M., June 23, 1975, are not the only, nor necessarily the best, judges of *La vie mode d'emploi.* As Nelson Goodman reminds us, "knowing is as much remaking as reporting" (1978:22). But my claim of competence goes further. I not only see what I have studied with the understanding that an ethnologist attains in fifteen years of studying some particular culture. I have learned to see shamanic events in the same ways that shamans themselves learn to see them, by learning texts. Within their own terms, I can submit my competence to their own evaluations, since they judge their pupils foremost by how many texts have been mastered. By now, I know more shaman texts than does any shaman in Nepal. In Chapter 4, when discussing the opening passages of public recitals, I noted that Karṇa Vīr knew and used at least five different openings, the most of any shaman in Jājarkoṭ. In comparison, I use more than two dozen examples to inform my analysis of openings. Every shaman possesses some version of Tilīkarmā, the most important of recitals, used to manipulate fate for the most seriously afflicted patients and to reshape shamans themselves at critical points in their careers. I possess ten versions of that recital. Admittedly, I have memorized them imperfectly and must improvise when reciting, but this is also true of every shaman that I have ever heard. They never hold such lapses against their pupils. They would agree, too, that in the current context, any resulting imperfections do not endanger the (perfectly shamanic) goals to which I here put those texts, making a public display of specialized knowledge to reshape understandings and relations in the world, reordering disorder, and offering therapeutic clues to some general social afflictions, most notably our persistent confusions that language is unproblematically denotative while art is purely mimetic. I, too, struggle to create a new world, where we no longer suffer from treating words as though they were pictures, of treating truths as though they froze in place fixed correspondences between words and things and thoughts.

Somewhat exaggeratedly, I might claim to know more about how to be a shaman than any single shaman himself knows. This has had practical consequences, since anthropology, unlike philosophy, never leaves the world just as it finds it. It is not just that writing down previously oral material can interfere with its historic development by creating falsely canonical, ahistorical texts, as Pynchon reminds us with black humor in *Gravity's Rainbow*. My ritual of writing performs a process similar to a shaman's performance, imparting meaning through selective emphasis, struggling against the inevitable indexicality and reflexivity of both language and method. In my ceremony, this manifests itself most thoroughly as grammar. Other than prosody, there are, of course, no indications of punctuation in these oral texts. Pronouns are rare, for Nepalis avoid using them almost as much as they do personal names. Frequent passages of unattributed reported speech present possibly deliberate ambiguities not resolved by context. Through my diacritics, I dilute the metaphysics of a living, immediate presence with shadows of the transcendental signified that haunts Western thought. Shaman texts do not just describe ideal situations; they impose their ideal, atemporal, divine performance on the accidental, time-bounded, and thoroughly human actions of the particular shaman who invokes them. The texts must be heard by those who recite them as directions which shape and inform the course of their activities, standing to everyday life as *langue* does to *parole* (Saussure 1966). Through these texts spirits not only attend the ritual; they are tamed, reshaped, reanimated, and given sociable presence each time. In every performance, shamans reveal and triumph over an "underlying menace of a chaos as decisive as it is dangerous" (Artaud 1958:51), a menace most deeply experienced as possession. Grotesque physical clues that spirits are present, paradigmatically the trembling that accompanies their arrivals, are given orderly shape by both the rhythmic breathing of reciting and the precise, powerfully concrete, transformational images of the recitals. Spirits are discursive events. Without speech they lack presence. To have a special existence, they require a special language. Unable to sing those singular, contrary dictions to my readers, I can only provide a printed score whose richest chords may be impossibly elusive.

There are other, less ponderous, directions that my interference takes: Some months after I last visited him in 1989, one of my key informants, Gumāne, died. During the last days of his father's life, Gumāne's third eldest son, Śiva Bahādur, began preparing to become a shaman (6.8). When I returned in 1992, he was eager to recover everything that his father had taught me. He memorized directly from my collection of tapes and transcripts, traveling with me for two weeks to make sure he got them right. I have, it seems, gone further than most ethnomethodologists, having not just uncovered native methods of constructing sense, but applying those methods to help members make sense of their lives.

Knowing many texts, knowing their contexts of application, and having a firm sense of their meaning meet specifically shamanic standards of shamanic understanding. More problematic are standards by which may be judged my understanding of particular passages, my attempts to go "beyond" the words themselves. That shamanic texts are oral introduces levels of indeterminacy that exceed the "ordinary" plurivocality of any expression. Mispronunciations, distractions, and problems of memory must occur, compounding ambiguities found in written documents. Audiences cause interruptions. Delayed preparations may require time-killing repetitions or expansions. Often, when I listen to a tape again, I hear new allusions, puns I had previously missed, echoes to Sanskrit texts, metonyms that suddenly unfold in new ways. Two versions of lines taped a decade apart may differ by, say, a phoneme, or a performance may wildly alter a dictated version. Each new variation undermines the quality of my previous translations. In each case, I try to answer whether the difference is deliberate wordplay or only a malapropism, a sign of manipulative technique or just a lapse from fatigue, contempt, giddyness, or distraction. Paraphrasing Aristotle, Höfer observes of such situations: "One is caught in the dilemma as to whether to accept this formulation as a kind of performative truth in its own right or to treat it as a denotative that grasps an untruth. Can the impossible be trustworthy and preferred, in certain cases at least, to what is untrustworthy even though possible?" (1992:161). Such problems, I suspect, admit no solution. Sacks remarked that "there is order at all points" (1984:22), suggesting, as an extreme reading, that every slip of the tongue be treated as a technical accomplishment. Given our predilection for sense making, perhaps it is, though such a widened definition of sensibility may swallow itself endlessly. Choosing what is significant is finally a matter of aesthetic preferences.

Paralleling the problems found within any corpus of texts, each rereading of my own translations reveals nuances within my choice of English words that I would never claim for the originals. Many things slip through the net of my impressions, their places taken by new problems, ambiguities of English replacing ambiguities of Nepali. Such problems are inevitable and insurmountable; but if translation is given up as impossible, then the endeavor of ethnography must also be abandoned, for the two are inseparable. Moments of indeterminacy probably often slip past the shamans themselves, and are certainly lost to their clients. I have sometimes, with effort, shown to a shaman a pun in his "own" text of which he was unaware, or have introduced to them solutions of riddles in their texts, based on other texts, that they had not even heard as riddles. In Chapter 3, I mentioned their disapproving reaction to such apparent disrespect toward the pure text. To challenge the accuracy or authority of any text, even a variant, is, as I argumentatively discovered, to challenge the shaman himself in the depth of his identity. Semantics become, for shamans, at one extreme pure pragmatics, at the other, pure syntax, a result of the shamanic metaphysics discussed in Chapter 5. To me, such contested moments clearly affirm my theoretical preference for separating issues of intentionality from any form of mentalism. Shamanic texts must be treated like archaeological monuments, having broken free of the subjectivity of individual authors. Meaning is overproduced at all points, with bottomless subtlety, but it is a production that is free from its immediate ennunciator. I have taken entirely seriously a dramatic subjunctive from Lévi-Strauss's passage of *The Raw and the Cooked* in which he memorably declares that he has shown not how individuals think in myths, but the ways that myths operate in minds that are unaware of it. "[I]t would perhaps be better to go still further and, disregarding the thinking subject entirely, proceed as if the thinking process were taking place in the myths, in their reflections upon themselves, and their interrelation" (1969:12). I have not sought, however, neo-Kantian homologies and isomorphisms, the key characteristics of the structuralist method. I have not tried to show how "myths" operate in some fictitious construct called "Mind." Instead, I have demonstrated their social operations within a more transparent fiction, "Discourse." By emphasizing the ways that texts are used to inform and make significant events and lives, I show how to play the game in which they are the glass beads.

The sacredness of the material has been of direct assistance for my demonstration, for as Walter Benjamin observed, "Where a text is identical with truth or dogma, where it is supposed to be 'the true language' in all its literalness and without the mediation of meaning, this text is unconditionally translatable" (1968:82). My translations have been found, as he predicted, "between the lines." This claim must, however, be taken on trust. Benjamin's assurances do not lessen the individual problems posed by each word, but to recount sets of endless options and the paths to my "final" choices would burden my analysis with labyrinths of excessive detail.

In this work, I have sought a context in which my translations sound plausible, read coherently, and are internally consistent. Anything more is, I insist, beyond our abilities, for we will never find some position outside language from which we can evaluate, with privileged certainty, remarks made within it. My goal has been to limit the plurivocality of particular language events, to give them a clear speaking voice. I do not seek a certitude that I believe nonexistent. I would dismiss the ultimate incommensurability of intentional worlds not by having uncovered hard evidence to the contrary, but because the boredom of such a conclusion seems to me unsustainable.

Were I to climb to the top of an initiation pole, summon bloodthirsting spirits and satisfy them by drinking blood from the neck of a living piglet, I might see some things differently than I do now. However, I would still use the same words to describe what I see, for every shaman expresses his experiences in the phrases of the texts that he has memorized. Beyond those phrases, with which and of which we can speak, one must, as the bottom line of the *Tractatus* taunts us, remain silent. There are worlds, but no meanings, outside language.

It may be asked, if I have really obtained a thorough perspective, why the conclusions that I have drawn aren't far more extensive. First, there is the "aura of normalcy" which shamanic texts and shamanic practices have increasingly attained the longer I examine them. I try to reciprocate the trust that I expect from readers regarding my translations with expectations that they, too, will see the obvious. "Hand a knowing person the leaves, don't say, 'make leaf dishes,'" instructs a Nepali proverb. Second, whenever I have gone beyond translating texts and offered extratextual conclusions, I have always begun by asking what the shamans who taught me their texts would say about my exegesis of them. Through return visits, I have endeavored to outline my conclusions to them. Echoes of their laughter sometimes haunt me, but I generally feel that they can see most of my conclusions as plausible and reasonable. Throughout, my goal has been to create the text, to play the language-game, that accounts for the words and actions of shamans in a way that I could translate back to them. From whatever future vantage points, I hope to be able to look back on this as a successful playing of the game, as a coherent explanation of how it is played, with no more dissonance than I feel contributes to its composition. However, as Wittgenstein warned: "You must bear in mind that the language-game is so to say something unpredictable. I mean: it is not based on grounds. It is not reasonable (or unreasonable). It is there-like our life" (1969:73e) So, too, is any text.

Taking a pragmatic approach to language diminishes the temptation to choose between alternate perspectives of interpretation, or to take particular symbols too seriously. Once it is accepted that the best way of conceiving "truth" is as "warranted assertibility" (or any other provisional status) and that the history of philosophy is the history of tropes, there is little compelling reason to substitute one set of metaphors for another set, so long as that original set remains potent and still retains its ability to create a lifeworld. Only when metaphors have grown stale and "paint their gray on gray" need we overthrow them for fresh ones. For any of my audiences, Nepalese or Western, ethnologist or shaman, the metaphors found in these texts remain, I believe, remarkably potent, still capable of reconstituting reality through their images. By refashioning the narrative, choosing between alternate passages those that I find most striking, I select those tropes that I expect to engage readers most thoroughly. The picture of man, freshly fashioned from ash and chicken dung, immediately cursed with death for his incoherent mumbling is as good an onto-theological anecdote as any with which I might replace it, in little need of a philological, psychoanalytic, structuralist, interpretive, or any other gloss.

Designed to battle entropy, to slow and momentarily reverse the Kali Yuga despite its inevitable decay of everything from the cosmos to individual lives, shamanic texts resist indexicality and reflexivity. They are, as I have observed, artfully constructed to reproduce their own reality in whatever context they are invoked. They themselves become their own context. They are still relatively capable of this production, despite the inevitable decay of language and of the social connections that assist their effectiveness. In discussing the issue of history as disintegration, I once translated for Jājarkoṭ's leading shaman Rousseau's charming remark that the first speech was all in poetry, reason came only much later

(*D'abord on ne parla qu'en poésie; on ne s'avisa de raisonner que long-temps après,* Rousseau 1974:97). Karṇa Vīr unhesitatingly and enthusiastically agreed, adding that this follows from Mahādev's being the first speaker, not men. Our efforts at imitating divine poetry are feeble, but our worlds remain sometimes responsive to them. To be a shaman is to achieve a practical mastery over language, like a blacksmith's mastery of fire. The shaman pounds on his words just as he pounds on his drum, as if to shatter them, testing the elasticity of language, pulling it apart to reveal within it the vulnerable points of the world, where it may be most susceptible to manipulation. As metal is hammered on an anvil, words are tempered on a shaman's tongue until they crack to reveal an unspeakable, divine presence. Shamanic texts must be heard also as winks and nudges *(Winke und Gebärden),* as provisional instruments for grasping at things they can never entirely contain or express (Heidegger 1959:117). They belong to entirely different realities than do signs and ciphers. They are not definitive, precise, eternally complete, and confrontationally defensible concepts, for such concepts do not exist. Finally, shamans fail, they and their patients die, since neither natural world nor human life proves fully containable within semantic structures. Not every breath is a sound, nor every sound a phoneme. Shaman ontologies prove insufficient to efface all metaphysics. But before we wrestle with chimeras at the limits of ontology, we need to listen carefully to the details, to words themselves, without which any discourse becomes a sea of murmuring babble.

As I have shown, shamanic recitals acknowledge but do not focus on organic symptoms of illness. They address, shape, and manipulate fundamental ontological conditions that permit illness and social disorder. Upholding and tampering with ṛtā (cosmic order), shamans do not simply affirm the seamlessness of the natural and the supernatural, the extravagant and the prosaic, the ordinary and the extraordinary. They undertake to refashion the tension in those seams, to tighten relations, to revitalize lives and social ties that have loosened into unrelenting daily drudgery, into dull hopelessness. Shamans, like Prometheus, return from their journeys, their crises, simultaneously dramaturgic and "real," with a gift of hope, promising a healthier, better, purer, more harmonic and balanced world. Disorder in the world is countered through orderliness in language. Each shamanic performance affirms that reality truly is socially constructed through the medium of language. Consequently, only words have any genuine effect on the world and its participants. Shamans affirm that knowledge and power, syntax and pragmatics form sets of synonyms. Though admitting (4.7) that anyone's knowledge is imperfect, that no one can control fully all the forces that require control, shamans undertake, through language, to repair and refashion the cosmos. Through endless series of inversions and displacements, they return time to timelessness, corruption to wholeness, death to life. They accomplish this with grammar. In *The Twilight of the Idols,* Nietzsche voiced his fear that our belief in god remains inevitable, so long as we still believe in grammar. Shamans affirm the ties of grammar and divinity fearlessly, with faith that semantics and theology are a final set of synonyms.

Echoes of several "philosophers" in just the preceding two paragraphs undermine my claim to have left philosophy to one side. What has appealed to me most about neopragmatism is Rorty's characterization of philosophy as "just another literary genre," one that instructs us about alternate ways of seeing the world exactly as a good poem or a good novel—or a good shamanic recital—instructs us. For Rorty, philosophy is all about keeping going an interesting conversation, of seeing "human beings as generators of new descriptions rather than beings one hopes to be able to describe accurately" (1979:378). That is what I see this work as undertaking. I offer new ways of describing some of us, those who make the "rulings of the night," those who resist the world's ongoing deterioration, who authoritatively create and maintain a life-world in and through their words. Shaman recitals both create shamans and change ("cure" and "curse") others. They seem to do this by establishing what Nagel has called "an objective phenomenology not dependent on empathy or the imagination" (1974:449), a practical, self-grounded ontology. They make sense of what they and their world are *really* like, not just how they appear, playing a language game that is a total way of living, of being and staying alive. Their field is consciousness presided over by Vāc, their tokens are minds and hearts and bodies.

If, perhaps, through my description of these texts, we catch new glimpses of ourselves, of our struggle against the limits of death, disease, and decay that bound our lives, and of the simultaneous moments of transcendent sublimity for which we strive, then my text has become a shamanic one. Through another of its reflections, my goal may then be seen as not only to make sense of lives in Nepal, but also to come to terms with our own, my own, life. Provisional goals, provisional answers: a continuing conversation, in which, for now, here, I stop my pen.

> This possible feast has been rejected,
> from my child you've been deflected!
> To the Time of Death,
> to the Messenger of Death,
> I give sacrifice.
>
> (7.2)

Glossary
References
Index

Glossary

Since each Nepali word has a short gloss on its first appearance, this list does not include words that occur only a single time in the text. Words are listed in the order of the Roman alphabet, but with long vowels following short ones, dental consonants following retroflex ones.

Transliteration follows the method of R. L. Turner (1980).

agni. Fire; the god of fire.
aiṭhān lāgnu. Paralytic loss of breath in the night.
akṣeta. Pure uncooked grains of rice for sacred purposes.
andhaviśwās. Superstition.
aṅg bandhnu. To protect the body.
baknu. "Speaking," consultations with a shaman.
banpā. Forest spirits.
barāṅg. Spirits of inanimate forces.
bāhun (variant: *bābān*). A Brāhman.
bāyu (often in the compound *bāyu burmā,* sometimes *bāyu batās*). Spirit of a human who died by accident or suicide, or whose corpse was polluted.
bhed (usually in the compound *ched bhed*). Secret knowledge.
bhoṭo. An archer's wristguard.
bhut (archaic plural: *bhutān*). Ghost.
bīr. Spirits of animals.
boksī. Witch. Diminutive: *boksinī.*
boksī lāgnu. To bewitch.
cakra katāunu. To cut a circle or pentagram.
cal. Move. Causative: *calāune.*
celā. Pupil.

chāl. Trick.
chānamā. Grain scattered to conclude a ceremony.
ched. Secret action; deceit.
chiṇḍo. A bottle gourd.
choko. Ritually pure.
curmi. A shaman's assistant.
ḍaṁkī. Most powerful type of witch; spirit of a dead witch. Diminutive: *ḍaṁkinī.*
daijo. Dowry.
deutā. Deities; major local spirits of nonhuman origin.
deutā bolāunu. To summon the spirits.
deutā lāgnu. Possession by spirits.
deva. A god.
devī. A goddess.
dhaṅgrī. A dhāmī's assistant, also called a *pujārī.*
dhām. A spirit's power; the spirit itself.
dhāmī. Spirit medium; oracle.
dhāmījhā̃kri. "Standard" Nepali for any spirit medium or shaman.
dhāminī. Female medium.
dhuwā. Minor spirits that inhabit crossroads.
dokh. General afflictions.
dṛṣṭī. Sight, especially mystical seeing.
gauḍā. A star obstruction; block; difficult pass.
gauḍā lāgnu. To have a crisis, to reach an impasse; to suffer a star obstruction.
gel. A tree planted in a shaman's tomb; the spirit of the dead shaman.
guru. Teacher.
gyān. Knowledge.
gyānī. Seer.
haṁsa maṭṭ. Monument for a shaman's spirit.
herneharu. Seers; ritual experts.
jaiśī. Astrologer.
jal toyo. Literally, water blood; preliminary offerings at an initiation ceremony.
jantar (Sanskrit: *yantra*). Amulet; ritual diagram.
jap. To repeat over and over a spell; the spell itself.
jādu. Tricks of a magician.
jhagrenī. Wife of a shaman; a female shaman.
jhāṅgarī (Standard Nepali: *jhā̃kri*). Shaman, locally derived from *jhārnu.* To exorcise. Vocative: *jhāṅgrīyau.*
jhāṅgarī lāgnu. To "shamanize." Past tense: *jhāṅgarī lāgyo.*
juṭho. Ritually impure.
kamnu (also *karnu*). To tremble, to be possessed. Causative: *kamāunu.*

kapṭī. Minor witch. Often in the diminutive, *kapṭinī.*
kāmī. Blacksmith caste.
kānphaṭa. A follower of the sect of Gorakhnāth.
khaḍgā. Astrological crises of children.
khelnu. To play.
khetī. A recital.
klaṅkenī. An experienced hag (not exactly a witch, but an old woman who is dangerous).
kūl deutā. Family lineage gods.
laṭṭā. Topknot.
lāgu. Threats and problems.
lāgu pharkāunu. To return malevolent effects to their sources.
lākh. A hundred thousand.
lāmā. Tibetan priest or monk.
lāṭo Congenital cretin. Male: *lāṭā.* Female: *lāṭī.*
liṅga. Phallic emblem representing Mahādev.
malāmi. Funeral goers.
maṁsa maṭṭ. Tomb for a shaman's physical body.
mancit. Heartmind.
mandāmī. The seven levels of this world.
mantar (Standard Nepali: *mantra*). Ritual formula; spell.
masān. Spirits of dead humans.
māilo herne. "Looking at dirt," a diagnostic technique.
māī. Locally used as polite address for any goddess; more specifically, an epithet of Sitālā Devī, goddess of smallpox.
māṅgal. Auspicious hymns to the god.
māphī. Bloodthirsty spirits.
melā. A recital (also called *dhūr, khetī,* and *okhā*).
moc. Malevolent skyfallen object that causes reproductive problems.
mul. Water source; root.
mūl. A severe astrological disturbance.
mūl nakṣatra. One of twenty-seven houses of the lunar elliptic.
nām garnu. To address someone with his or her personal name.
nāyak. Local chief of the traditional aristocracy.
nyāulo. A drongo bird.
paṇḍit. Brāhman priest.
parelī. Formal recital of a god's personal history.
pārkī. Pulse readers; fortune-tellers.
pirā. Wooden seat.
pitār (variant: *piṭṭṛ*). Spirit of a patrilineal ancestor.
prakil. Counselor.

prasād. Blessed food.
pret. Ghost.
pun purus. Life force; life breath.
putlā. Debris found inside the body.
putlā tānnu. To remove substances that a witch has put inside someone.
pūjā. Worship ceremony.
pūrṇimā. The full moon.
ṛtā (Sanskrit). Cosmic order.
rammā (Kham). Shaman.
rāh (variant: *rāi*). Spirit of a dead child.
rāh mārne. Ritual to kill rāh.
rākṣas. Demon.
rāyā sarsu. Two varieties of mustard.
richaṅg phālne. Leaf-throwing diagnostic ritual.
rog. Physical diseases.
rudrākṣa. Berries of the *Elaeocarpus* tree.
sadān. Type of tree, resembling sandalwood, and bleeding thick red bloodlike sap when cut.
sapanā bigriyo. A dream has broken.
sat byū. Seeds of truth.
sāto. Wits; awareness.
sāto gāyo. To have lost one's wits.
siddha. A forest-dwelling Hindu ascetic; a perfected being.
simī-bhūmī. Minor local spirits of the soil and springs.
sirān. The head of a bed.
siyo (sometimes pronounced "*hiyo*"). Fragile, detachable part of one's life-force. Needle; border.
siyo mārne. Ritual to kill siyo.
suwā. Pole climbed at a shaman's initiation; a class of spirits (variant: *sawā*) involved in that climb.
syāunyā. Spirits who hover in the air at graveyards, similar to *masān.*
ṭikā. Forehead dot.
toyo (variant: *toyan*). Blood feeding; name of the initiation ceremony.
vāi. Malevolent forces resulting from witchcraft.
vāṇ. Arrows; supernatural assistants.
veda. Book knowledge.
veta. Cane.
vidhī. Ritual techniques.
viprālī (diminutive of the Vedic term *vipra,* one who trembles; a particular kind of priest). Shaman.

References

Abu-Lughod, Lila

1986 *Veiled Sentiments: Honor and Poetry in a Bedouin Society.* Berkeley: University of California Press.

1990 Shifting Politics in Bedouin Love Poetry. In Lutz and Abu-Lughod 1990:24–45.

Adhikari, Surya Mani

1988 *The Khaśa Kingdom. A Trans-Himalayan Empire of the Middle Age.* Jaipur and New Delhi: Nirala Publications.

Allen, N. J.

1976 Approaches to Illness in the Nepalese Hills. In J. B. Loudon (ed.), *Social Anthropology and Medicine.* London: Academic Press. 500–552.

1978 Sewala Puja Bintala Puja: Notes on Thulung Ritual Language. *Kailash* 6.4:237–56.

Alper, Harvey P. (ed.)

1989 *Understanding Mantras.* Albany, N.Y.: State University of New York Press.

Aristotle

1987 [335 B.C.] *The Poetics I.* Translated with notes by Richard Janko. Indianapolis: Hackett.

Artaud, Antonin

1958 *The Theater and Its Double.* New York: Grove Press.

Atkinson, Jane Monnig

1989 *The Art and Politics of Wana Shamanship.* Berkeley: University of California Press.

1992 Shamanisms Today. *Annual Review of Anthropology* 21:307–30.

Austin, J. L.
1965 *How to Do Things with Words.* Cambridge: Harvard University Press.
1979 *Philosophical Papers.* Oxford: Clarendon Press.

Bawden, C. R.
1962 Calling the Soul: A Mongolian Litany. *School of Oriental and African Studies Bulletin* 25:81–103.

Benjamin, Walter
1968 [1955] *Illuminations.* New York: Harcourt, Brace, and World.

Beyer, Stephan
1973 *Magic and Ritual in Tibet. The Cult of Tārā.* Berkeley: University of California Press.

Bilmes, Jack
1986 *Discourse and Behavior.* New York: Plenum.

Borges, Jorge Luis
1964 *Other Inquisitions.* Translated by Ruth L. C. Simms. Austin: University of Texas Press.

Bourdieu, Pierre
1977 [1972] *Outline of a Theory of Practice.* Translation by Richard Nice of *Esquisse d'une théorie de la pratique.* Cambridge: Cambridge University Press.

Briggs, George W.
1989 [1938] *Gorakhnāth and the Kānphaṭa Yogīs.* Delhi: Motilal Banarsidass.

Caraka Saṁhitā
1981–83 Sanskrit text with English translation by Priyavrat Sharma. 3 vols. Varanasi: Chaukhamba Orientalia.

Coulter, Jeff
1979 *The Social Construction of Mind.* Totowa, NJ: Rowman and Littlefield.

Das, Sarat Chandra
1881 Dispute between a Buddhist and a Bon-po Priest for the Possession of Mt. Kailas and the Lake of Manasa. *Journal of the Asiatic Society of Bengal* 50:206–11.

Desjarlais, Robert R.
1992a Yolmo Aesthetics of Body, Health, and "Soul Loss." *Social Science and Medicine* 34.10:1105–17.
1992b *Body and Emotion. The Aesthetics of Illness and Healing in the Nepal Himalayas.* Philadelphia: University of Pennysylvania Press.

Dumont, Louis
1970 *Homo Hierarchicus.* Chicago: University of Chicago Press.

Eliade, Mircea
1964 [1951] *Shamanism: Archaic Techniques of Ecstacy.* New York: Bollingen Foundation.

Evans-Pritchard, E. E.
1937 *Witchcraft, Oracles, and Magic among the Azande.* London: Oxford University Press.

Favret-Saada, Jeanne
1980 [1977] *Deadly Words: Witchcraft in the Bocage.* Translation by Catherine Cullen of *Les mots, la mort, les sorts.* Cambridge: Cambridge University Press.

Flaherty, Gloria
1992 *Shamanism and the Eighteenth Century.* Princeton: Princeton University Press.

Foucault, Michel
1972 [1969] *The Archaeology of Knowledge and the Discourse on Language.* Translated by A. M. Sheridan Smith. New York: Pantheon.

Frege, Gottlob
1970 On Sense and Reference. In Peter Geach and Max Black (eds.), *Translations from the Philosophical Writings of Gottlob Frege.* Oxford: Oxford University Press.

Friedrich, Paul
1979 *Language, Context, and the Imagination.* Stanford: Stanford University Press.

Fürer-Haimendorf, Christof von (ed.)
1974 *Contributions to the Anthropology of Nepal.* London: Warminster.

Gaborieau, Marc
1975a Les Bāyu du Népal central. Puruṣārtha: *Recherches de sciences sociales sur l'Asie du Sud* 1:67–90.
1975b La transe rituelle dans l'Himalaya central: folie, avatar, méditation. *Puruṣārtha: Recherches de sciences sociales sur l'Asie du Sud* 2:147–243.

Gadamer, Hans-Georg
1965 *Wahrheit und Methode.* 2d. ed. Tübingen: Mohr.

Gaenszle, Martin
1991 *Verwandtschaft und Mythologie bei den Mewahang Rai in Ostnepal.* Wiesbaden: Franz Steiner Verlag.

1992 Ancestral Types: Mythology and the Classification of "Deities" among the Mewahang Rai. *Collection Puruṣārtha* 15:197–217.

Garfinkel, Harold
1967 *Studies in Ethnomethodology.* Englewood Cliffs, NJ: Prentice-Hall.

Geertz, Clifford
1966 Religion as a Cultural System. In Banton, Michael (ed.), *Anthropological Approaches to the Study of Religion.* London: Tavistock. 1–46.
1973 *The Interpretation of Culture.* New York: Basic Books.

Ginzburg, Carlo
1985 [1966] *Night Battles. Witchcraft and Agrarian Cults in the Sixteenth and Seventeenth Centuries.* Translation by John and Anne Tedeschi of *I benandanti.* New York: Penguin.

Goodman, Nelson
1978 *Ways of Worldmaking.* Indianapolis: Hackett.

Greve, Reinhard
1981/82 A Shaman's Concept of Illness and Healing Ritual in the Mustang District, Nepal. *Journal of the Nepal Research Centre* 4.1:99–124.
1982 Deu Basne und Antibiotika: Schamanistische Heilrituale und westliche Medizin in Austauch. In Manfred Brinkmann and Michael Franz (eds.), *Nachtschatten in Weissenland: Betrachtungen zu Alien und neuen Heilsystem.* Berlin: Verlagsgesellshaft Gesundheit. 257–68.
1989 The Shaman and the Witch: An Analytical Approach to Shamanic Poetry in the Himalayas. In Mihály Hoppál and Otto J. von Sadovszky (eds.), *Shamanism Past and Present.* 2 vols. Budapest: Hungarian Academy of Sciences. 219–23.

Hamayon, Roberte N.
1990 *La chasse à l'âme: esquisse d'une théorie du chamanisme sibérien.* Nanterre: Société d'ethnologie.
1993 Shamanism and Pragmatism in Siberia. In Mihály Hoppál and Keith Howard (eds.), *Shamans and Cultures.* Budapest: Akadémiai Kiadó. 200–205.

Hardman, Charlotte
1981 The Psychology of Conformity and Self-Expression among the Lohorung Rai of East Nepal. In P. Heelas and A. Lock (eds.), *Indigenous Psychologies: The Anthropology of Self.* London: Academic Press. 161–179.

Harré, Rom
1985 The Language Game of Self-Ascription: A Note. In Kenneth J. Gergen and Keith E. Davis (eds.), *The Social Construction of the Person.* New York: Springer-Verlag. 259–63.

Hatto, A. T.
1970 *Shamanism and Epic Poetry in Northern Asia.* London: School of Oriental and African Studies.

Hegel, G. W. F.
1966 [1807] Preface to the Phenomenology of Mind. In *Hegel: Texts and Commentary,* translated and edited by Walter Kaufmann. Garden City, NY: Anchor.
1975 [1835] *Aesthetics. Lectures on Fine Art.* Translated by T. M. Knox. Oxford: Clarendon Press.

Heidegger, Martin
1959 *Unterwegs zur Sprache.* Pfullingen: Neske. (*On the Way to Language,* translated by Peter D. Hertz [New York: Harper and Row, 1972].)
1972 [1968] Time and Being. Included in *On Time and Being.* Translated by Joan Stambaugh. New York: Harper and Row.

Held, G. Jan
1935 *The Mahābhārata, An Ethnological Study.* London and Amsterdam: Kegan, Paul, Trench, Trubner.

His Majesty's Government of Nepal
V.S. 2022 (1965) *Śrī Panc Surendra Bikram Śāh Devakā śāsan kālamā baneko Muluki Ain* (Legal code enacted during the reign of King Surendra Bikram Shah). Kathmandu: Kānūn tathā Nyāya Mantrālaya (Ministry of Law and Justice, Law Books Management Committee).
V.S. 2031 (1974/75) *Meci dekhi Mahākāli. Khaṇḍ 4: Sudīr Pascimañcal Bikās Kṣetra.* Kathmandu: H. M. G. Printing Office.

Hitchcock, John T.
1967 A Nepalese Shamanism and the Classic Inner Asian Tradition. *History of Religions* 7.2:149–58.

1974a A Shaman's Song and Some Implications for Himalayan Research. In Fürer-Haimendorf 1974:150–58.

1974b A Nepali Shaman's Performance as Theatre. *Artscanada*. 30th Anniversary Issue: 74–80.

1976 Aspects of Bhujel Shamanism. In Hitchcock and Jones 1976:165–96.

Hitchcock, John T., and Rex L. Jones (eds.)

1976 *Spirit Possession in the Nepal Himalayas*. New Delhi: Vikas.

Höfer, András

1979 The Caste Hierarchy and the State of Nepal: A Study of the Muluki Ain of 1854. *Khumbu Himal* (Innsbruck) 13.2.

1981 *Tamang Ritual Texts I: Preliminary Studies in the Folk Religion of an Ethnic Minority in Nepal.* Wiesbaden: Franz Steiner Verlag.

1985a Tamang Ritual Texts: Notes on the Interpretation of an Oral Tradition of Nepal. *Journal of the Royal Asiatic Society* 1985.1:23–28.

1985b Review of Larry Peter's "Ecstasy and Healing in Nepal." *American Anthropologist* 87.2:422–23.

1992 On the Poetics of Healing in Tamang Shamanism. In Bernhard Kölver, (ed.), *Aspects of Nepalese Traditions*. Stuttgart: Franz Steiner Verlag. 155–70.

Höfer, András, and Bishnu P. Shrestha

1973 Ghost Exorcism among the Brahmans of Central Nepal. *Central Asiatic Journal* 17.1:51–57.

Holmberg, David

1989 *Order in Paradox: Myth, Ritual, and Exchange among Nepal's Tamang*. Ithaca and London: Cornell University Press.

Hoskins, Janet

1988 The Drum is the Shaman, the Spear Guides His Voice. *Social Science and Medicine* 27.8:819–28.

Hultkrantz, Äke

1973 A Definition of Shamanism. *Temenos: Studies in Comparative Religion* 9:25–37.

Husserl, Edmund

1960 [1929] *Cartesian Meditations: An Introduction to Phenomenology*. Translated by Dorian Cairns. The Hague: M. Nijhoff.

Hutchins, Edwin
1987 Myth and Experience in the Trobriand Islands. In Naomi Quinn, and Dorothy Holland (eds.), *Cultural Models in Language and Thought*. Cambridge: Cambridge University Press. 269–89.

Jackson, Anthony
1979 *Na-Khi Religion: An Analytic Appraisal of the Na-Khi Ritual Texts*. The Hague: Mouton.

Jakobson, Roman
1981 [1959] Linguistics and Poetics. In *Selected Writings*, Vol. 3: *Poetry of Grammar and Grammar of Poetry*. The Hague: Mouton. 18–51.

Jośī, Satyamohan
V.S. 2028 (1971/72) *Itihās*. Vol. 1 of *Karṅālī Loka Saṁskṛti*. Kathmandu: Nepāl Rājkīya Prajyā-Pratiṣṭhān (Nepal Royal Academy).
V.S. 2032 (1975/76) Kehī Nepālī Loka-Deutāharuko Bhūmikā. In Tulasī Devas (ed.), *Nepālī Loka-Saṁskṛti-Saṁgoṣṭī*. Kathmandu: Nepāl Rājkīya Prajyā-Pratiṣṭhān. 127–33.

Kirk, G. S., and J. E. Raven
1963 *The Presocratic Philosophers. A Critical History with a Selection of Texts*. Cambridge: Cambridge University Press.

Kristeva, Julia
1989 [1981] *Language: The Unknown*. Translation by Anne M. Menke of *Le langue, cet inconnu*. New York: Columbia University Press.

Kundera, Milan
1980 *The Book of Laughter and Forgetting*. New York: Knopf.

Lacan, Jacques
1968 [1956] *The Language of the Self*. Translation by Alan Sheridan of *Fonction et champ de la parole et du langue en psychanalyse*. Baltimore: Johns Hopkins University Press.

Laderman, Carol
1991 *Taming the Winds of Desire: Psychology, Medicine, and Aesthetics in Malay Shamanistic Performance*. Berkeley: University of California Press.

Lecomte-Tilouine, Marie

1987 Hommes/divinités de la forêt. A travers le miroir au Népal central. *Études rurales* 107–8 (July-Dec.): 55–69.

1991 Pouvoir tribal et hindouisme en Himalaya: le symbolique et ses transformations chez les Magar de Gulmi (Népal central). Thèse de l'Ecole des Hautes Etudes en Sciences Sociales, Paris.

1993 The Proof of the Bone: Lineage and Devālī in Central Nepal. *Contributions to Indian Sociology* (n.s.) 27.1:1–23.

Lévi-Strauss, Claude

1963a [1949] The Sorcerer and His Magic. In *Structural Anthropology,* translated by C. Jacobson and B. G. Schoepf. New York: Basic Books. 167–85.

1963b [1949] "The Effectiveness of Symbols." In *Structural Anthropology.* New York: Basic Books. 186–205.

1969 *The Raw and the Cooked.* Translated by John and Doreen Weightman. New York and Evanston: Harper and Row.

Levine, Nancy E.

1987 Caste, State, and Ethnic Boundaries in Nepal. *Journal of Asian Studies* 46.1:177–88.

Levy, Robert I.

1987 How the Navadurgā Protect Bhaktapur: The Effective Meaning of a Symbolic Enactment. In Neils Gutschow and Axel Michaels (eds.), *Heritage of the Kathmandu Valley.* Sankt Augustin: VGH Wissenshaftsverlag. 105–34.

1991 *Mesocosm: Hinduism and the Organization of a Traditional Newar City in Nepal.* Berkeley: University of California Press.

Lok-Falck, Éveline

1977 A propos du terme chamane. *Études mongoles et sibériennes* (Nanterre) 8:7–18.

Lutz, Catherine

1988 *Unnatural Emotions: Everyday Sentiments on a Micronesian Atoll and Their Challenge to Western Theory.* Chicago: University of Chicago Press.

Lutz, Catherine, and Lila Abu-Lughod (eds.)

1990 *Language and the Poetics of Emotion.* Cambridge: Cambridge University Press.

Macdonald, Alexander W.

1962 Notes préliminaires sur quelques *jhā̃kri* du Muglan. *Journal Asiatique* 250.1:107–39. (Translation: Preliminary Notes on Some *jhā̃kri* of Muglan, in Hitchcock and Jones (1976:309–41.)

1976 [1968] Sorcery in the Nepalese Code of 1853. Translation of "La sorcellerie dans le code népalais de 1853," in Hitchcock and Jones 1976:376–81.

Malinowski, Bronislaw

1923 The Problem of Meaning in Primitive Languages. In C. K. Ogden and I. A. Richards, *The Meaning of Meaning*. New York and London: Harcourt Brace Jovanovich.

1965 *Coral Gardens and Their Magic II: The Language of Magic and Gardening*. Bloomington: Indiana University Press.

Marriott, McKim, and Ronald B. Inden

1977 Toward an Ethnosociology of South Asian Caste Systems. In Kenneth David (ed.), *The New Wind: Changing Identities in South Asia*. The Hague: Mouton. 227–38.

Maskarinec, Gregory G.

1992 Shamanic Etiologies of Affliction from Western Nepal. *Social Science and Medicine* 35.5:723–34.

1993 Flatter, Promise, Threaten, Kill: Shamanic *Mantar* as Speech Acts. In Charles Ramble and Martin Brauen (eds.), *Anthropology of Tibet and the Himalaya*. Zürich: Völkerkundemuseum der Universität Zürich. 198–207.

McHugh, Ernestine

1989 Concepts of the Person among the Gurungs of Nepal. *American Ethnologist* 16.1:75–86.

Messerschmidt, Donald A.

1976 *The Gurungs of Nepal: Conflict and Change in a Village Society*. Warminster: Aris and Phillips.

Miller, Caspar J.

1979 *Faith Healers of the Himalayas. An Investigation of Traditional Healers and Their Festivals in Dolakha District of Nepal*. Kirtipur: Centre for Nepal and Asian Studies, Tribhuvan University.

Mironov, N. D., and Sergei M. Shirokogoroff
1924 Śramana Shaman: Etymology of the Word "Shaman." *Journal of the Royal Asiatic Society, North China Branch (Shanghai)* 55:105–30.

Mumford, Stan Royal
1989 *Himalayan Dialogue: Tibetan Lamas and Gurung Shamans in Nepal.* Madison: University of Wisconsin Press.

Nagel, Thomas
1974 What Is It Like to Be a Bat? *Philosophical Review* (Oct. 1974):435–50.

Nakazawa, Shinichi
1986 The Zero Logic of Disease—A Critique of Violence. In *Monumenta Serindica 15* (Anthropological and Linguistic Studies of the Kathmandu Valley and the Gandaki Area in Nepal). Tokyo: Institute for the Study of Languages and Cultures of Asia and Africa. 117–66.

Naraharī Nāth, Yogi
V.S. 2012 (1954–55) *Itihās Prakāś,* vol 1. Kathmandu: Itihās Prakāś Maṇḍal.

Nietzsche, Friedrich
1973 [1873] Über Wahrheit und Lüge im aussermoralischen Sinne. In *Nietzsche Werke 3.2: Nachgelassene Schriften, 1870–1873.* Berlin: Walter de Gruyter.

Oakley, E. S., and Tara Dutt Gairola
1977 [1935] *Himalayan Folklore: Kumaon and West Nepal.* Reprinted with an introduction by Marc Gaborieau. Kathmandu: Ratna Pustak Bhandar.

Obeyesekere, Gananath
1981 *Medusa's Hair: An Essay on Personal Symbols and Religious Experience.* Chicago: University of Chicago Press.
1990 *The Work of Culture: Symbolic Transformation in Psychoanalysis and Anthropology.* Chicago: University of Chicago Press.

Oppitz, Michael
1986 Die Trommel und das Buch: Eine kleine und die grosse Tradition. In Bernhard Kölver, (ed.), *Formen kulturellen Wandels und andere Beiträge zur Erforschung des Himālaya.* Sankt Augustin: VGH Wissenschaftsverlag. 53–125.

1991 *Onkels Tochter, keine sonst.* Frankfurt am Main: Suhrkamp.

1993 Wie heilt der Heiler? Schamanische Praxis im Himalaya. *Pyschotherapie. Psychosomatik Medizinische Psychologie* 43:387–95.

Ortner, Sherry B.

1978 *Sherpas through Their Rituals.* Cambridge: Cambridge University Press.

Overing, Joanna

1990 The Shaman as a Maker of Worlds: Nelson Goodman in the Amazon. *Man (n.s.)* 25:602–19.

Padoux, André (ed.)

1989 *Mantras et diagrammes rituels dans l'hindouisme.* Paris: Editions du CNRS.

1992 *Vāc: The Concept of the Word in Selected Hindu Tantras.* Delhi: Sri Satguru Publications.

Pandey, Ram Niwas

1970 The Ancient and Medieval History of Western Nepal. *Ancient Nepal: Journal of the Department of Archeology* 10:53–60 and 11:45–60.

V.S. 2032 (1975/76) Paścamī Nepālko Śaiv-Śākta Paramparā. In Tulasī Devas, (ed.), *Nepālī Loka-Saṁskṛti-Saṁgoṣṭī.* Kathmandu: Nepāl Rājkīya Prajyā Pratiṣṭhān (Nepal Royal Academy). 134–58.

Parish, Steven M.

1991 The Sacred Mind: Newar Cultural Representations of Mental Life and the Production of Moral Consciousness. *Ethos* 19.3:213–351.

Parmenides. See Kirk and Raven 1963

Paul, Robert.

1976 Some Observations on Sherpa Shamanism. In Hitchcock and Jones 1976:141–51.

Pears, David

1970 *Ludwig Wittgenstein.* New York: Viking.

Perec, Georges

1978 *La vie mode d'emploi.* Paris: Hachette.

Pignède, Bernard

1966 *Les Gurungs: une population himalayenne du Népal.* Paris and The Hague: Mouton.

Plato

1952 [370 B.C.] *Phaedrus.* Translated with introduction and commentary by R. Hackforth. Cambridge: Cambridge University Press.

Purājulī, Budhisāgar (ed.)
V.S. 2036 (1979/80) *Srīswasthānī Bratakathā*. Kathmandu: Ratna Pustak Bhaṇḍār.

Pynchon, Thomas
1973 *Gravity's Rainbow*. New York: Viking.

Quine, W. V.
1969 *Ontological Relativity and Other Essays*. New York: Columbia University Press.

Raheja, Gloria Goodwin
1988 *The Poison in the Gift: Ritual, Prestation, and the Dominant Caste in a North Indian Village*. Chicago: University of Chicago Press.

Reinhard, Johan
1976 Shamanism and Spirit Possession: The Definition Problem. In Hitchcock and Jones 1976:12–20.

Rgvedā Saṁhitā
1977 Sanskrit with English translation in 13 volumes by Svami Satya Prakash Saravati. New Delhi: Veda Pratisthana.

Ricoeur, Paul
1976 *Interpretation Theory: Discourse and the Surplus of Meaning*. Fort Worth: Texas Christian University Press.

Rorty, Amélie Oksenberg
1992 The Psychology of Aristotelian Tragedy. In A. Rorty (ed.), *Essays on Aristotle's Poetics*. Princeton: Princeton University Press. 1–22.

Rorty, Richard
1979 *Philosophy and the Mirror of Nature*. Princeton: Princeton University Press.
1989 *Contingency, Irony, and Solidarity*. Cambridge: Cambridge University Press.

Roseman, Marina
1988 The Pragmatics of Aesthetics: The Performance of Healing Among Senoi Temiar. *Social Science and Medicine* 27.8:811–18.
1991 *Healing Sounds from the Malaysian Rainforest: Temiar Music and Medicine*. Berkeley: University of California Press.

Rosu, Arion
1986 Mantra et yantra dans la médecine et l'alchimie indiennes. *Journal Asiatique* 274.3–4:203–68.

Rouget, Gilbert
1985 [1980] *Music and Trance: A Theory of the Relations between Music and Possession.* Chicago: University of Chicago Press.

Rousseau, J. J.
1974 [1755] *Essai sur l'origine des langues.* Paris: Aubier Montaigne.

Ryle, Gilbert
1949 *The Concept of Mind.* New York: Hutchinson's University Library.

Sacks, Harvey
1984 Notes on Methodology. In J. Maxwell Atkinson, and John C. Heritage, *Structures of Social Action: Studies in Conversation Analysis.* Cambridge: Cambridge University Press. 21–27.

Sales, Anne de
1989 Gendres des esprits: les chamanes Kham-Magar. In Véronique Bouillier and Gérard Toffin (eds.), *Puruṣārtha* 12: *Prêtrise, pouvoirs et autorité en Himalaya.* Paris: Éditions de L'École des Hautes Études en Sciences Sociales. 101–25.

1991 *Je suis né de vos jeux de tambours: la religion chamanique des Magar du nord.* Nanterre: Société d'ethnologie.

Saussure, F. de
1966 [1916] *Course in General Linguistics.* Translation by W. Baskin of *Cours de linguistique générale.* New York: McGraw Hill.

Schutz, Alfred
1962 *Collected Papers,* vol. 1: *The Problem of Social Reality.* The Hague: M. Nijhoff.

1964 *Collected Papers,* vol. 2: *Studies in Social Theory.* The Hague: M. Nijhoff.

1966 *Collected Papers,* vol. 3: *Studies in Phenomenological Philosophy.* The Hague: M. Nijhoff.

Śarmā, Bāl Candra
V.S. 2019 (1962) *Nepāli śabdakoś.* Kathmandu: Nepāl Rājkīya Prajyā-Pratiṣṭhān (Nepal Royal Academy).

Sharma, Prayag Raj
1970 A Study of the Vayu Cult in a Village of Central Nepal. *Vasudha* 13.8:31–35.

1971 The Matawali Chetris of Western Nepal. *Himalayan Review* 4:43–60.

1972 Preliminary Report on the Art and Architecture of the Karnāli Basin, West Nepal. *Recherche Coopérative sur Programme 253 C.N.R.S.* Paris: Centre National de la Recherche Scientifique.

1974 Divinities of the Karnali Basin in Western Nepal. In Fürer-Haimendorf 1974:244–59.

Shirokogoroff, Sergei M.

1935 *Psychomental Complex of the Tungus.* London: K. Paul, Trench, Trubner.

Śreṣṭha, Biharikṛṣṇa

V.S. 2028 (1971/72) *Jan Jiwan. Diyargaũkā Ṭhakuriharu.* vol. 3 of *Karnālī Loka Saṁskṛti.* Kathmandu: Nepāl Rājkīya Prajyā-Pratiṣṭhān (Nepal Royal Academy).

Shweder, Richard A.

1991 *Thinking through Cultures. Expeditions in Cultural Psychology.* Cambridge: Harvard University Press.

Stein, Rolf A.

1959 *Recherches sur l'épopée et le barde au Tibet.* Paris: Presses Universitaires de France.

Stone, Linda

1976 Concepts of Illness and Curing in a Central Nepal Village. *Contributions to Nepalese Studies* 6 (special issue):55–80.

1988 *Illness Beliefs and Feeding the Dead in Hindu Nepal: An Ethnographic Analysis.* Lewiston, NY: E. Mellen.

Strickland, Simon S.

1982 Belief, Practices, and Legends: A Study in the Narrative Poetry of the Gurungs of Nepal. Ph.D. Diss., Cambridge University.

1985 The Gurung Priest as Bard. *Kailash* 10.2:227–64.

1987 Notes on the Language of the Gurung *Pe. Journal of the Royal Asiatic Society* 1:53–76.

Tambiah, Stanley

1985 *Culture, Thought, and Social Action.* Cambridge: Harvard University Press.

Taylor, Paul Michael

1988 From *Mantra to Matarάa:* Opacity and Transparency

in the Language of Tobelo Magic and Medicine (Halmahera Island, Indonesia). *Social Science and Medicine* 27.5:425–36.

Toffin, Gérard
1984 *Société et religion chez les Néwar du Népal.* Paris: Editions du Centre National de la Recherche Scientifique.

Trawick, Margaret
1990 *Notes on Love in a Tamil Family.* Berkeley: University of California Press.

Tucci, Giuseppe
1956 *Preliminary Report on Two Scientific Expeditions in Nepal.* Rome: Serie Orientale Roma.

Turner, Ralph Lilley
1980 [1931] *A Comparative and Etymological Dictionary of the Nepali Language.* New Delhi: Allied Publishers.

Unbescheid, Günter
1986 Göttliche Könige und königliche Götter: Entwurf zur Organisation von Kulten in Gorkhā und Jumlā. In Bernhard Kölver (ed.), *Formen kulturellen Wandels und andere Beiträge zur Erforschung des Himālaya.* Sankt Augustin: VGH Wissenschaftsverlag. 225–47.

Underhill, Ruth Murray
1938 *Singing for Power. The Song Magic of the Papago Indians of Southern Arizona.* Berkeley: University of California Press.

Watters, David E.
1975 Siberian Shamanistic Traditions among the Kham Magars of Nepal. *Contributions to Nepalese Studies* 2.1:123–68.

Winch, Peter
1958 *The Idea of a Social Science and Its Relation to Philosophy.* London: Routledge and Kegan Paul.
1970. Understanding a Primitive Society. In B. R. Wilson (ed.), *Rationality.* Evanston: Harper and Row.

Witherspoon, Gary
1977 *Language and Art in the Navajo Universe.* Ann Arbor: University of Michigan Press.

Wittgenstein, Ludwig
1953 *Philosophical Investigations.* Oxford: Basil Blackwell.
1958 *The Blue and Brown Books.* New York: Harper.

1963 [1921] *Tractatus Logico-Philosophicus.* London: Routledge and Kegan Paul.

1967 *Zettel.* Berkeley: University of California Press.

1969 *On Certainty.* Oxford: Basil Blackwell.

1975 *Philosophical Remarks.* Oxford: Basil Blackwell.

1979 *Remarks on Frazer's Golden Bough.* Retford: Brymill Press.

Index